The Handbook of Logistics Contracts

The Handbook of Logistics Contracts

A Practical Guide to a Growing Field

Joan Jané

and

Alfonso de Ochoa

First published 2006 by
PALGRAVE MACMILLAN
Houndmills, Basingstoke, Hampshire RG21 6XS and
175 Fifth Avenue, New York, N.Y. 10010
Companies and representatives throughout the world

PALGRAVE MACMILLAN is the global academic imprint of the Palgrave Macmillan division of St. Martin's Press, LLC and of Palgrave Macmillan Ltd. Macmillan® is a registered trademark in the United States, United Kingdom and other countries. Palgrave is a registered trademark in the European Union and other countries.

ISBN 13: 978–1–4039–9868–2 hardback
ISBN 10: 1–4039–9868–X hardback

This book is printed on paper suitable for recycling and made from fully managed and sustained forest sources.

A catalogue record for this book is available from the British Library.

Library of Congress Cataloging-in-Publication Data
Jané Marcet, Joan, 1966–
   The handbook of logistics contracts : a practical guide to a growing field / by Joan Jané Marcet and Alfonso de Ochoa Martinez.
      p. cm.
   Includes bibliographical references and index.
   ISBN 1–4039–9868–X (hdb.)
      1. Contracting out. 2. Business logistics–Law and legislation. I. de Ochoa Martínez, Alfonso, 1965– II. Title.
K1005.J36 2006
658.50068'7–dc22   2005044655

10   9   8   7   6   5   4   3   2   1
15 14 13 12 11 10 09 08 07 06

Printed and bound in Great Britain by
Antony Rowe Ltd, Chippenham and Eastbourne

To my wife Lourdes and my sons Joan Pau,
Josep Oriol and Jordi Lluis
J. Jané

To my wife Cristina and my sons Alvaro and Pablo
A. de Ochoa

Contents

Foreword

In 1995 I was sitting in the office of the Logistics Director of a major oil company. We had been working for a few months on evaluating their secondary distribution network and had just presented our final proposals to the top officials of the company.

The company was using ten dedicated truck fleets owned by different regional transport groups and was offering a daily service to some 2000 oil stations and thousands of direct clients (industries, hospitals, schools, ...).

Our plan was to push for an evolution in the system by reducing the number of subcontractors, incorporating new tracking and tracing technologies, and addressing issues like quality and safety. In short, we were aiming to completely overhaul the relationship between the oil company and its logistics operators.

The meeting went without a glitch. Our graphs and tables proved our point, and few questions were asked. By the end of the afternoon, we had the green light.

Back in the Logistics Director's office we exchanged a quick smile, dropped our slides and files, and had a coffee. And then, while having this cup of coffee, the Logistics Director looked straight into my eyes and said to me: 'Now, tell me the truth: are you really sure about all this?'

He was basically telling me: 'This is no case study in an MBA class; this is the real thing, and if this does not work I'll be out of work in no time.'

I calmed him down, repeating most of the arguments he had just used in front of his bosses. Nevertheless, I knew he had a point. Logistics contracts of this nature are risky, and even though volumes have been written on their overall suitability, little has been said on their implementation.

Anyone that has been involved in this type of contract knows what I am talking about and will probably agree that drafting the final contract is one of the key steps in the process.

I have participated in many seminars and discussed logistics cases in front of thousands of executives, and in these settings it is very common to hear how futile contracts are (in some cases one would think that contracts are just three or four pages one has to sign and then stow away in a drawer).

Yet my experience negotiating real, major third-party contracts tells me this is not so in real life. Agreeing on the final form of the contract is always a painful process, and one really appreciates the efforts made at this stage when problems arise (and they usually do: accidents, thefts, lack of service, …).

That is why I truly believe that the book written by Joan Jané and Alfonso de Ochoa will be of great help to all practitioners.

Their work covers in full detail all the aspects that should be addressed by any logistics contract. In fact, I am convinced that this book will help many of its readers to consider issues that might otherwise have been forgotten. Years of experience designing, negotiating and drafting logistics contracts are condensed in this fine piece of work that will soon become a reference for all European logistics directors.

Federico Sabrià
Professor
IESE Business School
University of Navarra

Preface

There is a long history of books about logistics. All of them have focused mainly on the technical and management issues of logistics activities, which led us to conclude that there was a need for a book devoted to examining the content of logistics contracts.

The goal we hope to achieve with this book is that it will be useful not only to practising lawyers, but also to all professionals working in logistics, both logistics services providers and their customers, and individuals with an interest (practitioners or scholars) in learning about logistics contracts. Through this book, we aim to provide a general but comprehensive overview of all the issues related to logistics contracts from a legal and economic as opposed to technical standpoint.

Because of the diversity of our audience, we have avoided the use of complex and confusing legal vocabulary wherever possible. In order for the book and the opinions contained in it to be applicable around the world, we have attempted to avoid referring to any particular national legal system and instead have taken a general legal approach applying the general principles of law. Therefore, the book and the opinions contained in it can be applied not only in the European market, but also in the US and the rest of the world.

The authors are aware that the steady growth and development of both the industry and the global market we operate in mean that this book and the references contained herein will surely need to be updated and modernised in the very near future. Therefore, our commitment is to keep this book up to date and improve and fill in any gaps in a second edition.

Acknowledgements

Writing a book is a very rewarding experience but also quite a daunting project. Many are the people who encouraged us to undertake the joint venture of writing this book, and many also those that have contributed and supported us during this journey. There are so many that, regretfully, it is impossible to mention them all. Nevertheless, there are some whom we would especially like to thank for their support during the writing of this book.

First of all, we would like to thank the research contributors. Maya Dori, who participated in the design and contributed to the research conducted for the book, has done an outstanding job. Sergio Colina also helped us in the research phases. Our thanks also go to Julio Lopez-Quiroga, not only a great companion and expert lawyer in this field, but also a close friend. All of them helped us by providing innumerable references, articles, and notes which have been very useful and without which this book would have never seen the light of day. It goes without saying that any error is exclusively attributable to the authors.

Secondly, thanks to Hewlett-Packard for the continued support to Joan Jané and the commitment to research in the field of logistics. Thanks also to Federico Sabrià for his disinterested friendship, his thoughts during the early stages of this book, his enthusiasm for the overall project, and his willingness to write the Foreword.

Last but not least, we want to thank the International Centre for Logistics Research at IESE Business School (CIIL) for sponsoring this book and for its outstanding contribution to research into logistics.

To all of them and all our friends, companions, and collaborators who throughout this time have shown an interest in the work and have encouraged and advised us, our most sincere gratitude for their support and friendship.

Joan Jané
Alfonso de Ochoa

1
Outsourcing Contracts: Outsourcing of Logistics Services

1.1 Introduction

Rapidly or slowly, globally or locally, outsourcing has already penetrated all sectors of business and value chains. Outsourcing has been one of the most commonly used management practices during the last decade, and the outsourcing business continues to grow and expand significantly across all value chains. However, we believe that there is still no true consensus as to the understanding of outsourcing and its implications. More precisely, there is confusion as to outsourcing contracts in general and their legal nature in particular. Therefore, we believe that it is best to begin a handbook on logistics contracts with a review of outsourcing terminology and outsourcing contracts prior to dealing with logistics outsourcing contracts.

Since a logistics contract may be used as a basis for outsourcing, and since there is a multitude of activities carried out in outsourcing, the problems arising from logistics contracts are similar to those arising from outsourcing contracts. From among the various potential definitions, a logistics contract can be defined as a commercial contract under which one party, known as the third-party logistics (3PL) provider, provides services of a logistical nature to a customer in exchange for payment of an economic amount. EU legislation has so far failed to provide specific regulations on logistics contracts; as a result, an in-depth review of their legal nature and framework is in order.

The 3PL business has grown at a rate of more than 20 per cent per year in the last decade and has developed as a result of the increasing demand for advanced logistics services. New 3PL players from different fields are entering the market and competing with the traditional transport and warehousing firms. At the same time, the market is evolving from being highly fragmented to more consolidated, with very few 3PL players controlling the global market. Nevertheless, some general requirements must be fulfilled by all 3PL providers in order to provide their services in European countries.

The aim of this chapter is to provide an overview of logistics contractual relationships in the context of a growing and developing logistics industry. In the first part, we will review the fundamental issues in outsourcing strategy and outsourcing contracts in general. In the second part, we will review the 3PL business and the legal nature and framework of logistics contracts. Finally, we will review in detail the general requirements that must be met to provide 3PL services in Europe.

1.2 Outsourcing contracts

1.2.1 The definition, history and development of outsourcing

1.2.1.1 Outsourcing terminology

Before we embark on an in-depth analysis of the practices and trends of logistics outsourcing it is important to first provide a formal definition of outsourcing and contracting in general terms. 'Contracting'[1] refers to the design and implementation of contractual relationships between buyers and sellers. 'Outsourcing'[2] refers to the process whereby activities traditionally carried out in-house are contracted out to external providers.[3]

We often use the term 'contracting' in a generic sense to describe not only the process of outsourcing, but also the process and means of finalising the contractual relations required to support such activities.

Therefore, by combining these two understandings of the term, we are able to provide a definition of the outsourcing contract as the reciprocal agreement between the purchaser and the supplier that regulates the relationship of the process and the act of providing the services externally by the supplier.

As expressed by Carlos Bertrán (1998), outsourcing may be defined as 'contracting by a company of one or several external suppliers to provide, by the employment of assets different from the internal structure of the company, a service previously performed by an internal department of that company'.

The term 'contracting' is also often used to describe a situation where an organisation will call for tenders and the internal service provider is allowed to bid. If the in-house team wins the competitive tender, then we cannot strictly speaking describe it as a case of 'contracting out'. However, this still counts as a form of contracting, because the relationship between the client and the provider is made explicit through an internal agreement, even though it is not an agreement that has the force of law. An organisation cannot legally enforce a contract with itself, even though it can implement a set of agreements with internal manufacturers or service providers. In this sense, the main advantages of contracting can be seen as the sense of discipline that is imposed by introducing an element of competition, and the resulting performance management.

1.2.1.2 A historical view of outsourcing

We must go back to the eighteenth and nineteenth centuries to find the first common examples of outsourcing being practised in Europe. To take an example from the private sector, there are well-documented historical accounts of the contracting out of specialist areas of metal manufacturing in nineteenth-century England.[4]

Outsourcing involves contracting an outside organisation to carry out specific activities, which were previously carried out by the firm itself. These activities may vary from administrative services, such as payroll processing or providing security guards, to entire fields of activity such as information technology, accounting, order management, customer service, logistics, contract manufacturing and even design. It constitutes a form of restructuring, since it often involves fundamental changes in strategy, organisation and workforce. While the concept of outsourcing is not new, the ways companies outsource, and the strategic importance of outsourcing in business, are recent developments. Specialised service companies have demonstrated that they can provide better services in terms of quality and price, and that they are more reliable, particularly in the case of activities that require a specific set of skills that differ from the mainstream business of the company.

The theory of organisations has always attempted to explain the different factors that the manager or entrepreneur needs to consider when choosing between external market transactions and internal production. Already in 1937, Ronald Coase named those inefficiencies associated with large size, 'diseconomies of scale'. When Oliver Williamson, in 1985, came up with the concept of 'transaction costs economics', more attention was paid to attempting to understand the conditions in which both firms or markets could become more effective as modes of organisation. Up until the early 1980s many academics and management gurus advocated patterns of vertical integration and conglomerate diversification. The argument was that they yielded efficiencies in terms of economies of scale and corporate synergies. Since then the message has completely changed, to 'stick to the knitting' (Peters and Waterman, 1982) and get back to the 'core business'.

Today, outsourcing is a business practice that has penetrated all business activities and industries. Indeed, Peter Drucker already predicted back in 1995 that most organisations would enter into some type of outsourcing contract. 'In 10 or 15 years, organisations may be outsourcing all work that is "support" rather than revenue-producing ... In many organisations a majority of the people who work for it might be employees of an outsourcing contractor' (Drucker, 1995).

1.2.1.3 Trends in outsourcing

In the late 1980s academics began to develop new concepts of business organisation such as the 'shamrock organisation' and the 'virtual corporation' (Domberger, 1998). Charles Handy (1989) defines his concept of the shamrock organisation as 'a form of organisation based around a core of essential executives and workers supported by outside contractors and part time help'. This is very similar to Davidow and Malone's (1992) definition that 'the virtual corporation will appear less as a discrete enterprise and more an ever-varying cluster of common activities in the midst of a vast fabric of relationships'. The virtual organisation is described as an organisational form in which there is a group of core activities always carried out in-house by full-time employees, while the rest of the activities are contracted to external organisations or individuals. Benetton, the Italian clothing company, is often cited as a classic example of a virtual organisation.

Strategic networks and alliances have become popular variants of the modern organisational structure. Research in the field reflects this trend: 'The strategic network is claimed to be capable of achieving the efficiency benefits of contracting, while retaining the informational and technological advantages of vertical integration' (Domberger, 1998), 'These companies act simultaneously as large integrated companies and as companies that concentrate on only a few things and subcontract the rest' (Jarrillo, 1993). There is a high degree of cooperation with these contractors who form part of the network. These network contractors are also called 'business partners', or team members working towards a common goal. To a certain extent there is no difference between a strategic network and a strategic alliance, the latter being defined as 'a relationship between firms in which they cooperate to produce more value (or a lower cost) than is possible in a market transaction. To create that value, they must agree on what it is, on their need of each other to achieve it, and on sharing in the benefits' (Lewis, 1995). The modern phenomenon of 'partnering contracts' involves creating an atmosphere of trust between the contracting parties, through open communication, sharing of information and working together towards a common objective. The partnering relationship is achieved through agreeing to work together in a spirit of trust and cooperation. However, partnering does not replace the traditional contract, which legally binds the parties in the transaction. As long as the partners display a sense of cooperation and act accordingly, there will be no need to invoke the formal contract.

Toyota is often described as offering the best example of a strategic network on the basis of their own particular way of structuring their relationships with suppliers. To quote a further example, Marks & Spencer have been building up an organisational network involving cooperative relationships with their suppliers for nearly 50 years.

1.2.1.4 Core competencies

Whenever outsourcing is discussed there is always an implicit reference to the core competencies that companies decide to retain. A firm should be able to differentiate between its core activities and the rest of its activities that can be outsourced to third parties. However, many executives are still confused about what the concept of a core competence actually means. Recently, management theorists have introduced the concept of 'strategic sourcing', in an attempt to describe the fact that taking decisions about contracting involves identifying and securing the core competences, and that it therefore constitutes an integral part of formulating the strategy of the organisation. A core competence is defined as 'the collective learning in the organisation, especially how to coordinate diverse production skills and integrate multiple streams of technology' (Prahalad and Hamel, 1990). Theorists describe a core competence as 'a bundle of corporate skills that can be put to work in producing different products, both current and future'. Prahalad and Hamel mention as examples of core competencies Sony's capability to miniaturise components and audio-visual products, and Philips's optical media expertise and its applications. Prahalad and Hamel conclude that most companies cannot realistically identify and take on more than five or six core competencies, and that therefore careful assessment is required before any activity is outsourced.

The benefits of outsourcing essentially derive from using markets in such a way that companies can create strategic networks through successful contractual relationships. Companies decide to concentrate on their core competencies and outsource strategically, because in this way they can gain additional benefits such as flexibility, cost savings, specialisation and market discipline. In this way companies can focus most of their time and resources on business strategy and tactics rather than on administrative issues.

1.2.1.5 Benefits and costs of outsourcing

Outsourcing is often directed and driven by a corporate strategy. However, it is also worth mentioning that corporations must evaluate both the benefits and costs that implementing an outsourcing strategy (Domberger, 1998) will incur. The main benefits of outsourcing are flexibility, specialisation, market transaction, financial return, cost structure and cost savings.

Flexibility is understood as the ability to adjust the scale and scope of the activity upwards or downwards. Organisations that network with outsourcing providers can adjust more quickly, and at lower cost, to changes in demand as compared to integrated organisations. Therefore, virtual corporations are able to respond with greater flexibility to market dynamics.

Outsourcing fields of specialisation to providers yields economic benefits. The provider is able to exploit the principle of economies of scale and, subsequently, provide efficient and value-added services to the contracting organisations. Contracting organisations rely on the technology and expertise provided by the outsourcing providers.

Market transaction is concerned with the existence of a formal contractual transaction between the purchaser and the provider. This allows the purchaser to focus on output rather than input, competition among suppliers, choices by purchasers and innovative work practices. For the contracting organisations, this benefit usually bears fruit in the mid and long term, after the outsourcing transition is over and there is a successful change management in place.

Financial return is associated with the return on assets (ROA) ratio that indicates the financial efficiency of the corporation. Outsourcing strategies will allow some of the corporate assets and infrastructure to be dismantled and/or sold, and these will be replaced by variable expenses generated by the outsourcing providers. Although corporate benefits can be slightly reduced, management would expect the corporate efficiency (ROA) to significantly improve.

A further significant benefit of outsourcing is in the cost structure, because for the corporation some fixed costs are replaced by variable costs. This means that the new cost structure of the corporation after the outsourcing strategy is in place will be more closely aligned with the generation of revenue and fluctuations in demand. In this sense, this will reduce the risk of having to absorb higher fixed costs in lower demand periods.

Finally, to add to the previous outsourcing benefits, international studies indicate that outsourcing usually results in cost savings. However, cost savings will depend to a large extent on the specific industry, the type of outsourcing activity and the initial cost structure of the contracting organisations. Nevertheless, it is important to understand that every gain in efficiency need not necessarily lead to lower quality.

On the other hand, there are several costs ensuing from outsourcing that must be taken into account, such as the costs of transaction and monitoring, the loss of control, and the loss of in-house skills, corporate knowledge and innovative capacity.

Transaction costs cover the costs of searching for and selecting contractors, as well as the costs of writing and negotiating contracts. Contracts will never foresee all possible contingencies, so resources have to be earmarked for negotiation. In addition, there may be implicit or explicit costs associated with exiting or replacing contracts.

Organisations will have to dedicate resources for the monitoring of contractors in order to ensure the best value for money from the contract. Therefore, the costs of monitoring form a significant part of the outsourcing costs.

The sense of a loss of control that is experienced by the management when outsourcing in-house activities is an outsourcing cost that is directly linked to the loss of in-house skills. However, the real challenge faced by an organisation is not to lose the ability to be a smart purchaser and to excel in managing strategic networks of business partners, much in the same way as is currently done by many successful organisations that are very 'hollow', for example, Benetton, M&S, Virgin or HP.

The risk of losing corporate knowledge refers to the fact that collective knowledge within the organisation can disappear due to outsourcing. There is a similar risk of losing innovative capacity and finding that technical progress is compromised in the long run, because the contractor is not rewarded for innovation, especially when contracts are awarded solely on the basis of the lowest winning bid.

Finally, it is worth mentioning that contractual relationships based on a low level of trust and confidence are fragile and likely to fail. The importance of trust between contracting parties adds motivation to the concept of 'partnering contracts', where outsourcing costs such as transaction and monitoring costs are minimised.

1.2.1.6 Controlling the risks of outsourcing contracts

Risk as a concept refers to the possibility of an adverse outcome that causes loss, damage or injury. Outsourcing is often perceived as being higher risk, because control over activity-related input is transferred to the provider. The greatest risk in an outsourcing contract is non-performance (Domberger, 1998).

Usually there are contractual instruments in place to ensure that performance remains within acceptable limits: incentives for superior performance and penalties for poor performance. Incentives and penalties, together with performance-monitoring systems designed to detect deviations in performance, can help minimise the risk for the client organisation. However, it would be a mistake to assume that performance risk stems entirely from the supplier's side. How the client behaves can have a decisive impact on whether the contractor performs or not. In order to minimise such risks for the contractor, the contract usually contains some safeguards that specify aspects such as minimum volumes or fluctuations in demand generated by the client.

Each client will incorporate in their contract the safeguards that they regard as most appropriate for minimising risk. This topic has generated extensive debate among practitioners as to whether incentives are more effective than penalties, or vice versa. According to one pioneer in decision analysis, 'The major driving force is loss aversion. It is not so much that people hate uncertainty – but rather, they hate losing... People are much more sensitive to negative than to positive stimuli' (Tversky, 1990). From this statement one might conclude that penalties are likely to be more effective than incentives. However, the right balance between penalties and incentives in fact is determined by the type of contract and level of trust between the parties.

1.2.2 The legal nature of outsourcing contracts

As mentioned above in section 1.2.1.1, in which we provided some definitions of outsourcing, we are referring here to a management technique rather than to a specific type of contract. It could, therefore, be said that outsourcing contracts as such, with their own specific classification, do not exist. The varied and diverse types and structures of agreements and contracts that the generic term 'outsourcing contract' seems to encompass does not correspond to one single legal entity. Such an overwhelming variety could be attributed to any standard relationship that we may wish to establish in an abstract sense. Hence, when we speak of outsourcing contracts, we are not trying to refer to a specific type of contract, but rather we are using the term in order to address the legal problem that arises from the practical application of outsourcing as a management technique.

On this basis, a legal analysis of outsourcing contracts will stress that:

- an obligation exists on the part of the supplier to provide a service to the client;
- the usual supplementary agreements exist in addition to those particular to the provision of services, which are basically concerned with the transfer of assets and assignment of workers.

In order to establish the legal nature of an outsourcing contract, it is necessary to first determine the immediate objective of the communication of the supplier concerning the service provided. The reason for this is that the supplier, on the basis of this objective, has an obligation to provide either the service itself, or the result of that service, determining a particular element of a services or work leasing contract, respectively. Once this issue is determined, it will be necessary to deal with the essential nature of the contract of additional agreements, in order to determine whether it is worth maintaining the contract within the legislative classification established beforehand (works or services).

If the obligation of the supplier is considered to be the provision of a result, then the supplier shall be responsible to the client if they fail to provide that result (regardless of what that result is), while if the obligation is the provision of a service, then the supplier is responsible for undertaking the work it has committed to (regardless of the result). Therefore, determining the type of contract is relevant, in order to establish the legal regime applicable to the contract and, hence, the applicable regulations for resolving any conflicts that could arise between the parties.

If we consider the objective of the contract, it would appear apparent in principle that the obligation of the supplier consists in providing a service and not undertaking a work. Therefore, what the supplier is obliged to provide is the actual provision itself, regardless of what the result of this provision may be. Nonetheless, doubts may arise concerning the scope of the clauses which set out the level of services or the standard of quality required from the supplier in the provision of these services.

In our understanding, the fact that the contract lays out certain minimum levels of service does not imply that the supplier is bound to produce a specific result. Rather, it is a way of accepting, in contractual terms, an objective criterion for measuring the degree of compliance with the obligation (i.e. that of providing a service). Thus, for example, when an outsourcing contract establishes the minimum number of data to be processed daily, or the maximum acceptable percentage of losses, the actual meaning of this is an agreement that the supplier will be in breach of obligation if it does not attain these minimum levels. However, this does not mean that a fixed result has been agreed upon (the number of data or percentage of losses may vary once the minimum has been exceeded). Neither does fulfilling the minimum levels mean that the supplier is in compliance with the obligation (which is the provision of the service in itself).

The fact that the obligation on the supplier to provide a service to the client is an obligation to perform and not one to provide a result, leads us to recognise the existence, in the outsourcing contract, of the particular elements of a contract of leasing of services. This is defined as being a contract in which the one of the parties is bound to provide the other one with a certain service. This can be differentiated from a contract of employment, in the sense that while the lessor is bound to the provision of a service in itself and not the result that arises from that provision in the first, in the contract of employment it is bound to provide the result without considering the work that creates this result.

Once the existence of the elements of the contract of leasing of services has been identified, we have to analyse whether the existence of agreements that are additional to those pertaining to this type of contract is essential from the point of view of the nature of the contract. In such a case we would find ourselves with a mixed, linked or complex contract, depending on the relationship between the elements of the different types of contracts involved. Alternatively, this essence is unaffected (in which case, we would have a typical contract of leasing of services).

As has been mentioned above, it is not possible to provide a general response in abstract terms. Rather, each contract must be analysed individually in order to determine its legal nature. This is because the variety of structures included in the general term 'outsourcing contract' does not correspond to one single legal form, but rather to several. These legal forms range from a typical contract of lease of services (as would be the case with simple outsourcing not involving any transfer of assets) to linked contracts (for example, contracts involving, in addition to the provision of a service, an agreement concerning the transfer of assets that will not be used in the service to the client, as in this case the contract of leasing of services and the contract of sale are juxtaposed) or complex contracts (for cases in which the assets acquired are used in the provision of a service to the client). A contract can also contain elements of more than two types of contracts (for example, in the case of an outsourcing contract with the transfer of assets, some of which are owned and others rented, and in addition to the elements of the contract of leasing of services, there are other particular elements dealing with sale and leasing).

In addition to such contracts mentioned here that relate to sale and leasing, also frequent are contracts of outsourcing particular to company contracts (e.g. contracts dealing with the incorporation and functioning of joint ventures) and contracts of deposit and transport (for contracts of logistics outsourcing, where the merchandise is deposited in stores owned by the supplier, to be subsequently distributed by the suppliers themselves). Given the diversity of structures and services, agreements of a different nature cannot be excluded.

In any event, as Garcia Villaverde (1990) points out, we should not lose sight of the fact that what is at issue here is an attempt to place in order the rules that could come into play. If these appear in the form of a mixed contract (i.e. a contract formed by the union of provisions supplied under typical contracts of a different nature), Garcia Villaverde proposes that to achieve this end, use should be made 'as a final point of reference, of the function sought by the parties with the new contract, which is associated with the intent declared by the latter in overall content of the same'. In the case of a union of contracts (in other words, contracts with independent provisions which, as a whole, seek to attain a specific result without merging to the point that they form a single contract), it is the unity of purpose which will be considered in turn.

1.3 Logistics contracts

1.3.1 The definition and development of logistics

Logistics as a term, often used indiscriminately,[5] had almost become a common phrase in language by the end of the twentieth century. Used to refer to services that go beyond the simple provision of transport and warehousing, the term covers all the steps that make up the process of production and distribution.

Today, logistics is defined as: 'The process of strategically managing the procurement, movement, and storage of materials, parts and finished inventory (and the related information flows) through the organisation and its marketing channels in such a way that current and future profitability are maximised through the cost-effective fulfilment of orders' (Christopher, 1998).

The Council of Logistics Management, for its part, has defined logistics as:

> The part of the process of supply chain management that sees to efficiently and effectively planning, implementing, and monitoring the storage and direct and reverse flow of goods, services, and all the information related to them, between the point of origin and the point of consumption, with the aim of fulfilling the consumer's expectations.

In a wider sense of the term logistics, the Institute of Logistics has defined it as 'the time relating to the positioning of resources' or simply as 'the efficient management of the supply chain'.[6]

However, we can conclude that, as logistics is a constantly changing and evolving activity, it is difficult to establish any clear definition of the term as it quickly becomes outdated and obsolete.[7]

Supply chain management is a concept that has come to gain considerable support as managers increasingly recognise the importance of logistics as the last cost-cutting frontier. Major changes, such as globalisation, lead time reductions, customer orientation and outsourcing have, amongst others, contributed to this interest in logistics. The supply chain reflects the network of organisations that are involved, through upstream and downstream linkages, in the different processes and activities that produce value in the form of products and services in the hands of the end customer. Integrating the supply chain has become a key means for different industries to gain competitive advantage.

Supply chain management can be more accurately defined as 'a network of connected and interdependent organisations mutually and co-operatively working together to control, manage and improve the flow of material and information from suppliers to end users' (Aitken, 1998, cited in Christopher, 1998).

The members of the Global Supply Chain Forum redefined supply chain management in 1998 as 'the integration of key business processes from end user through original suppliers that provides products, services, and information that add value for customers and other stakeholders' (Lambert et al., 1998).

The concept of supply chain management incorporates two important ideas:

1. It is a collaborative effort that combines many parties or processes in the product cycle; and
2. It shows that the supply chain can cover the entire product cycle, from the introduction of raw materials to the point at which the consumer purchases the product.

Supply chain management can form a loop that commences with the customer and ends with the customer. Through this loop flow all materials and finished goods, all information, even all transactions.

As many companies move into supply chain management strategies, they decide to outsource their logistics activities either partially or completely to companies referred to as third-party logistics (3PL) providers. In the following section, we will provide an overview of the legal nature of logistics contracts, while in section 1.3.3 we will describe the development of the 3PL provider business, and the types of relationships and contractual agreements that can be established between 3PL providers and their clients and partners.

1.3.2 The legal nature of logistics contracts

Any comment that may be made about the concept of logistics, from a legal point of view, is faced with the absence of its own legal regulation on the matter whenever the concept is understood, as we do, from a comprehensive point of view – in other words, as an operation that integrates a series of activities of an extremely diverse nature.

Regulations referring expressly to the term 'logistics' are scarce. And yet, logistics activity is without doubt one of the fundamental pillars of industry and service companies at the turn of the century.[8]

It is difficult to define, in law, the concept of logistics. The concept has arisen more in military and economic fields, and the legal concept being offered (if an exclusively legal concept can be offered) has been a simple development of the economic phenomenon.[9]

In etymological terms, the term derives from the French word *logistique* and originates from the unit in armies that are commissioned with the movement and supply of troops on the field.

As there is no legal definition of the term 'logistics', the European Logistics Association[10] has defined it as:

The organisation, planning, monitoring, and execution of the flow of goods from the development and purchase, through production and distribution, until it is at the disposal of the final consumer in order to satisfy the demands of the market at the minimum cost and capital.

A contract to provide logistics services necessarily presupposes that a company hires logistics operations from 3PL providers. In other words, if it is the company itself that, through its own means, carries out the logistics activity, it will undoubtedly turn to third parties who supply specific goods or services that tend to facilitate this activity (leasing of premises, IT contracts, etc.) but will not *self-contract* the execution of logistics activities.

Therefore, we move into what we can call 'employed or public logistics', which is what the professional 3PL provider carries out in respect of the merchandise of contracting third parties. In contrast, 'independent or private logistics' is what is carried out by the company itself as a necessary complement to the main activity of the company (e.g. manufacturing) and with which, logically, there is no contract to provide logistics services.

The provision of logistics services to third parties by the 3PL provider has to suit the needs of this third party. We have already mentioned at the beginning of this section that the diversity of elements forming the logistics activity makes it difficult to make an appropriate form of logistics agreement.[11] Obviously, not every entity that requires logistics services needs the same provisions; likewise, the treatment given to different goods differs greatly because, to quote an example, the logistical handling is substantially different for a finished vehicle than for dairy products. In addition, the means available to them also have to be different for each type of product.

A contract to provide logistics services is a commercial contract. It is onerous, bilateral and reciprocal, of consecutive and complex redemption. It does not need to be in writing, although there are many advantages to it being formalised.

Conceptually, it can be defined as a contract under which one party, called the 3PL provider, undertakes before another[12] to provide those services of a logistical nature that the latter needs, in exchange for payment of an economic consideration. It is important to keep such a broad definition, due to the multiplicity of operations that may be included, the range of merchandise for which the service may be required and the loose nature of the term 'logistics' itself.

Despite their complexity, contracts to provide logistics services can be grouped into the following categories:[13]

- Contract of transport of merchandise[14]
- Contract of deposit storage (warehousing)
- Other accessory contractual forms

To some extent, each contract to provide logistics services is 'tailor made' for the needs of the user. Yet, even when taking into consideration the specific needs of each user and the national or international nature of the contract, we can still establish a general form of agreement that is most often stipulated in logistics service contracts.

1.3.3 Third-party logistics outsourcing

The third-party logistics (3PL) provider business is developing as a result of the emerging demand for advanced logistics services. New firms from different fields are entering the market, competing with the traditional transport and warehousing firms.

Furthermore, there is a trend to outsource more logistics activities in all industries. The key drivers for this trend are:

- 3PL providers tend to be experts in logistics and, therefore, outsourcing the function permits an organisation to increase focus on its core competencies.
- 3PL providers can scale their labour, warehouse and transportation needs on the basis of the client's demands and market changes.
- Clients can expect improvements in lead-time, fill rates, back orders, inventory and labour costs.
- 3PL providers also facilitate improved capabilities in postponement, merge-in-transit, order-point processing, reverse logistics and other value-added services.

Logistics outsourcing implies the delegation to a 3PL provider of all or part of the logistics services that, previously, were carried out by the company. In other words, it implies the participation of a 3PL provider in the supply chain of the product for the main purpose of:

- Lowering the logistics cost for the company, with the consequent reduction in the price of the product, which is to the user's advantage as it also makes the product more competitive in the market. In addition, the company is able to reroute the resources that were, until then, used for logistics services, into the expansion or improvement of the company's own activity.
- Optimising and improving the supply chain, because these services are entrusted to an entity whose object is precisely to provide these services. This should generally suppose an increase in the quality and a decrease in the price of the product, providing more advantages for the final consumer.

The outsourcing of logistics services should translate into a better price, better service and better quality for the product, which is to the advantage of the final consumer, and which means an improvement of the competitiveness of the company in the market.

As we can see, the specialisation and competitiveness of the current economy have created an important growth in outsourcing logistics services by companies whose main objective is production, manufacturing and distribution. In short, these companies are able to concentrate all of their resources and efforts into their own activity of which, therefore, they are extremely knowledgeable, staying away from the important and rapid advances taking place in logistics management, in favour of using 3PL providers.

In recent years, logistics outsourcing has received a great deal of attention from logistics scholars. Researchers have reported on the outsourcing of logistics functions from several different perspectives (Boyson et al., 1999; Lieb et al., 1993; Lieb and Randall, 1996; Murphy and Poist, 2000). There continues to be an extensive and important focus on logistics outsourcing, mainly due to the fact that the adoption of 3PL providers is expanding in scope (Leahy et al., 1995; Murphy and Poist, 1998; Razzaque and Sheng, 1998).

A 3PL provider is an external provider who manages, controls and delivers logistics activities on behalf of the customer. Modern 3PL providers have emerged as a result of transportation deregulation in the 1980s, along with the customer emphasis on 'core competencies' in the 1990s. According to several studies, in the last decade the 3PL business has grown at a rate of more than 20 per cent a year. Recent studies also show that while 37 per cent of high-volume shippers outsourced transportation in 2000, 82 per cent expect to do so by 2006.

Typical services outsourced to 3PL providers are transportation, warehousing, inventory management, value-added services, information services and design, and re-engineering of the supply chain. Companies that outsource logistics activities to 3PL providers can apply different logistics outsourcing models (Gould, 2003):

1. Acting as a traditional shipper and maintaining internal control of all aspects of logistics design and management.
2. Outsourcing operational control of particular logistics functions of the supply chain.
3. Outsourcing the management and execution of entire portions of the supply chain; retaining control of solutions/systems design, information integration and overall supply-chain strategy.
4. Outsourcing supply-chain management, execution and information integration; retaining control of solutions/systems design and overall supply-chain strategy.
5. Creating overall supply-chain strategy; outsourcing all other aspects of the supply chain.

6. Adopting a turnkey solution, where the logistics partner manages all aspects of the customer's supply chain.

Depending on the individual case, the relationship between the customer and the 3PL provider can be formal or informal. However, this relationship has changed over time, and has moved from focusing solely on the contract, to become more strategic and based on partnership. In addition, in many cases a strategic alliance is created between the 3PL and the client. However, even in cases where strategic alliances are created between the parties, there is usually a contract that supports and regulates the relationship between them.

In research, 3PL providers have been classified by their type of alliance to customers, for example the scope of the partnership, design and management, the degree of customisation and dedication, the knowledge level of shippers and providers, and the material flow characteristics. A further way of differentiating between 3PL providers is to examine the extent to which they themselves are outsourcing certain logistics services.

A logistics alliance can be defined as a long-term partnership arrangement between a customer firm, usually a shipper, and a 3PL provider, in which the latter provides a wide array of logistics services including transportation, warehousing, inventory control, distribution and other value-added activities (Bagchi and Virum, 1996). In a logistics alliance, the parties would ideally consider each other as partners, and their collaboration is based on understanding and defining the customer's logistical needs. According to various studies (Anderson, 1995) the main benefits of logistics alliances are the improvement of economies of scale and scope, efficient operations, bargaining power, range of services, faster learning, network with other providers, knowledge of various kind, fast implementation of new systems, access to markets, restructuring supply chains, reduced investment base and smoother production.

In section 1.3.4 we outline the future trends of logistics relationships and the development of the 3PL business.

1.3.4 Developments and future perspectives

Having examined the historical development of the 3PL business we can confirm that 3PL providers have evolved both in knowledge and technology over time. The first wave of growth of the 3PL business took place in the 1980s, when traditional transport firms developed into 3PL providers. During the second wave, from the early 1990s onwards, firms coming from the parcel service became 3PL integrators.

In the latest wave, the players who enter the 3PL business are consultancy, financial, manufacturing and/or IT management firms. At the same time the times we live in are witnessing a massive consolidation of the logistics industry. In the past three years we have seen mega-mergers: Deutsche Post–AEI–Danzas–DHL–Exel, Kuehne&Nagel–USCO, UPS–Fritz and Exel–T&B–MSAS–Mark VII. However, recent studies on the logistics market (Armstrong & Associates, BG Strategic Advisors Analysis, 2003) show there is still extensive fragmentation in the logistics industry, with significant available market share for small 3PL providers. The available market share for certain logistics activities, such as value-added warehousing, freight forwarding and dedicated contract carriage, ranges from 30 to 80 per cent. Given the fact that these logistics activities are growing at an annual rate of 15–25 per cent, we can predict that the combination of fast growth and extensive fragmentation makes the logistics industry ripe for consolidation (Gordon, 2003). A growing market can support a broad range of successful companies that attract expansion-minded buyers. At the same time, fragmentation translates into a bunch of small acquisition opportunities for larger companies. Furthermore, as the market inevitably matures, businesses that were accustomed to more than 20 per cent growth are likely to supplement their organic operations with mergers and acquisitions.

There are three main underlying reasons for powerful consolidation:

1. The development of a new type of logistics management company, called the lead logistics provider (LLP).
2. The development of new, sophisticated and expensive technology solutions that only the strong 3PL providers can afford.
3. The emergence of cash-rich buyers seeking logistics targets and acquisitions.

The LLPs offer shippers a wide range of outsourcing services through a single point of contact (also named one-stop shopping). They also provide broad geographical coverage, as well as sophisticated technology capabilities. Typically, the LLP relies on a network of smaller 3PL subcontractors to deliver these services.

Pioneers in using LLPs are General Motors and Nortel, both of which by 2001 decided to outsource billions of dollars in logistics spending. General Motors sought an LLP with the technological capabilities to cut dealer order-entry cycles from 60 days down to 15. This LLP was formed through a joint venture between General Motors and Menlo Logistics where both companies now share board seats and equity stakes. Nortel, meanwhile, looked for a logistics partner to help it free up hundreds of millions of dollars in working capital and inventory.

Few companies can actually meet the LLPs' broad range of capabilities (Gordon, 2003), which include:

- Multimodal expertise in services including truckload, less than truckload, intermodal, air, ocean and warehousing.
- A global geographical scope that covers all locations relevant to the client's supply chain.
- Complex management skills to perform 'master contracting' solutions, where the LLP manages other smaller 3PL providers in subcontracting relationships.
- Analytical know-how to provide shippers with a thoughtful, strategy-led approach that identifies opportunities for outsourcing to add value.
- Powerful technology systems to manage massive flows of data, synthesise them into meaningful reports and recommend courses of action.
- The financial resources to provide solutions such as the upfront purchase of a shipper's logistics division, combined with a willingness to enter into risk and reward-sharing contracts.

In the electronics and high-tech industry there are major original equipment manufacturers (OEMs) that have recently started seeking outsourcing partners able to provide the combined roles of contract manufacturing (CM) and LLP. As a result, 3PL providers are being asked to perform more advanced technical services for their electronics and high-tech customers, while contract manufacturers are increasing their logistics services, further blurring the line between these two types of service providers (Hannon, 2002). As well as 3PL providers expanding their CM services, there are contract manufacturers moving into the sphere of logistics. In fact, major contract manufacturers are increasingly taking the role of an LLP within the electronics industry, with a great need for top-tier 3PL partners that provide global solutions in freight, warehousing, value-added services and IT connectivity (Coia, 2003). The result will be participants in the 3PL and the CM industries meeting halfway, and creating a new type of company that offers a blend of CM and supply chain management services. Moreover, channel partners are also becoming important players in the supply chain, aiming to provide global supply chain solutions to OEM customers. All the above cases reflect the trend of 3PL providers, contract manufacturers and channel partners seeking to become one-stop shops or lead supply chain (LSC) providers for the OEM customers.

In a context where customers want complete supply-chain capabilities, we can see the next generation of supply-chain outsourcing in the form of the fourth party logistics (4PL) providers. The 4PL provider integrates the supply chain: they assess, design, implement and execute global solutions, combining their own experience with the experience of other suppliers. The 4PL provider reflects the way in which the supply is evolving, in that they bring together the capabilities of the 3PL providers, technology service providers and business process consultants, in order to provide value-added solutions for the entire organisation. The term 4PL was coined by the consulting firm Accenture in the 1990s and it was originally used to describe the act of using a consulting firm – the fourth party referred to – to integrate and manage a company's logistics resources and providers, including 3PL providers and transportation companies.

At first it was believed that the 4PL provider had to be a consulting firm, which indeed it often is. However, there are several LLPs coming from the 3PL business which, due to their system capabilities, service offerings and geographic scope are taking on the role of the 4PL provider quite successfully for some of their clients. 3PL providers that are in the process of evolving into 4PL providers focus on specialist niches for a few customers, where knowledge can be both adapted and developed to a large extent, and can still be used for coordinating the customers' activities (Hertz and Alfredsson, 2003). If a company is looking for a neutral 4PL provider that has no interest in providing any of the services, then a consulting firm may be the best choice as the 4PL provider. On the other hand, if a company is looking for a 4PL provider that understands the nuances of providing supply-chain services based on its own experience in logistics, then the choice should be an LLP. Nevertheless, it seems important for some of the LLPs aiming to be 4PL providers to detach themselves from their parent firms and become separate units, allowing their customers to trust them to play a more neutral role.

One conclusion that can be drawn from the current and future trends in the outsourcing of logistics, is that logistics contracts between shippers and 3PL providers, LLP or 4PL providers may be relatively complex from both a legal and business point of view. Most logistics contracts reflect a combination of warehousing, multimodal transportation and any other value-added activity of the supply chain such as inbound logistics, postponement, distribution, reverse logistics, etc. Contracts of this type are most likely to be contracted between 3PL providers and clients located in more than one country, while their respective legal entities could well be located in yet different countries. To look further at this aspect, section 1.3.5 will offer a review of the legal framework of logistics contracts, with reference to the international perspective and legal implications.

1.3.5 The legal framework of logistics contracts

A logistics contract may be used as a basis for outsourcing, and because there is a multitude of activities that are carried out in outsourcing, similar problems can arise from logistics contracts as those arising from outsourcing contracts. The lack of specific regulations regarding logistics contracts means that the parties must apply the regulations (national or international) that govern the activities that are going to be carried out by the 3PL provider (or similar activities) by analogy.

On this basis, the principle of freedom of contract applies to any contract to provide services, such that the parties are free to establish rights and obligations, as well as the legislation that shall regulate their relations. However, as this situation is not desirable, the parties usually agree as to which law will apply to their relations, regardless of the scope of the contract (i.e. national, international or multi-jurisdictional), respecting imperative laws at all times. Typical examples would include contractual provisions concerning the regulation of tax and employment matters.

In these circumstances, assuming that there is a multi-jurisdictional relationship, we believe that the ideal structure would be for the parties to agree on a framework contract that sets forth the basic rules and guiding principle, which will subsequently be developed or modified by local contracts in each of the countries where the services are going to be carried out.[15] This approach should be adopted, unless the specific circumstances of the given situation mean that this would not be advisable. Moreover, the proposed structure (framework agreement and local contracts) encourages and facilitates the exercise of control.

1.3.6 General requirements for developing the activity

In accordance with the circumstances described above, a 3PL provider or *logistics operator* would be an individual who is professionally devoted to the provision of logistics services to third parties.

As indicated above, there is no general regulation or legal definition of the 3PL provider or logistics operator within European market legislation; moreover, overall the tendency is for the legislative initiative to focus more on the transport market as a whole rather than on the logistics market.

Nevertheless, we can still find some definitions of logistics or logistics operators in certain EU national regulations. For example, in Spain, an indirect definition[16] can be found in the land transport legislation which, while not referring expressly to 'logistics operators', does refer to the 'warehouse owner-distributor':[17]

> Storage-distribution companies are the private individuals or legal persons that receive external merchandise or goods on deposit at their storerooms or premises. In relation thereto, they carry out the functions of storage, opening of loads and other complementary functions that may be necessary, and they undertake or administer the distribution of the same, in accordance with the instructions of the depositing parties.

Also, in Portugal, the definition of the *freight forwarder* contains a specific reference to the activity of logistics. The law stipulates that the freight forwarder activity include the carrying out of logistical and operational services:[18] 'The forwarding activity consists of performing logistical and operational services which include the planning, monitoring, co-ordination, and management relating to the expedition, receipt, warehousing, and distribution of merchandises...'

Overall, in almost every European country it is stipulated in some way that any activity carried out by one of the above-mentioned entities (freight forwarders, warehouse owners-distributors or transport companies) is subject to the prior obtaining of an administrative authorisation. This authorisation can be obtained from the competent public authority upon meeting the requirements concerning merchandise transport agencies, forwarding agents or warehouse owner-distributor companies. These requirements are summed up as follows:

1. The activity can only be carried out in a European country by a private individual or legal person who is a national of the country where the activity is to be carried out, or of a different member state of the European Union, or of a third-party state. In the latter case, the activity must be carried out in accordance with the principles of international conventional reciprocity.
2. The applicant must have accredited fulfilment of what is referred to as professional capability.
3. The applicant must have the required financial capability, and in some countries there is a requirement of honourability.

4. In order to be able to apply for an authorisation, the applicant must comply with and be up to date with all fiscal, employment and corporate obligations.
5. In some countries, the applicant has a further obligation to comply with the health, safety and hygiene requirements, as well as requirements regulating the conditions in general deposit warehouses. The applicant must also have premises available, which are open to the public, that are distinct from their private domicile.
6. Activities must be exclusively devoted to those relating to transport, and must comply with the legal provisions concerning the opening of premises. These premises must be suitable in terms of surface area and have the technical resources available for carrying out of the activity. Finally, the applicant must take out insurance to cover any damage that the merchandise could suffer during the period of storage.

To sum up briefly, we can state that the activities stated above can only be carried out by such persons who hold a permit. This permit can be obtained by submitting an application (usually on a standard printed form), accrediting that the documentation complies with the above-mentioned requirements.

In Table 1.1 we summarise the requirements of some European countries to carry out the activity.

Table 1.1   Some European countries' requirements for carrying out logistics

Requirements	Accrediting documentation
Accrediting personality	
Spain	• Fiscal Identification Number • Deed of incorporation, duly inscribed in the Companies Register and, as appropriate, • Deed of amendment or extension to the corporate purpose, in order to be able to carry out the activity
France	• Deed of Incorporation duly inscribed in the Commercial Registry • Certificate of Professional Capability • Certificate of non-bankruptcy • Certificate of financial capability • Financial balance sheet for the previous two years

24

Table 1.1 Some European countries' requirements for carrying out logistics – *continued*

Requirements	Accrediting documentation
Portugal	• By-laws • Deed of Incorporation, duly inscribed in the Commercial Registry • Police records for managers and managing directors • *Certificate de Insurance* for a third-part insurance policy

Professional capability

Spain	Document to confirm possession of a certificate of professional capability to carry out the activities of an agency, transport company or *storage company-distributor* by the individual who undertakes the effective management of the company, submitting the following documents: • Certificate of Capability • Power of attorney to represent both the availability of the accounts and the funds of the company in favour of the individual who provides the capability • Document substantiating that such an individual appears among the company workforce as a staff manager and that he is registered with the Social Security system or that he holds 15% of the share capital of the company
France	• Written examination • Diploma • 5 years of professional experience as a director of a company (*enterprise* or *commissionnaire de transport*) or a road transport (*routier*) company
Portugal	• A certificate from the General Directorate of Land Transport (DGTT) stating that a technical director has the professional capacity to carry out forwarding activity and effectively runs the company on a permanent and exclusive basis. The certificate can be obtained by means of a: – Written examination – Providing evidence of 5 years' professional experience as a director of a forwarding company and passing a specific exam determined by the *juri de exames* (tribunal)

Table 1.1 Some European countries' requirements for carrying out logistics –
continued

Requirements	Accrediting documentation
Honourability	
Spain	• A declaration of responsibility from each of the individuals who effectively run the company on a permanent basis
France	A declaration of responsibility. Any of the following: • The managers of companies of limited responsibility • The chair of the board of directors, the members of the board of directors and the general manager of public limited companies • The person who assures the permanent and real activity of the company
Portugal	A certificate issued by the Criminal Registry (*Certidao do registro criminal*) referring to any and all the directors, managers or general managers of the company
Economic capability	
Spain	Document justifying the availability of paid-up share capital and reserves of at least 60,000 euros. One of the following documents is to be submitted: • Accounting documentation of the company • Certificate issued by the secretary of the board of directors or equivalent body, with the approval of the chairman, relating to the share capital and reserves that appear in the latest official balance sheet
France	Availability of own capital or bank guarantee of at least 22,800 euros. The amount of the bank guarantees cannot exceed half of the total amount, i.e. 11,400 euros
Portugal	Document duly registered in the Commercial Registry confirming availability of 50,000 euros
Obligations of a fiscal nature	
Spain	Document confirming that the bearer is up to date with any fiscal obligations, submitting the following documents:

Table 1.1 Some European countries' requirements for carrying out logistics –
continued

Requirements	Accrediting documentation
	• Receipt of payment of the IAE (business activities tax). A new company must provide evidence of the corresponding registration • Certificate from the Spanish Inland Revenue that accredits: – Having filed the annual VAT return and the four most recent quarterly returns. If it is a new company, the corresponding registration must be submitted – Having filed the annual companies tax return and the last three declarations relating to payments on account. A new company must provide evidence of the corresponding registration
France	Not applicable
Portugal	Not applicable

2
Contract to Provide Logistics Services: a General Overview

2.1 Introduction

Any discussion about the concept of logistics from a legal standpoint is conditioned by the absence of regulations that specifically cover this concept in the most comprehensive sense of the word, i.e. as an operation that integrates a series of extremely diverse activities.

Regulations that expressly refer to the term 'logistics' are scarce. Yet logistics activities have undoubtedly been one of the fundamental pillars of industry since the turn of the century.

The absence of specific legal provisions, the diversity of the activities that a 3PL provider may carry out, and the diverse areas and products to which logistics operations can refer make it difficult to establish a priori a single model contract for logistics services. Nevertheless, professional experience shows us that when negotiating a contract the parties (customer and 3PL provider) pay little attention to its content aside from those matters related to the technical, economic or operative aspects of the contract. The parties' main concern, and without doubt the key to the success of any logistics contract, is the negotiation of the price and the performance levels that the 3PL provider must achieve while rendering the services. Nevertheless, there is more to a logistics contract, and these elements alone are not sufficient to ensure efficient and trouble-free relations during the contract. Parties do not pay much attention to other contractual clauses that, though in principle could be regarded as less important or of no importance whatsoever, may prove to be of great assistance in resolving disputes that arise between the parties.

27

The aim of this chapter is to determine and analyse what the basic content of a logistics contract should be, based on our own professional experience. We begin with the negotiations between the parties who intend to enter into a contract, briefly analysing how they are normally handled, the documents signed (in particular, letters of intent) and the consequences thereof. We will then undertake a comprehensive review of a contract by studying and analysing the contents clause by clause, from both a legal and an economic perspective. Finally, we will provide the reader with a model contract that we are aware will fail to meet all needs, although we hope it may prove to be useful when negotiating a contract.

2.2 Preliminary acts to concluding the contract: the letter of intent

Having proven the level of complexity that contracts entail in providing logistical services, and bearing in mind the numerous activities that their provision implies, it can be said that in principle, each service seeker would require an individualised form of contractual treatment, to fit the needs that they wish to cover.

The 3PL provider who wishes to conclude a contract with a person seeking his services has to be an expert in respect of the needs of his customer, in order to design the logistical operation in such a way that it satisfies those requirements in terms of service, cost and quality. In fact, it is the fulfilment of these very requirements that defines logistics.

The number and importance of logistical requirements will determine the length and complexity of the negotiation process prior to concluding a definitive contract. During the negotiation process both parties will establish the most important foundations for what will be concluded when the contract is finalised.

Therefore, in order to clarify the future contractual relationship, especially in logistical contracts that have a certain complexity (i.e. the acquisition of assets of the company seeking logistics, construction of warehouses) parties often conclude, prior to the contract, a so-called *letter of intent*.[1]

The letter of intent is generally defined as the document in which the parties set out their wish to enter or conclude a contract, without it being binding for either party. This, however, is a definition which is, by any standards, imprecise and based exclusively on a literal interpretation of the term, and which on numerous occasions stands in contradiction to the actual content.[2]

The obligatory, hence binding nature of the conditions established therein by the parties will depend on the content and scope that the parties wish to grant to the letter of intent.

As has been stated above, what commonly occurs in practice is that the letter of intent only reflects the desire of the parties to negotiate on the basis of some specific circumstances and conditions, with the intention that if it becomes feasible, a definitive contract may be signed, but after further negotiation.

A letter of intent may, therefore, be (i) a simple document in which the parties limit themselves to recording what has been agreed so far, without any firm undertaking to conclude a definitive contract in the future, with the clear assumption that for the negotiations to be successful the conditions established in the letter cannot be modified, in other words, if a contract is to be signed, then the agreements established in the letter of intent have to be reflected in that contract[3] or, on the other hand, (ii) an authentic undertaking, in order words a pre-contract[4] to concluding the definitive contract.

As contracts to provide logistics services do not need to be in writing, it is clear that this letter of intent is not, in any way, a compulsory requirement for the signing of a contract to provide logistics services. As a consequence, the parties do not have to produce such a letter if they do not consider it to be necessary.

2.3 General premises of the contract to provide logistics services

One aspect that specifically characterises the contract to provide logistics services is that of collaboration between the 3PL providers and their customers. If one ignores this perspective, it is difficult to understand the subcontracting of logistics services and, consequently, the contractual relationships that must bind both parties.

From the fact that collaboration and mutual support are essential between the parties, it is easy to deduce what the most fundamental aspects of the content of the contract will be. The 3PL provider and the customer are not opposing parties but 'partners' in the same venture or, as expressed by P. Budgen (1999), the contract to provide logistics services implies a 'society' or 'association' between the 3PL provider and the customer. The logistics contract, therefore, may reach the point of signifying something similar to a 'partnership' for the parties that sign it.

Therefore, it is common, and without doubt to some extent advisable, that the contract to provide logistics services should contain clauses (called clauses on 'Representatives') stipulating the designation, by each of the parties, of a person responsible for following through the operation (*person responsible for the contract*), who will have decisive and binding powers in respect of the daily operations that the activity involves and, also, the formation of a *contract monitoring committee* made up of representatives of one party or the other, that should meet, in periodic or extraordinary meetings, to analyse and evaluate the development of the contracted activity, solve any small hiccups or difficulties that could arise from the logistics operation (claims, supplies or stocks, administration, etc.).

2.4 Content of the contract to provide logistics services

As mentioned previously, each logistics contract is tailor-made, making it difficult to establish a standard form of contract. However, we believe that any contract to provide logistics services must have a minimum content, this being subject, of course, to multiple variations, depending on the agreements reached by the parties, and on the services or activities requested by the customer and to be provided by the 3PL provider.

For this reason, and despite our assessment that a general and standard form of contract does not exist, in the following section we will try to determine and analyse the content of the contract that, from our point of view, should always appear in a logistics contract. Complementary to this comprehensive review of the contract, we will provide the reader with a model contract in Appendix 2. Finally, Appendix 4 shows the logistics contract structure and the usage in percentages of the main clauses in European logistics contracts (Jané, 2005).

2.4.1 Scope of the contract

When defining the scope of a 3PL's services, it is important to specify any assumptions, guarantees or limitations relating to the provision of these services. The scope of the contract should be able to provide answers to the questions of what services the 3PL is going to provide, and where, when and how the 3PL will provide these services. Therefore, it is vital to define, as precisely as possible:

(a) The products of the customer that the logistics activity provided by the 3PL provider deals with.

(b) The collection and delivery points of the products and their geographic location (i.e. stating the province, region, and whether they are national or international deliveries).

2.4.2 The logistics platform

The logistics activity as we understand it revolves around a platform, be it a warehouse, open area, terminal, etc., to which the 3PL provider has access, in any of the forms recognised by the law (ownership, leasing, dispensation, etc.).

The person or entity that provides this platform must also be reflected in the contract, distinguishing between the 'out of house' provision of logistics services, where the 3PL provider provides the platform, and, 'in-house' provision where the logistics services are carried out in facilities provided by the customer.

Therefore, agreements about the platform can be extremely diverse:

(a) The platform from which the logistics activity is carried out can be the property of the customer, in which case, the 3PL provider by virtue of what has been agreed may, for example, lease it from the customer, enjoy it in the capacity of precarious tenant, acquire the platform by means of a sale, or simply be authorised to carry out the activity on it.

(b) It may belong to the 3PL provider either because he is the owner, or because he has it under lease, dispensation, usufruct or any other right that allows him to use it.

(c) The platform may have to be constructed or purchased, reflecting the needs of the customer. In this case, as it represents an important investment, it will be necessary to specify who has to construct it, and under which terms, conditions, etc. and who will count as the owner.

In any case, the platform has to be suitable and meet the necessary requirements for the storage and handling of the products commissioned from the 3PL provider. For this reason, not all platforms are the same, in the sense that they do not all have a large building or warehouse, nor do they all have identical equipment: for example, shelving would be necessary for the logistics activity of some products, but not for others. For example, different conditions and means of storage are required for pallets, containers, vehicles, bulk cargo, gas or liquid products.

Similarly, in addition to the administrative authorisation required for carrying out an activity, depending on the products managed (pharmaceuticals, dangerous goods, goods destined for consumption,[5] etc.) it may be necessary to obtain another type of authorisation or to fulfil specific requirements.

Clearly, all of this implies not only significant technical activity, but also activity of a legal nature. But the truth is that the platform forms the nerve centre of any logistics activity.

2.4.3 Exclusivity

In the contract the parties may stipulate the exclusivity either of the 3PL provider, or of the customer or of both parties, limiting it to the products referred to in the contract to provide logistics services and the territorial scope in which these services must be provided.

It is important to point out that the agreement of exclusivity can entail a double 'risk' for the parties. For the 3PL providers, while on the one hand, it is guaranteed that the products defined by the contract, within the defined territorial ambit, are going to be solely provided by themselves without having to deal with competitors and obtaining, in principle, a remuneration that, although variable, can be qualified as stable, they are, at the same time, restricting their possibilities for attracting new customers with the same products – on the understanding that these are their speciality – within the same general area in which they are located. As a result, possibilities of expansion and income are greatly reduced, forcing them to find other areas of development.

Customers, for their part, have the advantage of being able to count on a 3PL provider that they have chosen for the value for money offered, which, in principle, gives them an advantage over their competitors. However, they will be exclusively bound to this 3PL provider, with the disadvantages that can result from a lack of competitiveness in a highly competitive market.

As mentioned above, the agreement of exclusivity can be limited to certain products, areas, named entities, specific contracted activities, etc. In this sense, it seems a good idea in all cases to limit the exclusivity to such obligations that are considered essential. In the case of transport, for example, it would appear logical that this exclusivity does not exist, so that the vehicles may be completed with third-party loads, and take advantage of the return journeys, in this way lowering the cost of the activity.

In any case, whether exclusivity exists or not, the fact is that the parties must comply with the agreement of confidentiality, which we will discuss later, to ensure that their competitors, in their respective areas of business, do not have access to the techniques, procedures, know-how, etc. developed by each of the parties.

2.4.4 Obligations of the 3PL provider: the services undertaken

2.4.4.1 Services and requirements

The complexity and diversity of logistics activities are reflected, basic-ally, in the variety of operations that the 3PL provider may undertake under the contract to provide logistics services.

We already mentioned some – and only some – of these, when we wrote that the 3PL provider carries out activities of transport and distri-bution of merchandise, storage, load-splitting operations, handling, administration, stock control (of the number of goods, class, reference, etc. and of its state, period of life, and expiry, etc.), preparation of orders and inventories, etc.

The fact is that in general, providing logistics services usually means that the 3PL provider assumes the following tasks and services which, in combination, define the logistics activity:[6]

(a) Reception of the products or merchandise in the customer's factory or warehouse either 'at loading bay' – in which case loading and packing the vehicle are the responsibility of the 3PL provider – or 'at vehicle' – in which case the loading is the cus-tomer's responsibility.

(b) Transport from the factory to the 3PL provider's platform or, as the case may be, reception of the product delivered by the cus-tomer to the 3PL provider's own warehouses, either 'at vehicle' – in which case the 3PL provider carries out the unloading – or, less commonly, 'at loading bay' – in which case the customer carries out the unloading after the 3PL provider has received the merchandise.

It is essential that the contract include the correct delimitation of the moment of reception (in the customer's facilities, in the 3PL provider's facilities, at vehicle, at loading bay, etc.), as this will be the moment at which the 3PL provider assumes custody of the merchandise and, consequently, it will mark the starting point of the 3PL provider's liability.[7]

In this sense, there are several aspects that must be reflected cor-rectly in the contract, among them:

(i) Delivery times to the platform and, if appropriate, notifica-tion of dispatch for storage.

(ii) Load units in which the product is received (e.g. pallets, con-tainers, boxes).

(iii) Deconsolidation operations of the loads or load units received.

(iv) Checking, at the time of reception, the state, quantity, qual-ity, etc. of the products that are received for storage and, if appropriate, noting down these details on the delivery notes and notifying the customer.

(c) Storage or deposit of the merchandise received at the platform, meaning the location of the merchandise on the platform, for which any number of specific areas, or shelf space, etc. may have been contracted. In any event, the 3PL provider must try to optimise the space available at the platform whenever that would have a positive economic impact for both parties.

Depending on the nature of the product, certain storage rules and practices will have to be observed. For example, storage in refrigerated chambers, which requires constant temperature monitoring, is not the same as storage of general merchandise.

Also, a space may be set aside for depositing products that were rejected at destination, or expired, defective, etc.

(d) Stock control, which means not only stocktaking at intervals agreed between the parties, but also other series of activities related to the stored merchandise, which could include confirming the reception of products, giving notification of incident, verifying the state of products, monitoring products entering and leaving, etc. so that, at any given moment, the 3PL provider can determine the merchandise available, the need for replacements, the state of the merchandise, etc.

(e) Preparing orders or 'picking' is one of the main logistics activities carried out by the 3PL provider. The contract must determine the system of rotation of the products (LIFO, FIFO, etc.), which fundamentally will depend on their nature (i.e. on whether they are products of high or low rotation).

Also, preparing products generally involves labelling of the packages, or even the product, producing the corresponding invoice or delivery note, etc.

(f) Distributing the orders to the delivery points (normally, the customers of the logistics customer organisation or, in the event of provision, the actual manufacturing factory). This requires first locating the orders and loading them onto the means of transport.

It is necessary to define the delivery periods, the delivery times at each point (in order to avoid the invariably inconvenient waits at the destination points), the way and time frame for the final recipients to make any claims, the procedures to be followed in the event of rejection of the merchandise by the recipient, etc.

There are infinite possibilities for the provision of logistics services. For example, the 3PL provider may provide, on behalf of the customer, other services, such as:

(i) Shelf-stocking or merchandising.
(ii) Preparing the necessary documentation, depending on the type of merchandise.
(iii) Labelling and packaging the products for sale.
(iv) Arranging customs clearance of the merchandise.
(v) Processing any claims.
(vi) Reverse logistics.
(vii) Repairing damaged merchandise.
(viii) Participating in the manufacturing process of the product.
(ix) Other services.

Given the range and variety of aspects to be regulated between the parties, often many of those concerning the provision of services are regulated by adding an annex that refers to a manual of operations or procedures.[8]

Each activity to be carried out requires close collaboration and co-operation and, without question, a constant flow of information between the 3PL provider and the customer of the services, irrespective of what the logistics processes and systems utilised may be.

We should not forget here to highlight the vital role played by information technology, not only as a means of managing the warehouse itself, but also through allowing a constant flow of information that must exist between the parties in order for the contract to provide logistics services to be put into correct and optimum practice – notifications of the receipt of merchandise, requests to prepare orders, notification of incident, etc.

2.4.4.2 Service level agreements

The obligation of the 3PL provider is to provide the logistics services to the customer as previously described in terms of scope, platform and operating requirements in order to meet a certain service level. Therefore, in conjunction with the contract, by means of an appendix or a specific clause, the customer often chooses to introduce a mechanism for managing expectations and checking and reviewing whether the service obligations undertaken by the 3PL provider have been fulfilled. This is commonly called the *service level agreement* (SLA).

SLAs are mutually agreed upon between the parties and usually refer to qualitative logistics service specifications according to type of service. Therefore, both parties reach agreement on a list of key performance indicators (KPIs), meaning logistics service variables, together with their corresponding goals and limits.

By virtue of executing an SLA, the customer is seeking primarily to create a common understanding concerning the services, priorities and responsibilities of the 3PL provider, with the aim of protecting itself against the worst-case scenario. One researcher has pointed out that an SLA is nothing more than an insurance policy and therefore does not guarantee levels of service but rather provides compensation should things go wrong.

However, on many occasions the parties do not pay close attention to the details. Thus, it is quite common for either of the parties to try to impose its standard agreements on the other. This common practice should be avoided, and the parties would be well-advised to take all the time and effort needed to develop the SLA that fits with the specific business or services to be performed.

Nevertheless, there are certain basic elements that can always be found in an SLA in order for it to be effective, namely, it must include two sets of basic elements referring to both services and management.

The service elements clarify services by conveying information such as:

(a) The services provided (and perhaps certain services not provided)
(b) Conditions of service availability
(c) Service standards, such as the time frames for services to be provided
(d) Both parties' responsibilities
(e) Cost/service trade-offs
(f) Escalation procedures
(g) Protections and remedies to be implemented upon repeated failures

The management elements focus on issues such as:

(a) Tracking service effectiveness
(b) Reporting and addressing information about service effectiveness
(c) Resolving any service-related disagreements
(d) Reviewing and revising the agreement

Aside from reflecting the above-mentioned elements, and along the lines of viewing the SLA as an insurance policy which provides compensation should things go wrong, the agreement should foresee the consequences of failure by the 3PL providers to meet defined SLAs. Penalties can be applied every time an SLA is not met, meaning that the lowest acceptable limit of a certain KPI is not reached. Depending on the main goals of the agreement, penalties can be related to KPIs in quality, delivery, material supply, inventory control and so forth. Penalties are usually calculated as a percentage over revenue, that percentage having a variable value depending on how far the actual KPI is compared to the lowest acceptable limit. In terms of frequency, penalties can be calculated every agreed period, with monthly or quarterly being the most common. The longer the calculation period, the smoother the impact on the penalty amount because the average value can absorb short-term poor performance.

In addition to penalties, other agreements can also include so-called *rewards* or *bonus*. Rewards usually have the same principle as penalties with the sole difference that they benefit the 3PL provider should certain SLAs exceed the highest agreed goal for a given KPI. A contract that includes both penalties and rewards is usually called a *bonus/malus* contract.

2.4.5 Obligations of the customer: paying the price

The customer, in paying the 3PL provider, provides the remuneration for the provision of the services undertaken and, therefore, this is the customer's most important obligation.

As in most contracts, the parties may freely stipulate the price. However, the overall complexity of contracts to provide logistics services – which sometimes prevents the determining of an initial price – has created certain systems of payment which, although not exclusive to logistics contracts, do fit the provision of logistics services.

There are two main remuneration systems for outsourced logistics contracts, these being the fixed remuneration system and the variable remuneration system. Each remuneration system can be based upon different pricing models, as will be explained below. In addition, we will discuss 'gain sharing' as a complementary practice that can be used in conjunction with the selected pricing model.

2.4.5.1 Fixed remuneration system

The fixed remuneration system is the most popular and extensive remuneration system, where the customer firm agrees to pay the 3PL provider a fixed amount for providing logistics services. This remuneration system is applied in accordance with the pricing models agreed on by the two parties: transactional pricing or activity-based costing.

2.4.5.1.1 Transactional pricing or unit pricing. In the transactional pricing model the fixed amount to pay is worked out by applying the contractually agreed price or flat fee per unit of work. A unit of work can be contractually defined in different ways: it can be the number of pallets or boxes loaded, or the number of references or cases handled, or the weight of the merchandise managed, or the amount of space utilised in the warehouse (measured in shelves, shelf space, square or cubic metres, etc.), or the number of orders prepared, etc. Overall, it also depends on the function of the services contracted from the 3PL provider, which could be storage and management of stock, transport, picking, etc.

On the one hand the unit pricing structure is easy to design and implement; on the other 3PL providers tend to overestimate their unit price in order to minimise risk and guarantee that their fixed costs are covered.

2.4.5.1.2 Activity-based costing. In the activity-based costing model the customer firm agrees to pay a flat fee to cover the 3PL provider's fixed costs, including any leases, equipment, racking and management. They also commit themselves to a fee to cover variable costs such as labour, fuel and equipment maintenance, worked out on the basis of the unit pricing method explained above. The fixed remuneration system based on the activity-based costing model reflects more accurately the services rendered and expenses incurred, and 3PL providers do not need to augment the unit price to safeguard themselves against losses arising from their fixed costs.

Regardless of which pricing model the two parties agree upon, the fixed remuneration system is usually subject to the revision clauses, that generally have an annual frequency and make reference to the retail price index.

2.4.5.2 Variable remuneration system

If the payment of the 3PL provider does not involve payment of a fixed amount, then we can talk about the cost-plus pricing concept.

2.4.5.2.1 Cost-plus pricing. Cost-plus pricing, also known as open book, is a remuneration system consisting of a fee for the actual costs incurred by the 3PL provider for providing the logistics services, plus a mutually agreed upon mark-up or profit margin. Together with the cost-plus pricing system, the open book concept allows the customer firm to audit all invoices from operations carried out by the 3PL provider that have been charged to the contract account.

In summary, the cost-plus remuneration system implies, at least, the following:

(a) The customer pays the 3PL provider for the costs and expenses that are accrued by the provision of the hired services.

(b) The 3PL provider must usually open a specific account for each customer that is kept separate from other activities carried out, and that the customer has access to at any time. This also allows the 3PL provider to justify the amount of the charges passed on to that customer. With respect to the 3PL provider's general expenses, from which the customer also benefits, the rule of apportionment seems to be most appropriate – although, as we keep mentioning, every logistics operation is unique.

(c) The customer has to pay the 3PL provider an additional sum, usually established as a percentage of the costs incurred in the operation, this representing the 3PL provider's profit.

The cost-plus remuneration system is especially effective if the contractual assignment is changing in nature. To quote an example, a company that is starting new operations, launching a new product or undergoing some other transition that makes logistics requirements volatile.

The main advantage of the cost-plus pricing is that on one hand 3PL providers are guaranteed a profit over the operations, while on the other customer firms can exercise some control over the costs, and reduce the risk of the sort of overestimated fees that can arise with transactional pricing.

However, the cost-plus remuneration system itself does not encourage the 3PL provider to reduce costs, because each cost carries a specified profit margin, which is why it is not usually a viable long-term pricing model. Unless the contract includes additional 'gain sharing' clauses, the cost-plus remuneration system will presuppose the optimisation of means and resources by the 3PL provider, in his status as a logistics professional. Clearly, the 3PL provider will have greater incentive to reduce costs and expenses, in the case of mutually agreed 'gain sharing' practices applied in conjunction with cost-plus pricing.

Finally, it is worth mentioning that cost-plus pricing also involves another series of specifications of an economic accounting[9] nature which are beyond the scope of the simplifying and all-inclusive objective of this work but which without any doubt must be borne in mind when drawing up a cost-plus pricing contract.

2.4.5.3 Gain sharing

Regardless of which pricing structure is chosen, it is advisable to have some form of incentive for continuous improvement. Gain sharing is a system that allows both parties to share any benefits gained from optimising a logistics process or system. This practice entails a joint effort by both organisations to continuously bring down the costs and improve performance. Indeed, gain sharing agreements will help 3PL providers to invest in processes, technology and IT, in order to improve services and/or cut down on costs. In view of the fact that customer firms tend to outsource more complex and global logistics processes to advanced 3PL providers, lead logistics providers or 4PL providers, gain sharing becomes an excellent method for encouraging continuous improvements with respect to efficiency through a logistics contract.

Gain sharing works best in new relationships, where the learning curve is highest and there are many opportunities to work smarter. This does not mean precluding the use of gain sharing as an incentive in a long-standing relationship. Opportunities to drive improvement will always exist, but with gain sharing there is a point of diminishing returns.

To sum up, we can state that each outsourcing contract is unique, and the resulting remuneration system may be based on one or more of the pricing models outlined here in combination with other gain sharing or performance rewards. It may also happen that the remuneration system changes and different pricing models are agreed on during the life of the contract.

2.4.5.4 Payment

Without any specifications with regard to any other contract – except those arising from a cost-plus pricing contract – the method and period of payment, issues relating to accrued and effective taxes, etc., should be the object of detailed contractual regulation.

2.4.5.5 Non-performance of the obligation to pay

For the purpose of protecting the interest of the 3PL provider, and without prejudicing any option of imposing interest on the delay in payment or other penalties such as choosing to exercise the right of cancellation under certain circumstances, it is not uncommon to agree on specific measures that the 3PL provider can adopt in the case of non-payment by the customer. In practice, these agreements refer mainly to the following stipulations:

(a) The option of suspending the logistics services provided by the 3PL provider, and
(b) The option for the 3PL provider to retain any of the customer's merchandise that is in the 3PL provider's possession as a guarantee for the payment due by the customer.

From the customer's perspective, none of these options are acceptable, mainly because of the fact that the logistics process is an integrated part of the life cycle of a product and, therefore, it is essential that the product reaches its envisaged destination and to avoid any interruption in the production line, if the logistics services refer to the management of raw material or components.

In most cases the parties must be able to reach an agreement that is feasible for both of them. In the end, the parties usually include the right for the 3PL provider to retain or withhold goods, but they restrict this right to instances of serious and continuous non-payment by the customer.

2.4.5.6 Other obligations of the customer

Depending on the type of logistics contract, the customer is frequently obliged to deliver, to the 3PL provider, a minimum number or volume of merchandise (on, for example, a weekly, monthly or annual basis) for logistical handling. This is due to the fact that, as previously mentioned, the 3PL provider, in order to provide logistics services, is sometimes obliged to make important investments, which could only be redeemed through invoicing, and, therefore, at least a minimum amount can be foreseen from the beginning. This allows the 3PL provider to adjust his costs, and if the minimum volume is not fulfilled, he might agree penalties for the customer.

In any event, even if no volume has been agreed – because the volume could not depend on the logistics customer, but instead could fluctuate according to demands of the final consumers of the product – the customer should, with reasonable advance notice, provide estimates of the volumes that will be delivered within a specified period.

The opposite scenario is even more unusual: a maximum limitation of the products to be delivered to the 3PL provider. This situation may arise because the 3PL provider has limitations on available facilities, as a consequence of other commitments. The common practice, should the initially envisaged volume of merchandise be exceeded by a specific percentage, is that this should be communicated to the 3PL provider sufficiently in advance; furthermore, should this not be done, the 3PL provider is exonerated from all liability for non-performance for provision of the services.

Therefore, the 3PL provider has to know, from the very start, the forecast product movement, in order to be able to organise the logistics activity accordingly. This information should be provided by the customer and updated in case of any modification.

2.4.6 Liability[10]

There is no doubt that in temporary and general terms, the 3PL provider's liability is determined by his obligation of custody, in other words, it lasts from the moment he receives the merchandise until it is has been delivered to the agreed party and place.

In regard to the objective scope of liability, the events that generate liability for the 3PL provider may be summed up as any losses, shortages, damage, breakdowns or delays in delivery of the products for which he is responsible for logistics operations.[11]

Finally, in a subjective scope, the 3PL provider is answerable for any operative events of his liability caused, not only by his dependants, agents, employees, etc., but also for any caused by any person he involves in the act of providing the contracted services.

From a legal point of view, the 3PL provider carries out activities of a diverse nature (as we have already pointed out, the 3PL provider generally carries out, without prejudice to other additional services or contractual forms, at least activities included in a contract of deposit and others which due to their nature qualify as a contract of transport). For this reason, and for want of a uniform legal liability regime for the entire logistics chain, in principle it is necessary to take note and determine this liability, and of the moment in which it occurs (i.e. whether the operative event of the liability has its cause in the activities carried out in the warehouse, be it during loading and unloading or during transport). This is because the established legal liability regime differs substantially for each of the mentioned contracts.

In Chapter 3 we will discuss in depth the liability regime that applies to transport and deposit, here we will sum up the following differences:[12] in cases where the damage occurs during the period of deposit of the merchandise, the liability regime applicable to the 3PL provider will be the following:

(a) *System of responsibility*: in general, warehouse-owner responsibility starts from a presumption of error on the part of the 3PL provider, when the damage to the merchandise occurs under the custody of the receiver.

(b) *Operative events of the 3PL provider's liability*: the receiving 3PL provider is answerable both for any partial or total loss, and any breakdown and damage of the merchandise in his care.

(c) *Extension of liability*: the liability of the depositary lasts from the moment the merchandise is delivered for storage/deposit and custody up until the moment it is delivered to the depositor or another 3PL provider, as per instruction of the owner of this merchandise. Hence, the importance of the above-mentioned agreements regarding loading and unloading, and the contractual provision, if appropriate, of determining the exact moment from which the goods are understood to be in the custody of the 3PL provider.

(d) *Amount of liability*: the depositary of the merchandise is accountable both for the value of the merchandise (with the maximum legal limit of liability) as well as for the amount that could be demanded from him, corresponding to any damage and prejudicial consequences caused by the event for which he is liable, without any limited liability. In short, the depositary is answerable for all damages and prejudicial consequences (without limit).

(e) *Exoneration of liability*: there are no specific clauses to protect the depositary to exonerate him from liability. Therefore, the depositary is liable, in the event of fault, except for any loss or damage which is the result of unforeseeable circumstances or *force majeure*. Unlike the carrier, the depositary is answerable for any damage or loss that is the result of the nature and inherent vices of the merchandise, except in the case where the depositary has done everything possible to avoid damage and has also immediately notified the depositor of the damage.

Meanwhile, in the case of a transport contract, the liability regime for the 3PL provider differs from the depositary in the following ways:

(a) *Amount of liability:* unlike the depositary, the transport operator can benefit from established limits of liability, in this case laid out in 8.33 Special Drawing Rights (SDR) of the Geneva Convention of 19 May 1956 regarding the Contract for the International Carriage of Goods by Road (CMR).

(b) *Exoneration of liability:* in addition to the causes previously stated (*force majeure* and unforeseeable circumstances) the 3PL provider may be exonerated from the presumed liability if he can prove that the damage has been caused by the nature or inherent vice of the merchandise, which are another set of facts that have the effect of exonerating the carrier from legal liability.

However, the carrier cannot be exonerated from his liability – except through accreditation of misrepresentation in the declaration made by the consignor in the consignment note concerning the class or quality of the merchandise – although there may be cause for exoneration if the person with rights over the merchandise proves that the operative event of the liability is caused by negligence, or because he has not taken the usual precautions adopted by a diligent person.

This situation does not differ in any way from that established with regard to the deposit, so there is an assumption of liability of the carrier regarding any loss, damage or delay in delivery that occurs from the moment in which the merchandise is delivered for transport up until delivery to the destination; they are his liability and, as such, he must indemnify the aggrieved party for any damage.

In order to delimit the phase of occurrence of damage or losses it is essential to prepare delivery notes/control documents for each logistical phase of the product. There is no doubt that information technology is an essential instrument for this type of monitoring.

However, in addition to the legal regime mentioned above, it is worth pointing out that contracts to provide logistics services must establish a uniform regime of liability for the 3PL provider, although the legal regime outlined can be, in the majority of cases, contractually revoked or modified. In other words, it is a good idea to establish a regime which applies to any damage, loss or delay incurred while the merchandise is in the custody of the 3PL provider. The following notes give some general definitions of common agreements on such a regime:

(a) In principle, it is presumed that the 3PL provider is liable for any loss, shortage, breakdown, damage or delay in delivery, unless he can provide evidence that it is not due to any fault or negligence on his part.

(b) The liability lasts throughout the period during which the products are in custody of the 3PL provider, and applies to acts or omissions attributable to the 3PL provider, his employees, agents, dependants and subcontractors.

(c) However, there are clearly defined causes for which the 3PL provider is not liable. Some of these may be of a generic nature (force majeure,[13] etc.), others are specific to the contract to provide logistics services (IT system errors, delivery of expired products, etc.).

(d) The 3PL provider will be accountable for the value of the damaged merchandise, in other words, the stated limit will be applied. However, it is vital to specify which merchandise value is being referred to, whether it is the recommended retail price value, or the ex-factory value, or the value on the date of delivery to the recipient, etc., since there may be a significant difference in value between one concept and another for specific products.

The customer must always inform the 3PL provider of the value of the merchandise in advance. This aspect is also necessary for signing the insurance cover.

(e) Given the complexity of some logistics operations and the speed with which they may have to be carried out, a threshold is often contractually established in favour of the 3PL provider, with respect to any loss or shortage of stock in the warehouse or platform. The idea is, in short, to mitigate the common 'differences in stock or inventories' in all logistics operations. Thus, a *maximum acceptable limit of losses in stock* is often established (usually in the form of a percentage) which cannot be claimed against the 3PL provider. Whether or not inventory excess can be compensated with the losses will depend on the contractual agreements reached by the parties.

(f) In principle, the 3PL provider often requests exoneration of liability for indirect and consequential damage[14] or loss of profits, business or revenue and this is specified by means of a contractual clause. The grounds for this request is that such damages are not foreseeable and cannot be properly factored in when the contract is concluded. Although this argument does not lack force, the truth is that the customer has no chance of recovering any losses incurred as a result of any breach of contract by the 3PL provider. Therefore, customers are now requesting to add to the traditional recoverable losses such as wasted expenditure, damage to property and reprocurement costs, some foreseeable losses that may arise in the case of breach of contract, such as third-party claims or regulatory liabilities.

(g) Furthermore, it is always agreed that the 3PL provider will be held liable vis-à-vis the customer for any act or omission caused by his employees, servants or subcontractors hired to carry out any of the services.

2.4.7 Force majeure

Due partly to differences between legal systems, but mainly to the influence of the Anglo-Saxon legal systems, where the concept of force majeure is not a legal concept as is the case in many continental systems, but rather has been created by contractual innovation, the parties commonly agree to include a clause of force majeure which provides a detailed series of events which can be claimed to constitute force majeure. It is usually the 3PL provider that wishes to include a list of events or circumstances as broad as possible, as they are the party that shoulders the greater burden in carrying out most of the obligations.

It is quite common for the parties to include a list of events, not, however, with the intention of making the list exhaustive, thereby entitling the parties to invoke any other event not listed that may prevent, impede or delay the affected party in carrying out its obligations under the contract. The result of invoking and proving that an event of force majeure has occurred is that the affected party should be relieved from a liability which might otherwise arise upon failure by that party to carry out their contractual obligations.

The events commonly listed by the parties are the following:

(i)   The occurrence of natural catastrophes, such as fires, floods and acts of God.

(ii) Man-made interventions, such as war, strikes or legislative interference.

(iii) Change of laws, economic hardship or administrative inconvenience or order or regulations laid down by any authority whatsoever, unless these items are specifically excluded.

In addition to the scope of force majeure, the parties should establish an administrative framework to govern the obligations of each party, the common points being to regulate the following:

(i)   The obligation of the affected party to notify the other party within an early timescale that an event of force majeure has occurred, and to provide full details of the event and of the measures to be taken to overcome or mitigate the effects of the event as much as possible.

(ii) The remedies to be implemented by the parties during the duration of the effects of the event of force majeure. The right to implement the remedies may fall upon either party but it is usually the 3PL provider who has the task of overcoming it, and who is obliged to act as any reasonable and prudent person would do, by adopting any measure that may mitigate the effects, and thereby allowing, to some extent, the services to be continued to be carried out. On the other hand, the customer, in the case of an event of force majeure, is usually granted the right of partial non-payment of services and even, should the 3PL provider not act in accordance with the above-mentioned principles, the right to implement any measure to mitigate or abort the adverse effects of the event. This could include suspending the contract, and at a later stage may be allowed to engage, for the estimated duration of the event, the services of a third party that has not been affected by the event.

(iii) The affected party has the responsibility of proving that the event in question was beyond its reasonable control.

2.4.8 Insurance

With respect to the insurance clause, one should not yield to the temptation – as is prevalent in the sector – to assimilate insurance with liability, as this can have fatal consequences for any collaboration that may exist between the parties.

The parties have to decide which types of insurance to take out, although in general these must include at least the following:

(a) Insurance for damage to merchandise during transport.
(b) Insurance for damage to merchandise in storage (with coverage, if appropriate, for theft, fire, etc.).
(c) Public liability insurance.
(d) Liability insurance derived from damage by defective products.

Here we will concentrate on the first two types, as the third is often written in general terms by the parties, independently of the drawing up of the contract to provide logistics services. The final type is relevant for the customer and not for the 3PL provider.

With regard to the first two types (insurance of merchandise in transit and in storage) the parties will have to determine not only the extent and conditions of coverage (fully comprehensive, exemption, etc.) but also, more importantly, which party should take it out.

As mentioned above, it is essential to determine this point:

(a) If the 3PL provider takes it out, covering the cost with the fee paid by the customer, in the event of damage that is recoverable under the insurance policy, the insurer will either indemnify the 3PL provider or, if appropriate, the customer.
(b) If the customer takes it out, in the event of damage the insurer will indemnify the insured (customer), but will subrogate his rights. This means that unless there is express agreement in the insurance policy to exonerate the 3PL provider, the insurer can claim the indemnity paid to the insured (customer) from the 3PL provider. Therefore, if the parties intend to pass the consequences of an accident concerning assets on to an insurer, what will actually happen is that the 3PL provider will end up assuming these consequences (i.e. the amount arising from the accident).

Therefore, the various consequences that arise from which party takes out the insurance for merchandise must be borne in mind in order to avoid later 'surprises' which may jeopardise the relationship between the contracting parties.

2.4.9 Confidentiality

Starting from the fact that the logistics operation presupposes a close cooperation and mutual understanding between the customer and the 3PL provider, a confidentiality agreement between the parties would appear to be a good idea. The customer must inform the 3PL provider of the needs of the company, its objectives, its productivity and forecasts, etc., if they wish to optimise the service provided. It could also be said that the 3PL provider must be 'integrated' with the customer's company, in view of the importance that, for the latter, the logistics activity implies, and vice versa.[15] It follows that the 3PL provider has to know details of the customer's activities, and that the customer should provide the 3PL provider with any information about the company that could help this 3PL provider to carry out the assignment in a satisfactory manner for the customer.

Precisely because of this collaboration, that has to preside over the relationship between the 3PL provider and the customer, the obligation of confidentiality must extend to the customer with respect to the techniques used by the 3PL provider (their 'know-how'), as these techniques without doubt constitute an element that differentiates one provider from their competitors.

Also, if the parties have established, as a system of remuneration, the so-called cost-plus pricing system, then the obligation of reciprocal confidentiality is, if appropriate, essential for both parties.

It is clear that this obligation has to extend beyond the termination of the contract, and not be exclusively limited to the agreed duration of that contract.

Based on the above, the confidentiality clause is usually construed in such a way that all these items must be kept confidential, and any party wishing to disclose information must obtain the previous authorisation or consent of the other party, which cannot be unreasonably rejected, but also stipulating some circumstances in which the consent of the other party is not required (e.g. by legal provision, on the request of legal bodies or tax authorities, or to comply with Stock Exchange regulations and information to be provided). Except in the latter cases, where the information is required for purposes of public information or legal resolution, the consenting party usually requests that the third party to whom information is disclosed must enter into a separate confidentiality agreement with the disclosing party, or even with the consenting party.

2.4.10 Inspection and monitoring

Depending on the perspective, the powers of inspection and monitoring may refer to the monitoring of the logistics activity through some form of physical presence in the place where it is carried out (the platform), or the monitoring of the documents relating to the logistics activity:

(a) At the platform, the 3PL provider carries out a logistics activity that directly and essentially affects the company and activity of the customer. It may, therefore, be in the customer's interest to gain access to the platform to inspect the activity relating to the company's products that is being carried out by the 3PL provider.

Although it is in the customer's interest, and seems only fair, providing access to the customer may conflict not only with the 3PL provider's duties of custody and monitoring with respect to the goods deposited in the warehouse, but also with the provider's ability to carry out the operation correctly.

Contractually, therefore, they have to try to harmonise and balance the interest of both parties, the common formula being to grant the possibility of access to the customer but make it subject to four conditions: (i) that the 3PL provider is given prior notice; (ii) that it is conducted by an authorised representative of the customer; (iii) that they are always accompanied by a representative of the 3PL provider; and (iv) that they do not disturb any normal activity carried out in the warehouse.

(b) Similarly, in connection with their rights of control, inspection and monitoring, the customer has to have access to such documents as refer to the inventory or *stocks*, delivery notes, claims, etc. and, in the case of 'cost-plus' contracts, to all accounting, financial or contractual documents relating to the logistics activity.[16]

In any event, the 3PL provider, on request, also has to produce for the customer the documents accrediting the fulfilment of his employment and social obligations concerning his employees.

When the 3PL provider carries out and/or provides services at the customer's platform ('in-house'), certain incidents may arise with regard to liability for the disappearance of merchandise in store, with an increased likelihood if it is the customer who has contracted the services of monitoring and security. Such cases, which are not uncommon, raise the issue, which is difficult to solve, unless it has been expressly regulated in the contract, of determining whether this damage is attributable to the 3PL provider who handles the merchandise but is not able to contract the necessary security for its due custody or, on the other hand, to the customer as the person responsible for regulating access to the platform.

2.4.11 Ownership of the merchandise

The 3PL provider is obviously not the owner of the merchandise that is deposited in the warehouse. However, although this may seem obvious to the parties, it may not be so obvious to the 3PL provider's third-party creditors who may seek, in order to obtain any accounts due, to proceed against the goods that are in the 3PL's immediate possession.

For this reason we consider it a good idea to ensure that the contract expressly reflects who is to be considered as the owner of the deposited merchandise, a legal position that usually falls to the part of the customer – although this will depend on the contracts of sale that he has concluded with suppliers, dealers, purchasers, etc., all of these agreements having nothing to do with the 3PL provider – as well as the obligation of the 3PL provider to make this situation clear to anyone who intends to carry out some act that may disturb the ownership of the legitimate owner.

2.4.12 Assignment and subcontracting

Given the nature of association and close collaboration that should govern the relationship between the customer and 3PL provider, in addition to the fact that the customer has selected the 3PL provider on the basis of their particular skills, competency and other qualifications, the 3PL provider becomes an essential figure for the customer – an *intuitu personae* – and the contract usually provides a stipulation that prevents the contract being transferred or subrogated to third parties.

However, the contract commonly contains an exception, which stipulates that the 3PL provider has the possibility of subcontracting transport or distribution services, because 3PL providers sometimes lack the material resources or personnel to carry them out themselves, particularly when bearing in mind that the market for certain products is variable and depends on the time of year, and that therefore at some point the 3PL provider may have an excess or lack of means, both of which cases will be detrimental to providing the contracted logistics services. However, it seems logical that the 3PL provider should notify the customer of the subcontracted entities, for the purpose of granting them authorisation to access the agreed delivery points.

Furthermore, the contract often includes a provision in favour of the customer, stipulating that the parties agree to extend the terms of the contract to the customer's affiliates or subsidiaries, which will become either partially or fully bound by the terms of the agreement, depending on the extent of the services requested. In such cases it is worth providing clarification and agreement to the effect that the principal customer will not be responsible for the due fulfilment of the agreement by the affiliates and/or subsidiaries, and that neither the principal customer nor any of the other affiliates or subsidiaries will be in any way jointly and severally liable or responsible or guarantors for the due fulfilment of the obligations of any of the other parties of the contract.

Other clauses may be established concerning situations that could arise from a third-party acquisition of the majority of capital of one of the contracting parties.

2.4.13 Personnel

The issue of personnel is an essential topic in any discussion of logistics contracts. This is because, given the imperative nature and necessary rights of labour legislation, it is impossible for the 3PL provider and customer to draw up any agreement that contradicts any aspect of this legislation. Therefore, it is essential to establish appropriate guarantees and agreements to mitigate any situation that could arise. All the possible scenarios regarding personnel policy will be discussed in depth in Chapter 4.

Subcontracting companies to provide logistics services could be qualified, in some cases, as falling into the legal framework of *subcontracting of works and services*, bringing with it certain consequences for the customer. Subsequently, it is common to establish guarantees that protect the customer from any possible claims that may be made regarding the workers of the 3PL provider.

A situation may also arise where the 3PL provider may take on, for the purpose of providing the contracted logistics services, personnel that had previously been integrated in the customer's workforce; this situation is typified as 'company succession', and will be discussed further on in this book.

2.4.14 Duration and termination

2.4.14.1 Duration

The duration of the contract is determined by the complexity of the contract and the need to make investments to ensure the effectiveness of its contracted services. It would seem logical to assume, in view of what has been discussed so far, that although the parties may agree to a contract of minimum duration (e.g. in the event of a short-term need for the provisional services of a 3PL provider due to reforms or the destruction of a warehouse, or to cover excess demand), that the normal scenario would be to conclude the contract to provide logistics services on a longer-term basis. As mentioned above, there is neither a minimum nor maximum legal time limit for the duration of the contract, and the duration will be, therefore, determined by the stipulations agreed on by the parties.

The signing of the contract does not always coincide with the contract coming into force; the need to make certain investments – which, in principle, do not seem worth making until some form of contractual undertaking exists – suggests that, in complex operations, a certain period of time can pass from the signing of the contract that binds the parties until the 3PL provider begins to carry out the activity undertaken. In such cases it is a good idea to specify, in the contract, the date from which it becomes effective.

2.4.14.2 Termination

2.4.14.2.1 Causes of termination.   Neither contract will have perpetual existence. An agreement can come to an end either because the basic term has expired, and has not been extended, or because an event has occurred that entitles one party to terminate the contract during its lifetime, and that right of termination has been exercised.

Therefore, the causes of termination of a logistics contract can be categorised as follows:

(a) Expiry of the term agreed
(b) Mutual agreement
(c) Other events leading to termination:
    (i) Termination by one party because of the unremedied fault of the other party
    (ii) Termination of the contract by one party because of the other party's insolvency
    (iii) Economic termination of the contract
    (iv) Termination of the contract by applicable law
    (v) Termination of the contract for loss of consents or other agreements

2.4.14.2.2 Consequences of termination.   Upon termination of the contract, several issues will arise for consideration:

(a) *Continuing covenants and obligations:* the contract will typically stipulate that, notwithstanding the termination of the relevant agreement, the parties will continue to be bound by certain provisions. This would apply, for example, to any obligations of confidentiality, for which the contract would usually stipulate a certain period of time after the termination of the contract during which they would still remain in force.

The contract should also stipulate that the act of termination does not prejudice any rights or liabilities which may have accrued for or against a party prior to the date of, or as the result of, termination (but subject to the continuing limitation of liabilities of the parties in respect of these accrued rights or liabilities).

(b) *Damages and compensation:* when a contract is terminated, the parties may need to consider any rights they could have to claim damages or compensation from each other, on the basis of any losses accrued as a consequence of terminating the contract.

The starting principle is that the terminating party could require the ability to claim damages against the other party for breach of contract, where the contract has been terminated because of an alleged breach of contract by the other party, and where the damages to be claimed will typically be based on the 'contract measure' of restoring the terminating party to the position that it would have enjoyed if the terms of the contract had been carried out.

2.4.14.2.3 Specific consequences in logistics contracts.

As seen above, terminating a contract may be one of the most complex aspects of the logistics contractual relationship. Essentially, this is not due to the causes that lead to termination, which are hardly special in terms of the form of termination compared to other contractual forms (i.e. elapsing of the established duration, abandonment, rescission for non-performance, unforeseeable insolvency) but rather due to the consequences that can be incurred by the termination. Suffice it to say that, given the nature of the contract, its rescission must be an extraordinary 'remedy' in the event of non-performance by one of the parties.

There are complex questions which may arise from terminating, for whatever reason, the contract to provide logistics services. Therefore, some form of contractual regulation of these consequences should be determined by the parties at the beginning of the contract, covering the following points:

(a) Regarding any products that, on the termination date of the contract, may still be in the 3PL provider's possession – either in the warehouse or in the course of transport – and any monies collected for them: a specific time frame should be established for resolving this situation, as the 3PL provider may require the storage space for products of a new customer.

(b) Regarding any assets and other investments made by the 3PL provider with the consent and approval of the customer, and destined for providing logistics services to that specific customer: this is usually the case for contracts that are of a long duration, and which require the 3PL provider to accommodate certain specific demands of the customer, which could involve investing in assets, etc. that are especially designed to satisfy customer needs. In such cases it is common that the 3PL provider should wish to dispose of these assets, and that the customer – for whom the termination of the contract does not necessarily imply the discontinuation of the logistics activity – should purchase them at their current net value, in other words, after discounting depreciation ('book value'), because it would seem almost certain that these assets will be needed in order to continue with the logistics operation. Therefore, the contract often stipulates a bilateral obligation – on the part on the customer to purchase, and on the part of the 3PL provider to sell.

(c) Regarding certain contracts signed by the 3PL provider, with the consent and approval of the customer, that were required specifically for the provision of logistics services to the customer (leasing contracts for goods assigned for the activity, contracts for bank loan destined for the acquisition of goods or other investments, leasing contracts for the logistics platform, etc.): for the reasons set out above, the legal situation *ex parte* regarding such contracts is often stipulated, and are granted, if appropriate, to the customer who will subrogate the obligations – and rights – of the 3PL provider.

(d) Regarding any programs and other IT applications ('software') acquired with the consent and approval of the customer: the contract must determine the final destination for after the termination of the contract, and has to provide agreement with the supplier of these programs and IT applications at the time of contracting them, concerning the possibility of transferring licences, etc.

(e) Regarding any charges, encumbrances and other obligations granted over the assets to be transferred: it is necessary to take note of the manner in which they have been granted, in other words, whether they were granted with or without the consent of the logistics customer.

(f) Regarding any other fiscal, administrative, civil, etc. obligations accrued through the provision of legal services, and which appear after the termination of the contract: in principle, these will be the responsibility of the party they were attributed to, without prejudice that, to guarantee this performance, any relevant agreements may be established.

(g) Regarding any personnel employed to carry out the logistics activity signed with the customer: the termination of the contract supposes that the customer will commission another 3PL provider with this activity or, as appropriate, may decide to provide it himself with the material elements and personnel available in his own business organisation. In either of these cases, the assumption may follow of *company succession* regarding the workers employed by the 3PL provider. In this sense, the contract often stipulates guarantees by the 3PL provider, in favour of the customer and later 3PL providers to whom he may turn, in the event of claims against the customer or later 3PL providers, so that the 3PL provider is responsible for the employed workers before and during the performance of the contract[17] and for indemnities and other liabilities. None of this will prejudice the option of stipulating that the workforce assigned to the logistics activity is assumed by the customer on termination of the contract.

(h) Regarding the logistics platform: this will invariably depend on what the situation had been during the life of the contract. Therefore, if, (i) it is the property of the customer, this would require rescinding the contract that made it available to the 3PL provider, if appropriate; (ii) it is the property of the 3PL provider, or the platform is available to him through any other means, and the platform is the centre where the 3PL provider carries out logistics activity for other customers, it should continue to be in the possession of the 3PL provider; (iii) it is destined exclusively for the logistics activity provided to the customer, the situation will depend on whether the 3PL provider uses the platform through a leasing contract, in which case, it would seem logical that this contract be transferred to the customer; (iv) the 3PL provider has it within the capacity of owner, having built it with the sole purpose of being able to fulfil the terms of the contract, in which case, any agreement concerning the platform after the termination of the contract usually includes, as with any other asset, the obligation to purchase it from the 3PL provider at its 'book value'.

In any case, given the variety of situations that may arise, the parties should provide precise definitions to deal with the consequences of the termination of the contract to provide logistics services. These definitions should, similarly, cover the generic possibility of demanding indemnities – in the event of rescission for non-performance – or, if appropriate, stipulate fixed amounts as a penalty clause.

2.4.15 Data protection and intellectual property

2.4.15.1 Data protection

Data protection is not a matter that parties in many logistics contracts need worry about; however, the best way to approach this issue is to establish a general clause concerning data protection that the party processing personal data must comply with, in addition to providing a commitment to keep the other party informed of any change in the data processing system or file and/or changes in regulations.

The data protection regime derives from EU Directives 2002/58/EC, 97/66/EC and 95/46/EC which provide a harmonised legislation and a minimum standard, which subsequently each member state may expand on, offering greater levels of security.

2.4.15.2 Intellectual property

In many outsourcing contracts the parties may agree that intellectual property will be assigned to the customer when the contract comes to an end. Logistics contracts are no exception, and, due to the important role that IT systems play in carrying out the terms of the contract, here, even more than in other contracts, it is reasonably common to find an agreement to this effect, especially in cases where a system has been specifically developed for a certain logistics activity, and has been paid for by the customer. It can also be the case that the IT system and other systems were provided by the customer himself, therefore an agreement to facilitate their use should be included.

Although the assignment of such defined intellectual property needs specific requirements in each country, the following offers a summary of the requirements usually common to every country:

(a) The rights that are being assigned
(b) The field of exploitation
(c) The reason for the assignment
(d) The duration of the assignment

2.4.16   Dispute resolution and governing law

2.4.16.1   Dispute resolution

The frequently mentioned complexity of the contract to provide logistics services means that inevitably during the lifetime of a contract the
parties will have disputes over certain matters. This is particularly the
case for contracts where the level of complexity is aggravated by an
economic-accounting component (for example, in 'open book' or
'cost-plus' contracts). From our point of view, the parties should take
advice on this, and, when negotiating the terms of a contract, pay
attention to including a clause that provides a dispute resolution
scheme that is likely to resolve any disputes most quickly and ami-
cably. However, practice shows us that the parties usually overlook
such a clause, as they assume that it suffices to provide a very simple
clause stating the governing law and jurisdiction. Moreover, when a
provision concerning dispute management is included it tends to
contain very little attention to detail.

As stated, from our point of view, and taking into account the nature
of association and close collaboration that form the basis of logistics
contracts, the parties would be advised to make provisions in advance
for how to resolve any controversies that could arise, with the aim of
solving them quickly and effectively, and as far as possible without
upsetting the relationship between the parties, and to stipulate that the
parties must continue to fulfil their obligations as far as possible,
notwithstanding the dispute.

The most typical forms of dispute between the parties tend to arise
from issues relating to:

(a) The fulfilment of an obligation
(b) When the principle of *force majeure* is to apply
(c) The accuracy of statements or invoices

Although there are many ways of construing the clause, in our view
the most common and advantageous method is to decide on a system
for dispute resolution with different levels, each of which is determined by the importance and nature of the dispute. Possible levels
could be the following:

(i)   On the first level, in the case of minor or technical disputes,
      the parties could agree to finding an informal resolution of
      the dispute within a determined time frame. The usual agree-
      ment in such a case is to submit the dispute – depending on

whether it is of a technical or operational nature – to the appointed contract representatives of each party, the senior managers, or to an independent expert, with a view to discussing the dispute in good faith, and ultimately resolving it amiably, without the need to pursue the matter any further.

(ii) On the second level, before submitting the controversy for litigation or arbitration as may be agreed, the parties could agree on involving a third-party overseer as a means of providing a more formal mechanism for dialogue. This is a mechanism that is rapidly developing nowadays, and involves agreeing to use one of the alternative dispute resolution (ADR) methods. These methods, in spite of being more formal and structured processes, are perceived as being informal and do not preclude the option of the parties resorting to arbitration or litigation in the event that no settlement is reached.

(iii) On the final level, and when the methods of the previous levels have failed to bring about any agreement between the parties, or directly in the case of a major dispute, the parties should decide to address the dispute in a more formal way, be it through arbitration or litigation.

If the parties have recourse to arbitration, they should include the terms of the agreement clearly and comprehensively, to avoid the danger that the agreement be declared null and void or that it create uncertainty of the jurisdiction of the arbitral tribunal. Therefore, the terms the agreement should include are: the express will of the parties to submit all or any specific matter to arbitration, the mandate of the arbitral tribunal to act, the language of the arbitration, the arbitration body and the applicable procedural rules, and the number and procedure for the appointment of arbitrators.

It is also important to point out that submitting a dispute for arbitration is not incompatible with the right for a party to submit a petition to the courts for provisional or precautionary measures (an injunction) prior to, or during, arbitration, for the purpose in order to secure a position. Indeed, this right is even expressly foreseen in many arbitral rules.

If the parties decide to have recourse to justice, they can simply stipulate that any dispute which may arise will be settled in court. In this case, if there is any international aspect or element, it is a good idea to specify which country's courts will have jurisdiction over the agreement.

The contract should also stipulate whether the courts will have exclusive or non-exclusive jurisdiction. In the former case the parties are obliged to bring any action in the courts of the nominated jurisdiction; in the latter a party may bring action either in the courts of the named jurisdiction or in the courts of any other country having jurisdiction over the agreement, according to their own jurisdictional rules.

If any of the parties are domiciled outside the jurisdiction of the court nominated, it could also be a good idea to specify the appointment of an agent to provide legal services for that party in the relevant jurisdiction. This is intended as a means of overcoming the need to obtain a court order to carry out a lawsuit against a party domiciled outside an area of jurisdiction.

2.4.16.2 Governing law

In agreements with an international scope, the most likely scenario is that the parties will determine the applicable body of substantive laws to govern the agreement. The chosen law will be the judicial system to be applied for interpreting the content, execution and the effects of the agreement, in the event of any dispute involving that agreement.

Concerning the choice of the governing law, the parties usually tend to prefer a neutral law, English or New York law being the most popular choices for a neutral governing law.

In the unlikely event that there is no express choice of a governing law, a court may decide which governing law to apply to the agreement. This must be decided in accordance with the principles of the conflict of laws of the jurisdiction within which the court resides. The courts will in particular be guided by the application of the 1980 Rome Convention on the 'Law Applicable to Contractual Obligations'.

2.4.17 Rights of relevant transactions

Situations in which a customer, for whom the logistics activity up until then had formed an integrated part of his own business organisation, decides to externalise this activity to a third party – a 3PL provider – are not unusual; in fact, as can be seen above, this is the usual situation for *outsourcing operations*. This change in business policy may involve a series of operations, more or less complex, that essentially arise from the need of the customer to dispose of his logistics resources by granting or transferring to the 3PL provider:

(a) All shares or stakes of the company in the group that, until then, had carried out logistics activities, in accordance with the rules that govern company law, and without prejudice to the contractual agreements referring to the 'guarantee of liabilities' of the acquired company.

(b) The human and material resources assigned to the logistics activities, taking note of the nature of the asset, and of all rules and regulations. Similarly, and if appropriate, the 'transfer' of contracts with the employees, raising the above-mentioned problem that derives from 'company succession'.[18]

3
Contract to Provide Logistics Services: Carriage of Goods

3.1 Introduction

In a global and decentralised economy in which production, distribution and sale centres are usually separated by thousands of kilometres, transport (both of raw materials to factories, and from factories to distribution centres and then points of sale) has become a determining factor in the competitiveness of products and enterprises. Transport services are now one of the cornerstones if not the most important service provided by 3PL providers, such that experts in this area are of the opinion that logistics cannot be understood if the role of transport is not considered first. Therefore, in response to market demands, 3PL providers have entered the market to provide a global, door-to-door or multimodal transport service that competes with the traditional carriers, which only offer fragmented transport service.

The demands of the market mean that the current supplier of all-round services not only has to be an astute business person, but also an adviser and partner to his clients (their success directly determines his own). As a result, he must have extensive knowledge of the market and its requirements to be able to be in a position to advise his clients. The global transport provider must have in-depth knowledge of the market, physical operations and loading operations, be adept at processing the documents required for this type of transaction, and be fully aware of all the national and international rules and regulations that establish the conditions, requirements, restrictions and standards that apply to the services provided.

Therefore, the aim of this chapter is to present in a concise but precise and detailed manner the terms of the current international conventions, describing their scope and practical implications, and in particular, the liabilities that can arise from each type of transport, including road, sea, rail, air or multimodal.

3.2 Carriage of goods by road

3.2.1 Introduction: definition and legal regime

We have indicated previously how international transport is regulated by international conventions, either of reciprocal nature or multilateral scope. This latter group includes the Convention of Geneva of 19 May 1956 relating to the Contract of International Transport of Merchandise by Road (CMR), which was amended by the Protocol of Geneva of 5 July 1978.

In the international transport of merchandise by road, it is likewise worth highlighting – though this is not going to be considered below – the existence of forms of transport that fall under the regime of TIR ledgers. These offer a particularly singular feature, which is that they are not subject to customs inspections or payment of entry, departure duties or taxes, as long as they meet the conditions and the applicable international conventions.

3.2.2 Scope of application

In order for a contract of transport of merchandise by road to be subject to the CMR rules, it is necessary that the following requirements are met:

(a) That there is a *contract* that covers transport. If nothing is established in this respect in the agreement, a verbal contract would be sufficient.
(b) That transport is carried out by means of *vehicles*.
(c) That the contract be *onerous*.
(d) That the place of origin or of the loading of the merchandise and the place where it is planned for unloading to take place, stated in the contract of transport, are located in different states of which at least one is a signatory of the Convention.

The application of the Convention to contracts of transport is only dependent on the concurrence of the elements stated, regardless of domicile and nationality of the parties in the contract.

Likewise, the Convention applies to transport carried out by the state itself, institutions and governmental organisms, provided that these comply with the provisions thereof.

Regarding the object being transported, the following are expressly excluded from the scope of the Convention:

(a) Transport carried out under the regulation of international mail agreements.
(b) Funeral transportation.
(c) Removals transportation.

Also, pursuant to the first section of the Protocol of the Signature of the Convention, transport between the United Kingdom of Great Britain and Northern Ireland and the Republic of Ireland is excluded from the CMR regulations.

However, by means of private agreements, states can distance themselves from the Convention regulations by establishing a particular regime with respect to those *cross-border forms of transport*. Where such regulations do not exist, the rules of the CMR Convention shall apply.

The Convention also considers the case of merchandise transported during part of the journey by sea, rail, inland waterway or air, and where, except for situations prescribed by article 14 of the CMR, no breaking of cargo took place. In such a case, the CMR decides in this latter respect in favour of the application of the latter with respect to the whole of the transportation, unless it has been proven that the loss, damage or delay in the delivery has been caused during the journey by sea, railway, inland waterway or air, and clearly it has not been due to an act or omission by the company transporting it by road during this journey, but rather due to an event that could only occur in the course of and by reason of the transportation carried out by sea, railway, via inland waterway or air. In the case in which the company transporting by road is the same as the one undertaking the transport by any other means different from that, its liability shall be determined in accordance with the provisions set out above, it being considered for these purposes that we are dealing with different transport companies.

As regards the *subjective scope of the application of the Convention*, the transport company shall be liable for loss, damage or delay in the delivery of the merchandise that may be due to acts and omissions of its employees or of any persons that it involved in the transport, provided that they carried out the said acts and omissions in the performance of their functions.

3.2.3 Contractual documentation

The contract of transport regulated by the Convention is *consensual* in nature. In this respect, while the bill of lading constitutes a due document of the contract of transport, any irregularity, falsifying or loss does not affect the existence or the validity of the contract which remains, in any event, subject to the rules of the Convention.

The bill of lading is issued in three original copies that will be signed by the forwarding party or consignor and the transport company:

(a) The first copy will be delivered to the forwarding party.
(b) The second copy accompanies the merchandise transported.
(c) The third copy remains in the possession of the bearer.

The Convention states the content of a bill of lading that is considered to be the minimum and necessary. This is without prejudice to the fact that the parties to the contract may add any other statement that they deem appropriate in the bill of lading.

The bill of lading must contain the following terms:

(a) Place and date of drafting.
(b) Name and domicile of the forwarding party.
(c) Name and domicile of the transport company.
(d) Place and date on which the merchandise was loaded as cargo.
(e) Name and domicile of the recipient and place of delivery.
(f) Denomination of the nature of the merchandise and of the form of packing, as well as the usual name of the merchandise if it is dangerous.
(g) Number of packages, their particular markings and their numbers.
(h) Quantity of merchandise, stated in gross tonnage or in another form.
(i) Transport costs (price of the same, accessory costs, customs duties that may accrue from the conclusion of the contract until the time of the delivery).
(j) Instructions required by the customs formalities and others.
(k) A statement that the transport company is subject to the regime established by this Convention, even though there may have been a stipulation to the contrary.

In addition, where appropriate, it may contain:

(a) Express mention of the prohibition against transhipment.
(b) Costs the carrier is responsible for.
(c) Sum of reimbursement to be received at the time of the delivery of the merchandise.
(d) Value of the merchandise declared and the sum that represents the special interest on the delivery.

(e) Instructions from the carrier to the transport company concerning the insurance of the merchandise.
(f) Agreed period in which the transportation has to be carried out.
(g) List of documents delivered to the transport company.

As a general principle, it can be stated that the shipper is responsible for all of the damage that the transport company may suffer due to inaccuracies or insufficient data on the statements indicated in the bill of lading.

Likewise, and reaffirming the *imperative nature of the Convention*, it is established that all clauses that directly or indirectly abrogate the terms laid down in the Convention shall be rendered null and without effect. Nonetheless, the nullity of such clauses does not affect those set out in the contract.

In the case of a transport company delivering *hazardous merchandise*, the Convention establishes that the carrier shall have to specify the exact nature of the hazard that this represents and, as appropriate, shall indicate thereto the precautions to be taken. In the event of the warning not having been recorded on the bill of lading, the carrier or the recipient shall be responsible for proving by any other means that the transport company had knowledge of the precise nature of the hazard entailed by the transport of the merchandise in question.

At the time of the receipt of the merchandise, the transport company is bound to check:

(a) The number of packages.
(b) The apparent condition and packaging of the merchandise.
(c) Gross tonnage or quantity and content of the packages, if so requested by the shipper and to the account of the latter.

In the event of a disagreement between what is stated in the bill of lading and the checks made, the transport company shall record this on the bill of lading. However, this does not place any commitment on the shipper, unless the latter acquiesces.

Unless there is justified reason to do otherwise, the bill of lading is to record:

(a) The terms of the contract.
(b) The receipt of merchandise by the bearer.

Likewise, the consignor is responsible for:

(a) The costs incurred by the transport company due to defective packing, unless this condition was known to the latter.

(b) Attaching the necessary documents which have to accompany the merchandise for customs or other purposes, as well as regarding their veracity, authenticity and sufficiency. Nonetheless, the transport company, as the agent, shall be liable for the loss or improper usage of these documents. Such liability will not extend beyond that which may correspond in the event of the loss of the merchandise.

With regard to other matters, a broad *right of disposal* is established in favour of the consignor. The latter shall be empowered to make use of the merchandise, make the bearer halt the transporting, modify the planned delivery place and decide whether it should be delivered to a recipient other than the one initially designated. The same rights shall lie with the recipient if this is so stated in the bill of lading.

Nevertheless, this right of disposal shall not result in the division of the shipment, that is to say, the separation of the freight among two or more recipients when it was originally being shipped to a single one. The right of disposal terminates when:

(a) The second copy of the bill of lading is forwarded to the recipient.
(b) The merchandise arrives at the destination point. At this time, the recipient can require the provision of the second copy and the delivery of the merchandise against receipt.

Should the *merchandise be rejected* by the recipient, the Convention establishes that the carrier can make use of this without the need to use its copy of the bill of lading.

When the transportation cannot be carried out, or impediments to the delivery arise, the transport company – requesting instructions from the consignor – is authorised to unload the merchandise at the expense of the party that is entitled to it. The latter can then sell the merchandise when this is so justified by the perishable nature or the condition of the merchandise, when the costs of safeguarding it are disproportionate or when due instructions are not received from the consignor within a reasonable period of time.

Finally, with regard to the transportation price the Convention sets out the following rules:

(a) The merchandise is subject to the obligations and costs resulting from the bill of lading.
(b) Such obligations and costs must be deducted from the sum resulting from the sale of the merchandise.

(c) If such an amount is greater than that resulting from the sale, the bearer shall be able to demand that it be paid the outstanding difference.

3.2.4 Liability of the transport company

With regard to the liability of the bearer, the CMR Convention sets out the following rules.

3.2.4.1 General principle

In accordance with the norms of the Convention, the transport company is liable for the total or partial loss or for such breakages as may take place from the time of the receipt of the merchandise until the time of the delivery to the shipping agent, as well as for any delay in delivery. This is, accordingly, a liability for *presumed culpability*.

3.2.4.2 Exoneration from liability

The bearer shall be exonerated from liability if the loss, breakage or delay has been caused:

(a) By the *fault of the party that held the right over the merchandise.*
(b) Due to *an instruction from the latter* that does not derive from a blameworthy action by the transport company.
(c) Due to *faults particular* to the merchandise.
(d) Due to *circumstances that the bearer could not prevent and whose consequences it could not halt.*
(e) Due to *particular risks* inherent in one or several of the following facts:
    (i) Use of uncovered vehicles, when such use has been expressly agreed in the bill.
    (ii) Absence of or defect in the packing of the merchandise.
    (iii) Handling, loading or unloading of the merchandise and complementary operations carried out by the carrier or persons acting on behalf of one party or the other.
    (iv) Nature of certain merchandise, total or partial loss or breakage due to ruptures, mould, internal or spontaneous deterioration, drying or the activity of pests or rodents.
    (v) Insufficient or incomplete markings or numbers on the packages.
    (vi) Transport of live animals.

Defects in vehicles used for transportation, or the fault of the persons from whom the vehicle has been rented or used do not constitute reason for exoneration.

As regards the burden of proof concerning the circumstances of exposure, we must highlight a dual regime:

(a) If it is established that loss, breakage or delay occurred due to a cause mentioned in the foregoing paragraphs, the burden of proof is incumbent upon the transport company. In this way, the culpability of the latter is presumed.
(b) If the concurrence of any of the particular risks (i)–(vi) is alleged and demonstrated, then the burden of proof is reversed, it becoming incumbent on the complainant to offer proof to the contrary.

Total or partial loss: the party that has the power of disposal over the merchandise may, without need for proof, consider the merchandise to be lost – *legal presumption of loss of merchandise*:

(a) When 30 days elapsed from the date the delivery was due, or, in the absence of an agreement concerning the delivery date,
(b) Sixty days after the transport company took responsibility for the merchandise.

When, by virtue of the terms laid down in the Convention, the transport company accepts responsibility for a partial or total compensation for the merchandise, this compensation shall be calculated in accordance with the *value that the merchandise had at the time and place at which the transport company took responsibility for it.*

The value of the merchandise shall be determined in accordance with its Stock Exchange price listing or, in the absence thereof, according to the current market price, and in the absence of both of these markers, according to the current value of merchandise of the same nature and quality.

Nonetheless, it shall not be possible for the compensation to exceed 8.33 account units per kilogram of gross tonnage that is missing. However, the transport price, customs duties and the other unexpected costs arising from the transportation shall furthermore be reimbursed in full in the case of total loss and on a pro-rata basis in the case of partial loss. This shall not be the case for damages.

Breakage: in the case of breakage, the transport company shall pay in full the sum of the depreciation. This is to be calculated in accordance with the value of the merchandise, as this has been stated above. However, in any event, it cannot be possible for the compensation to be greater than:

(a) The corresponding sum in the case of total loss, if the entirety of the shipment as a whole suffers depreciation due to breakage.

(b) The amount that would apply in the case of loss of the depreciated part, if only one part of the shipment suffers depreciation due to breakage.

Delay: there is a delay in delivery:

(a) When the merchandise was not delivered in the agreed period or was not delivered at all.
(b) When the effective duration of the transportation exceeds the time that may reasonably be permitted to a diligent transport company in the case of a partial freight. This is estimated as the time necessary for a full cargo under normal conditions.

In the case of a culpable delay, if the party that holds the right over the merchandise proves that there is detriment arising from the delay, the transport company is bound to pay compensation for this. *Under no circumstances shall this sum exceed the price of the transportation.*

Extinguishing of the profitable use of the restriction: the transport company shall not enjoy a predominant right for disposals that exclude or limit its liability or that serve to reverse the burden of proof:

(a) If the damage was caused by *misrepresentation or a fault comparable to misrepresentation* on the part of the transport company.
(b) If the damage was caused by *misrepresentation or blame on the part of the employees of the transport company* or any other persons that the transport company may have employed for the purpose of transportation. Furthermore, provided that they were acting to perform their functions, these persons or employees shall not enjoy a predominant right – in terms of their personal liability – for the disposals which, under the Convention, exclude or limit their liability.

Complementary norms: the Convention establishes that the shipper may make a declaration for a *value of the merchandise greater than the limit* set by the rules of the Convention in the bill of lading, against the payment of an excess premium to be agreed between the parties. In such a case, this sum shall replace the stated limits.

It may also, by paying an excess price, set the sum for a *special interest on the delivery* of the merchandise at the destination and for the relevant purposes in case of loss, breakdown or delay in delivery. If this declaration of special interest exists, the carrier shall be able to claim a sum in compensation equal to the supplementary damage, without prejudice to the compensation due in accordance with the Convention, and in concurrence with the sum declared for special interest.

The party that has the right of disposal of the merchandise may, in turn, claim *interest on the compensation, which the Convention sets at an annual rate of 5 per 100* from the day of the written complaint to the transport company or the day on which the legal claim is filed.

Finally it should be pointed out that the Convention, along with the liability deriving from a breach or failure to precisely comply with the contract of transport, establishes the possible requirement of extra-contractual liability.

Insurance: only a brief mention of the question of insurance is made throughout the whole of the terms stated in the Convention. Thus, nullity in law of all the stipulations by which the transport company places itself as being the beneficiary of the insurance of the merchandise and other analogous clauses is declared.

3.2.5 Claims and actions

3.2.5.1 Study of the different actions

In accordance with the norms of the Convention, it is presumed that the recipient received the merchandise in the condition described in the bill of lading in the following cases:

(a) If the goods are accepted without checking their condition or making any complaints.
(b) With regard to *declared losses or breakages*, if no record is made upon delivery.
(c) With regard to *undeclared losses or breakages,* if no record is made in writing within seven days of delivery.

In any event, in order for a *delay* in delivery to give rise to compensation, it is necessary to have lodged a complaint in writing within 21 days of delivery.

3.2.5.2 Term to exercise actions

As regards the *time-barring* of actions set out under the Convention, and as a general principle, a general period of one year *dies a quo*, as stated in the Convention, is established.

Nevertheless, a time-barred period of three years is established when the action has been exercised as a consequence of a fraudulent act, or one equivalent to misrepresentation.

In both cases, there is a time-barred period rather than an expiry period. For this reason, and without prejudice to the circumstances laid down in the national laws relating to an interruption of the time-barred period, the *written extra-judicial document interrupts the prescription until the transport company replies to the claim in writing and returns the accompanying document.*

In order to comply with the interrupting act of the stated time-barred period, it is necessary for the following requirements to be met:

(a) That this is an authentic claim and not a simple comment on an event that occurred or a communication impossible to ascertain.
(b) That the claim is made in writing.
(c) That the claim is addressed to the transport company.
(d) That this is the first claim.

In any event, and without prejudice to the statements made above, the suspension or interruption of the time-barred period is subject to the law of the territory of the court or the tribunal that is considering the litigation.

3.2.5.3 Jurisdiction

Claimants can only exercise their rights before:

(a) The court or tribunal of the contracting state that the parties have expressly made themselves subject to; or
(b) The court or tribunal of the state where the respondent has their habitual place of residence; or
(c) The court or tribunal of the state where the respondent has their main domicile; or
(d) The court or tribunal of the state where the respondent has an agency branch office through which the contract of transport has been concluded; or
(e) The court or tribunal of the place where the transport company effectively accepted responsibility for the merchandise, and not that where agreement was reached; or
(f) The court or tribunal of the state of the place where, contractually, the delivery of the merchandise to the recipient was agreed upon.

The decisions issued by a court or tribunal of a contracting company could be exercised in other member states if the requirements stated in the CMR are met.

Notwithstanding all the statements made above, it is possible for the parties to the contract to be subject to an *arbitration tribunal*, if the following conditions are met:

(a) That this has been expressly agreed on in the contract of transport.
(b) That such a clause expressly envisages the application of the CMR Convention by an arbitration court.

3.3 Carriage of goods by sea

3.3.1 Legal regulations

(A) The Hague-Visby rules

(a) The Hague rules: The carriage of goods by sea arises from the approval of the 1924 Brussels Convention, which unified certain rules regarding the bill of lading.[1] The interests underlying the signing of the Convention were the protection of the forwarders through clauses exempting them from the liability that the carriers inserted into the bills of lading, in such a way that the legal regime proposed is one of *ius cogens*, and therefore cannot be repealed. These rules are also known as 'The Hague rules', since they are similar to those of the same name approved by the International Maritime Committee in 1921.

(b) The Protocols of Brussels of 1968 and of London of 1979: The Hague rules have undergone two amendments. The first was introduced by the Protocol of Brussels of 1968,[2] which dealt with the liability of the carrier, and its scope of application. As regards the scope of application, two further criteria are added on the basis of the criteria of The Hague rules (knowledge of which would have been extended to member states): that the freight be located at the port of a member state, and that the voluntary delivery of the parties is done by means of a paramount clause.

The second amendment was introduced by the Protocol of London of 1979[3] which replaced the gold standard, in order to establish a limit on liability, with the Special Drawing Right (SDR).

However, the ratification of this 1979 Protocol means, by application of section 1, the ratification of the original Brussels Convention.

(B) The 'Hamburg Rules' of 1978

The United Nations Convention of 31 March 1978[4] was approved at the Hamburg Diplomatic Conference. It has been ratified by over 20 countries and as such it is currently in force, though its scope is rather restricted since it has not been ratified by the more developed countries. This Convention contains rules of liability that are different from The Hague-Visby rules, and has given rise to opposition from large shipowners, which is one reason why it is not very widely ratified.

(C) Object of regulation in these special rules

Both The Hague-Visby rules and the Hamburg rules apply to international carriage of goods by sea and seek to regulate the liability of the carrier for loss or damage to the merchandise – as well as delays under the Hamburg rules – on the basis of liability for fault. The liability for fault regime is marked by two parameters:

- The causes of exoneration from liability of the carrier, and
- The qualitative limits on liability.

The carrier's liability under The Hague-Visby rules is based on the obligations that it assumes through the contract of transport before, during and after the voyage – which include the formality of ensuring the vessel is in seaworthy condition. On the other hand, there is also a list of causes of exoneration that the carrier may make recourse to. Overall, this amounts to establishing a system of liability for fault, in which the burden of proof on the carrier is eased, allowing the latter to appeal to a number of legal causes of exoneration from liability.

Under the Hamburg rules, the carrier is responsible for loss or damage to the merchandise, should this occur when the merchandise was in their custody. This applies under the proviso that the carrier, their employees or agents adopted all the measures that could be reasonably expected in order to prevent any loss or damage and consequences thereof (section 5.1 of the Hamburg Convention). This establishes an *iuris tantum* presumption of culpability on the part of the carrier, exoneration from liability now amounting to demonstration that all the reasonably necessary measures were adopted in order to avoid loss or damage. As far as the burden of proof is concerned, this is attributed to the party who, in all likelihood, had most knowledge of the said facts.

The liability for loss of, or damage to, the merchandise – and also for a delay in the case of the Hamburg rules – is subject to limitations. The amounts are set as follows:

- In the case of The Hague-Visby rules, 667.67 units of account per load or unit (in accordance with the 1979 Protocol).[5]
- In the case of the Hamburg rules, 835 units of account per load or other unit of freight transported, or alternatively, 2.5 units of account per kilogram of gross tonnage, at the choice of the shipper.

3.3.2 Determination of the applicable law: scope of application

The scope of application of these rules is laid down in section 5 of the Brussels Protocol. The 1924 Brussels Convention applies provided that the bill of lading was issued in a contracting state (section 10), and so it was only required for one of the states among those that undertook the carriage to be a member of the Convention.

According to the new draft of the Brussels Convention, The Hague-Visby rules will be applied to all contracts involving carriage of merchandise between two different points when:

(a) the bill of lading was formalised in a contracting state;
(b) or the carriage takes place from a port of a contracting state;
(c) or the bill of lading stipulates that the contract will be governed by the provisions of the Convention or the regulations of the state that applies them or carries them out, whatever the nationality of the vessel, of the carrier, of the forwarder, the shipping agent or of any other interested party. The insertion of this clause into the contract, traditionally known as a paramount clause, carries with it the application of The Hague rules, amended by the Protocols of 1968 and 1979 (hereinafter referred indistinctly to as The Hague-Visby rules or RHV), and with this the *ius cogens* rules laid down for the regime of liability, beyond any other clause that is contrary to or incompatible with this regime.

3.3.3 Scope of application

(A) Setting the limits of the object of carriage: merchandise

The Hague-Visby rules are only applicable to carriage of merchandise and not of passengers. The term 'merchandise' includes 'goods, objects, merchandise and items of any class, with the express exclusion of live animals and the freight which, in accordance with the contract of carriage, is declared to be placed on deck and transported in such a manner'.

(B) International carriage of merchandise

The requirement is that the transport be international, between ports of two different states. This excludes the national carriage of merchandise or piloting.

(C) International carriage of merchandise documented in bills of lading or similar documents

The Hague-Visby rules are applicable to the international carriage of merchandise documented in a bill of lading or any other similar document that may serve as a title for the carriage of merchandise by sea.

(D) Temporal application: the transport stage

Sec. 1 limits the application of these special rules 'to the time that has passed from the loading of the merchandise until they are unloaded;

these operations are carried out using the particular resources of the ship. It is considered that, when resources external to the same are used, the contract will come into force from the time that the merchandise is on board the vessel.'

Thus, delivery of merchandise to the carrier or its agent at the port is not covered by the rules, the custody, storage and displacement prior to loading being excluded from these regulations, along with the safe-keeping and storage of the load by the shipping agent until it is delivered to the recipient.

The operations involving the loading and unloading by resources external to the vessel are not affected by the liability regime set out in The Hague-Visby rules, the matters that the parties have agreed on being applicable, however.

The time span for the liability of the carrier is greater under the Hamburg rules, since these extend the points of reference of the loading of the merchandise to it actually being on board ship and the unloading, established in The Hague-Visby rules, to the actual delivery of the merchandise by the shipper and the receipt by the recipient (art. 4, Hamburg Convention, 1978).

3.3.4 International competence

Neither the 1924 Brussels Convention nor the subsequent 1968 and 1979 Protocols that amend it contain any provisions regarding the international competence concerning disputes arising from the carriage of merchandise under the bill of lading regime.

On the other hand, the Hamburg rules contain a specific rule concerning international judicial competence. When these rules are applicable, once the Convention has been signed and ratified, national courts will be invested with the power to deal with litigation cases, provided the claimant is subject to these rules and the case is lodged in a country where any of the following is located:

- the principal establishment or the residence of the respondent;
- the place where the contract is to be carried out;
- the port of loading, unloading or any other place designated to that end in the contract of carriage of goods by sea;
- in certain cases, the court or the place at which the carrier's vessel is loaded (art. 21).

Given the current absence of specific international regulations, in addition to the general rules laid down by national laws, the specific provisions contained in both the EC Regulation 44/2001 of the

Council, relating to judicial competence, recognition and judicial enforcement in civil and mercantile matters and the 1952 Convention on the arrest of seagoing ships apply.

3.3.5 Personal and material elements of the contract

3.3.5.1 Personal elements

There are fundamentally three parties that appear in a contract of transport under a bill of lading regime: the shipper, carrier and shipping agent.

(A) The shipper.   This is the party that contracts the carriage, whether directly or through a commissioning agent, and as such the shipper appears in the bill of lading. If it acts through another agent, the owner of the freight will have the status of shipper provided that there is a form of direct representation, and hence the commissioning agent contracts on their own behalf and that of an outside party, with the name of the owner of the freight appearing in the contract. However, if the commissioning agent is acting on their own behalf in subcontracting another party, they will appear as the forwarder in the contract.

The contracting of transport entails two activities: the placing of the merchandise at the disposal of the carrier, who will issue and deliver the bill of lading with the information provided by the shipper.

The status of the shipper, regardless of the legal title by virtue of which they possess the goods, grants the authorisation to bring a claim against the carrier in the case of a contractual breach and, specifically, damage to or loss of the freight.

Art. 1.3 of the Hamburg rules defines a shipper as the party that is responsible for the carriage, whether directly or though another agent that acts on their own behalf and on their account.

(B) Consignee or shipping agent.   This is the recipient of the freight, which holds the right to claim it at the port of destination. In the case of a bill of lading, this authorisation will derive from the possession of the title. Furthermore, if sea waybills have been used, it will have the status of consignee if its name appears on the sea waybill, even though this lacks the traditional title status. In any event, it is independent from that of the shipper. It is not an assignee and as such any exceptions that the carrier could hold with respect to the shipper cannot be opposed.

The Hamburg rules refer to the 'shipping agent' as the person authorised to receive the merchandise (art. 1.4).

(C) Carrier. The carrier is the party that assumes the obligation of undertaking the carriage, without necessarily being the one that completes the transport. This is the reason why the carrier does not always coincide with the shipowner, as is the case when the charterer is the party that contracts the shipper. Section 2 RHV defines a carrier as 'the ship-owner, shipping company or charterer that is bound with the shipper under a contract of transport'. Leaving aside the definitions of shipowner, shipping company or charterer that are subsequently made in section 3, it is possible to emphasise the service assumed under contract by describing the carrier as the party that assumes the formal or material obligation to transport the merchandise by sea under a bill of lading regime.

The Hamburg rules define carriers with greater precision (art. 1). They distinguish between the effective carrier and the contractual carrier, allocating joint responsibility to both to comply with the provision of carriage (arts. 1 and 10).

The obligation that the carrier assumes results from the transfer of merchandise to the agreed place, being therefore responsible for compliance therewith. If the contractual carrier does not coincide with the shipowner, there is good reason why the latter is exempt from liability in the case of a contractual breach caused by a delay, loss of or damage to the merchandise, even though The Hague-Visby rules do not expressly distinguish between the effective and the contractual carrier.

3.3.5.2 The bill of lading

Carriage of merchandise by sea subject to The Hague-Visby rules must necessarily be documented in a bill of lading or a similar instrument. The absence of the document does not determine the nullity of the contract, but rather the non-applicability of the legal regime of The Hague-Visby rules.

The Hamburg rules are applied to all of those contracts of carriage by sea by virtue whereof the carrier undertakes, against payment for freight, to transport the merchandise by sea from one port to another, without this necessarily being documented in a bill of lading (art. 1.6 Hamburg Convention). Nevertheless, 'when the carrier takes responsibility for the merchandise, it has to issue a bill of lading to the forwarder, should the latter so request' (art. 14.1 Hamburg Convention). The bill of lading is a document substantiating the contract of transport, the delivery of the merchandise to the carrier 'and by virtue whereof there is an undertaking to deliver these against the presentation of the document' (art. 1.7 Hamburg Convention).

The bill of lading is a document issued by the captain of the vessel or the party that arranges the carriage of the merchandise, in which it is recognised that certain goods have been received on board and there is an undertaking to transport them to the place of destination and deliver them to the authorised holder of the title.

Four copies of the bill of lading are to be issued, signed by the captain and the forwarder. The forwarder will retain one copy and will forward another to the recipient or shipping agent, authorising them to claim the merchandise. The captain will take two copies, one for himself and another for the shipping company.

(A) Content of the bill of lading.   Section 3.3 RHV contains the statements that the bill of lading has to contain:

- The name, registration and port of the vessel. The charter details are not as important, while the identification of the vessel is important. The bill of lading may contain a statement that the vessel has been replaced or that it has not been determined.
- The name and domicile of the captain. This is not compulsory and when it is included, it is in order to identify the shipowner carrier that the captain is acting on behalf of.
- The loading and unloading ports. This makes it possible to identify the sea stage of the carriage.
- The name of the forwarder.
- The name and domicile of the shipping agent, if the bill of lading specifies one. Should this be the carrier, this item is not essential, since possession of the certificate is sufficient to claim the merchandise upon delivery.
- The freight. This is the price of the carriage. Depending on whether the loads are due or have been paid, the receipt of the merchandise by the recipient will be levied with the payment of the freight.
- The main markings necessary for the identification of the merchandise, in the form that these have been provided in writing by the forwarder prior to this being loaded on board. This is done in such a way that the markings stated are printed or clearly written on the unpackaged merchandise, or on the boxes or packages that contain them, in such a manner that they can normally be legible until the end of the trip.
- The number of loads, parts, quantity or weight as may be the case, as recorded in writing by the forwarder.
- The state and apparent condition of the merchandise.

The carrier is required to check that the merchandise received corresponds to the declaration made by the forwarder regarding the markings, number, quantity or weight.

(B) Functions of the bill of lading. The bill of lading comprises a wide range of functions: in addition to being the instrument for the contract of transport it also functions as a security for the merchandise and acts as the background title to the carrier.

The Hamburg rules comprise this triple function, the bill of lading being described as

> a document that provides evidence of a contract of transport and substantiates that the carrier has taken the merchandise into its charge or loaded the same, and by virtue whereof, there is an undertaking to deliver the same against the provision of the document. Such a commitment is established in the provision included in the document whereby the merchandise are to be delivered to the order of a specific individual, to order or to the bearer. (section 1.7 Hamburg Convention)

(a) The instrument in which the contract of transport is documented. The bill of lading constitutes proof of contract content and fulfilment, without losing sight of the fact that the clauses limiting the liability of the carrier are null and void. The form of the contract has an *ad probationem* function, since its validity does not depend on this being formally processed, although it is necessary so that The Hague-Visby rules apply. The proof will extend to the content of the contract, and specifically to the identification of the carrier, forwarder and consignee – directly or through the clause to the bearer – the price of the carriage (freight); the merchandise object of carriage; and the determining of the port loading and unloading, in order to have knowledge of the transport stage involved under the regime of The Hague-Visby rules.

(b) Proof of delivery of merchandise to the carrier. This particular document constitutes proof of delivery of merchandise to the carrier, while at the same time it is proof of the obligations assumed by the carrier in the contract of transport under the bill of lading regime.

The issuing of the bill of lading by the carrier constitutes an *iuris tantum* presumption, which allows for proof to the contrary, that the merchandise was delivered to the carrier in the conditions described in the document. Nevertheless, with respect to a third-party holder of the bill of lading who claims the merchandise, this presumption does not allow for proof to the contrary, in so far as the exceptions deriving from the personal relations existing between forwarder and carrier cannot be opposed (art. 3.4 Brussels Convention, as amended by the 1968 Protocol).

(c) Security. The bill of lading incorporates a right of credit against the carrier in order to demand the delivery of the merchandise at the place of destination. This security can be nominative, to the order or to the bearer:

- It will be nominative when it expressly designates the individual that the merchandise is to be delivered to. This may be the forwarder or a third party – recipient or shipping agent. This bill of lading can only be transferred by assignment.
- It will be to the order when it is recorded that the merchandise will be delivered to the order of the forwarder or of a third party and of the successive endorsees.
- When it is issued to the bearer, the possession of the certificate will serve as identification and this can be transferred upon the material delivery of the document.

If the bill of lading is either nominative or to the order, in addition to possession of the document it will be necessary to justify its ownership, so as to validate the right of credit that it bestows on the carrier. However, mere possession of the document will be sufficient in the case of the issuing of a bill of lading to the bearer.

The bill of lading is also a document substantiating the background to the title. As well as legitimating merchandise description and content, it also allows for a replacement delivery to be made in the case of transfer. It is possible for acts of provision, particular to the ownership, to be made using the bill of lading.

3.3.5.3   Documents similar to the bill of lading

The following documents can be admitted.

(a) Bill received for shipment.   This is issued by the agent of the carrier when the merchandise is delivered prior to its shipment, and in principle it only represents the receipt of the freight by the carrier.

The bill of lading received for shipping – even though it is a provisional receipt – entitles its holder to remove the merchandise at destination, and to exercise the acts of responsibility as appropriate, as well as serving as a title substantiating the background.

(b) Delivery orders.   These assume the existence of a bill of lading and the claim to make a partial delivery of the merchandise or one by instalments.

To this end, the carrier issues a 'delivery order' and records it in the bill of lading. This delivery order confers security status to the merchandise or part thereof and legally entitles its holder to remove it during the trip or at the port of destination.

Along with these particular delivery orders, there are others that are known as improper, since they are issued by the holder of the bill of lading. Although these entitle their holder to remove the part of the freight that they refer to, they do not represent said merchandise and lack the status of security.

(c) Through bill of lading.   This is issued in the case of combined or cumulative carriage, in order to cover the transport made by several carriers, and entitles its holder to claim the merchandise at the place of destination.

Responsibility for issuing it lies with the first carrier. This bill of lading covers the whole of the carriage, even though there are stages undertaken by another carrier. In unitary transport, the first carrier or contracting carrier subcontracts some of the transport stages, but this does not cease to be one single contract and it is jointly liable for compliance with all of its stages. Should the carriage be cumulative in nature, the obligation to undertake it is assumed by all of the carriers that act on it, with all of these being jointly liable. In both cases, a through bill of lading issued at the time when the merchandise is loaded constitutes a security. In addition to representing delivery to the first carrier for its carriage, it authorises the recipient to remove the merchandise from the bearer at the place of destination.

(d) Sea waybill.   This frequently replaces the bill of lading, and constitutes a receipt for the delivery of the merchandise, as well as containing the special statements of the contract of transport. In this way, the sea waybill satisfies the purposes of substantiating the content of the contract of transport and the delivery of the merchandise to the carrier, and consequently entitles its holder to remove said merchandise at the place of destination. However, it does not have the status of a security, as it does not represent the merchandise transported or confer intermediate possession.

Case law states that even though these documents 'substantiate the carrier's obligation with respect to the recipient', the latter does not need to 'present the document in order to claim for the delivery of the merchandise and therefore it is sufficient for it to be identified as the initially-designated subject to be the beneficiary of the right to delivery'. These are issued when the transfer of merchandise is not envisaged and accordingly are not to be used in transport.

Strictly speaking, this is not a document similar to the bill of lading, since it does not have the status of being a security, and The Hague-Visby rules will not apply to these contracts, because these contracts often include a paramount clause.

3.3.6 Obligations of the parties

The Hague-Visby rules do not aim to thoroughly and completely regulate contracts of carriage by sea under a bill of lading regime. As has already been stated, these were proclaimed in order to protect forwarders with respect to carriers, making use of a minimum number of obligations on the carrier and the liability regime. This is laid down on a binding basis in order to prevent liability limitations being imposed due to one party having a dominant position in the contract. For this reason, the carrier's obligations seem to be perfectly well determined while those of the forwarder and shipping agent can be inferred from the foregoing and from other general rules that make up the nature of the contract.

3.3.6.1 Obligations of the forwarder, or the recipient

(a) Delivery of the merchandise to the carrier.   The forwarder that arranges the carriage of the merchandise under a bill of lading regime must place the same at the disposal of the carrier, in order for the obligation to arise for the latter to transport them to the arranged place. This delivery can be made at the side of the vessel in order to be loaded by the carrier using its own resources; or aboard the vessel when loaded by means other than those supplied by the carrier; or also at the stores of the carrier or of its agents, which will logically be associated with the issuing of a 'bill of lading received for shipment'.

(b) Description of the freight.   The forwarder supplies the carrier with information about the chief markings for identifying the freight, as well as the quantity, weight, volume or number of loads, which are to appear in the bill of lading issued by the carrier. This is all without prejudice to the declaration made by the carrier regarding the apparent condition and state that the freight is in. Furthermore, the forwarder will declare the financial value and nature of the freight if these are of interest thereto for the purposes of limiting liability.

It is worth noting that the forwarder has liability with respect to the accuracy of the written declaration provided to the carrier regarding the markings, number, quantity and weight of the merchandise, which is later transcribed in the bill of lading. The forwarder is liable to the carrier for the damages that such inaccuracies could give rise to as a consequence of the claims from the holder of the bill of lading.

(c) Freight payment.   From the perspective of a reciprocal (synallagmatic) contract, the freight payment properly refers to the consideration owed for the carriage of the merchandise assumed by the carrier. The Hague-Visby rules do not provide any regulations in this respect. Since this is a form of transport that ordinarily takes place on regular lines, the carrier usually sets the tariff for the price, and this depends on the characteristics of the carrier. The freight amount will appear in the particular terms of the bill of lading. Payment for the carriage may be made in advance by the forwarder, and it is exceptionally allowed for the shipping agent that receives the freight to pay this at the place of destination.

(d) Removal of the merchandise at the place of destination.   When the carrier complied with its obligation, the forwarder or the recipient of the freight shall remove it, upon presentation of the certificate that entitles it for this purpose (ordinarily the bill of lading).

If the holder of the bill of lading is a third party rather than the forwarder, and freight payment is outstanding or there are costs generated for the carriage that are incumbent on the freight, this shipping agent will not be bound to remove the merchandise with respect to the carrier.

3.3.6.2 *Obligations of the carrier*

The main service assumed by the carrier in the contract of transport of merchandise under the bill of lading regime is the transfer of the merchandise from the loading site to the unloading one. This is an obligation to provide a result, as there is an undertaking not only to carry out the activity but also to make the transfer. This is to be done in a manner which preserves the goods in proper condition during transport. Along with the main transport obligation, there are a number of obligations regarding resources assigned to this aim. All of these are framed within the temporal application of The Hague-Visby rules set out in section 1. They are not restricted to the time taken for the actual transport, but may commence with the loading of the merchandise, as applicable, and conclude with the unloading, provided that these two operations were not explicitly excluded in the contract.

Following the classification laid down by convention, it is possible to group these obligations on the carrier on the basis of the three stages of carriage: before, during and after the voyage.

The liability regime laid down in The Hague-Visby rules is set out on the basis of these obligations of the carrier.

3.3.6.2.1 *Carrier's obligations prior to the commencement of the trip.*

(a) Obligation of navigability of the vessel. The carrier must use a vessel suitable to the freight committed for transfer. This obligation extends not only to the fact that the vessel be in condition to sail and properly loaded, equipped and supplied (section 3.1.a)); but it also extends to the holds, cold chambers and refrigerators and other places on the vessel where merchandise is stored (section 3.1.b) and c)).

The Hague-Visby rules do not take this obligation on the carrier into consideration as a guarantee or as an obligation to provide a result, but rather as a duty of care. Section 4 stipulates that when there are losses or damage that arise from faulty conditions of navigation of the vessel, the carrier will only be liable if the lack of due care in placing the vessel in the conditions set out in the aforementioned sections can be attributed thereto.

(b) Loading and stowage of merchandise. The carrier's obligations listed in section 3.2 include: 'acting in an appropriate and careful manner with respect to loading, stowage ... of the merchandise'. The loading consists in placing the merchandise on board the vessel in order for it to be transported. Stowage is the last operation, specifically the proper placement of the merchandise within the holds or chambers of the vessel.

This obligation on the carrier – who assumes the liability deriving from proper compliance therewith and hence the consequences of defective fulfilment thereof – could be affected by the temporal application of The Hague-Visby rules. These rules will apply to loading and unloading operations provided that these are carried out using the particular resources of the vessel. However, even though this may imply the exclusion of the carrier's liability for loading and unloading operations, as long as they are carried out using resources external to the vessel, this is generally not the case. This is because in most bills of lading the carrier assumes the loading and unloading operations, even though it may entrust them to a third party. In this way, should damage arise in the performance of the operations, the carrier is at all times liable on the terms set out in The Hague-Visby rules. This is without prejudice to the extra-contractual liability of the third party that carried out the loading to those that suffered loss (forwarder, recipients and their insurers).

Even in cases where the undertaking of the loading and the stowing by the forwarder is agreed, case law states that the carrier will always be liable for the lack of care by the captain in his control.

(c) Issuing and delivery of the bill of lading to the forwarder. Section 3.3 imposes on the carrier the obligation to 'deliver a bill of lading signed by the carrier, the captain or agent of the carrier at the loading port, that sets out the terms stated therein, after having received the merchandise on board': identification of the vessel, the captain, the forwarder and shipping agent authorised to remove the merchandise; loading and unloading ports; the freight, the markings on the merchandise, the number of loads, quantity and weight, and their apparent condition and state.

3.3.6.2.2 *Carrier's obligations during the voyage.*

(a) To undertake the transfer of the merchandise in compliance with the arranged itinerary. The Hague-Visby rules justify a deviation in the route not only in the case of saving or attempt to save individuals, but goods as well. Whereas the saving of individuals can be justified for humanitarian reasons, the saving of goods can benefit only the shipowner who will be compensated in accordance with the maritime salvage laws, while the forwarder and/or recipient will be affected without any party being in the least liable for the delay. For this reason, the Hamburg rules have adjusted this provision, in such a way that measures of deviation from the route for the saving of individuals are always considered to be reasonable, while in the case of the salvaging of merchandise this depends on whether the measures taken are reasonable (section 5.6).

The carrier is to be liable for the loss or damage resulting from an unjustified deviation that leads to an infringement of the law or of the contract, along with the damage arising from a delay.

(b) Preservation, monitoring and care of the merchandise. The content of this obligation is particular to the deposit. In reality, the carrier is bound to deliver the merchandise, once its carriage is completed, in the same conditions in which it received them. The carrier presumes that it receives the merchandise in the conditions stated in the bill of lading, and unless there are reservations about their condition or appearance, it is to be considered that they were in good condition (section 3.6).

The carrier is liable for damage suffered by the merchandise from the time at which it is delivered until it is placed at the disposal of the recipient, unless any of the causes of exoneration from liability set out in section 4 arise.

3.3.6.2.3 Obligations of the carrier once the voyage has been completed.

(a) Unloading of the merchandise. The legal regime of this obligation shall be correlated to that which is already set out for loading. Its inclusion in the contract of transport under the regime of the bill of lading will depend on whether it is undertaken with the particular resources of the vessel or – which is more common in line transport – whether the carrier has assumed the loading and unloading operations.

(b) Delivery of merchandise to the recipient. When the voyage has been completed, the carrier must put the merchandise at the disposal of the recipient in the same conditions in which it received it at the time of loading. The service assumed by the carrier concludes with the delivery, and this is when its safekeeping obligations cease. This is the time at which the reservations or objections about apparent damage must be indicated, and the period for reporting those that are not apparent commences. Finally, the delivery constitutes the *dies a quo* in the calculation of the period of expiry of the claim for liability for damages against the carrier.

The delivery must be made to the party that appears as the holder of the bill of lading and can substantiate it. The form in which the bill is issued can be nominative, to the order or to the bearer. The carrier complies with its delivery obligation by placing the merchandise at the disposal of the party that appears as the holder according to the bill of lading: if it is nominative, of the party that substantiates being the designated individual; if it is to the order, of the party that justifies the holding of the title in accordance with a regular chain of endorsements; and if it is the bearer, of the holder of the document.

3.3.7 Carrier's liability regime

3.3.7.1 Nature of the liability regime established in The Hague-Visby rules

(A) *Binding legal regime.* The objective of The Hague-Visby rules is specifically to outline a binding set of regulations concerning the liability regime of the bearers, which impedes its exoneration through contractual clauses that are imposed, making use of its dominant position.

The imperative nature of these rules is relative, since this is a minimum liability regime for the carrier which, although it cannot be alleviated or reduced, it can be increased under contract. Thus, section 10 sanctions any clause, agreement or accord in a contract of transport that exonerates the carrier or the vessel of their liability for loss or damage relating to the merchandise, that arise from negligence, fault or breach of the duties or obligations stated in the preceding sections, or that may alleviate said responsibility in any other manner that is not one determined under this Act.

At the same time, section 13 permits the carrier to waive the liability limits and causes of exoneration, as well as increasing its liability with respect to the terms of the Act, provided that this is included in the bill of lading.

Nonetheless, this liability regime is quite favourable to the carrier since it allows for a broad range of causes of exoneration from liability, especially for nautical faults in the provision. The obligation of navigability is conceived of as a duty of care and, as appropriate, the liability is limited in a quantitative sense.

(B) General principle of liability for fault by the carrier due to the breach of its contractual obligations. No general principle of liability on the carrier is contained in the original draft of The Hague rules, compiled at the 1924 Brussels Convention. It limits itself to listing the cases of liability and the causes of exoneration.

The Hamburg rules codify the principle of liability for fault by the carrier, with respect to the damage and/or losses to the merchandise, and delays in its delivery, while they are in its safekeeping. Said fault is presumed, with a presumption that allows proof to the contrary (art. 5.1 Hamburg Convention).

(C) Presumption of liability of the carrier. The general principle is completed by another, which can be deduced from the rest of the regulations. According to this, the carrier's liability is presumed in the case of damage and/or detriment to the freight during the time in which there is an obligation for custody. The temporal phase of application of the special legal regime is ordinarily understood as being that which passes from the loading of the merchandise in the port of origin until the unloading at the destination.

This presumption of liability of the carrier is concerned with the breach of the duty of care in complying with its obligations. But this presumption allows proof to the contrary. On the one hand, the bearer can be exonerated from liability if it can substantiate having employed due diligence. This means, in general terms, transferring its consideration to judicial decision or the party that settles legal disputes relating to compensation for damages caused. On the other hand, in order to facilitate the exoneration of the carrier from liability, section 4.2 lists a set of cases in which this applies, with the carrier being exonerated from liability. The proof of the applicability of some of these causes of exoneration lies with the carrier, and these will be examined in a subsequent section.

In general terms, in the Hamburg rules there is a *iuris tantum* presumption of fault on the part of the carrier with respect to the damage and/or losses to the merchandise, or their delay in delivery (art. 5.1 Hamburg Convention). However, the burden of proof is reversed exceptionally and it is necessary to substantiate the fault or negligence of the carrier in the following cases: damage caused by fire (art. 5.4 Hamburg Convention), damage resulting from risks especially inherent to the transport of live animals (art. 5.5 Hamburg Convention), and damage arising from measures adopted for the saving of human lives (art. 5.6 Hamburg Convention).

3.3.7.2 Scope of this liability

(A) Objective scope of the liability.   In principle, The Hague-Visby rules extend the carrier's liability to 'the losses, breakages or damage suffered by the merchandise'. No express mention is made of the liability for delay in the delivery of the merchandise.

The extension of the objective scope of liability of the carrier is made very clear in the Hamburg rules. This will cover 'the damage resulting from the loss or damage of the merchandise, as well as a delay in the delivery' (art. 5.1). It is considered that there is 'a delay in the delivery when the merchandise has not been delivered at the port of unloading set out in the contract of carriage by sea within the expressly agreed period or, in the absence of such an agreement, within the period that could reasonably be required from a diligent carrier, having regard to the circumstances of the case' (art. 5.2). This is a question of liability for fault, which accepts contrary proof that both the carrier and its employees and agents adopted reasonable measures to prevent the fact and its consequences.

(B) Subjective scope.   In this manner, and with regard to the subjective scope of the liability set out in section 4 – damages to the freight occasioned by the breach on the part of the carrier of the legal and contractual obligations deriving from carriage by sea – extends to the contractual carrier. This is the liability that is agreed with the forwarder for the carriage of the merchandise. In the case of a 'through bill of lading', this liability corresponds to the first carrier and also jointly to

the rest of the successive carriers, if this has been agreed to, since otherwise these successive carriers will only be liable for each one of the stretches assumed.

The liability of the carrier extends, in principle, not only to the acts carried out by the carrier itself, but also to those carried out by its dependants. This liability may take on a joint form, in the case where a claim for direct liability against the dependants is anticipated, which is associated with the possibility of the dependants of the carrier opposing the same causes of exoneration and limits on liability set out for the carrier in the Convention. This is expressly established in art. 4 bis. 1 of the Brussels Convention amended by the 1968 Protocol and extends not only to the exercising of claims deriving from the contract of transport, but also to the exercising of extra-contractual public liability claims.

However, the carrier's liability for the activity of its dependants, which is logical in all carriage respects, can be mitigated by the part played by the causes of exoneration from liability under section 4, and specifically the nautical faults, which exclude the carrier from liability when they arise. This precept exempts the carrier from liability in the case of damage and/or loss to the merchandise, when they stem from 'acts, negligence or fault by the captain, seamen, pilot or the staff employed by the carrier in the navigation or the administration of the vessel'. This exoneration from liability is unusual under the general regime of contracts of transport, in which the transport company is always liable for the damage caused by its dependants, and does not extend to commercial faults. These are understood as being those that are concerned with the handling and care of freight.

In this respect, the Hamburg rules eliminate this possible exemption from liability for nautical faults (art. 5).

There may be third parties subcontracted by the carrier in order to carry out the loading, stowage or unloading operations. The forwarder or the recipient do not have a contractual claim with respect to these third parties, without prejudice to the carrier being liable for damage caused to the freight as a consequence of the improper undertaking of these operations. This liability of the carrier contractual for the damage occasioned by the subcontracted companies is subject to the liability regime of The Hague-Visby rules, and specifically the quantitative limits of liability.

The forwarder would only have an extra-contractual public liability action against these autonomous third parties subcontracted by the carrier, hence not against dependants. The Hague-Visby rules would not apply in the exercising of this claim. Therefore it would not be possible to oppose the quantitative limits of liability. This would be the case unless the appearance of these autonomous third parties has been envisaged in the contract of transport so as to make use of The Hague-Visby rules through a paramount clause.

(C) Temporal scope.   The temporal scope of the liability of the carrier is determined by the legal provision concerning the scope of temporal application of The Hague-Visby rules. In principle, this temporal scope coincides with the transport stage which starts with the loading of the merchandise on board the vessel and concludes with its unloading, provided that these loading and unloading operations are undertaken with the particular resources of the vessel. In other circumstances, these loading and unloading operations would not be covered by the liability regime. Nevertheless, as we have already indicated, it is common for the carrier to include these loading and unloading operations in the contract, without prejudice to these not being undertaken with the particular resources of the vessel should these services be contracted out to a third party.

In this manner, in principle and unless there is a contractual clause that extends the liability of the carrier to these stages, the liability regime set out under The Hague-Visby rules does not apply: either upon delivery of merchandise to the carrier or to its agent at the port, until it is unloaded; or to the safekeeping, storage and displacement prior to the loading; or to the safekeeping and storage of the freight with the shipping agent until it is delivered to the recipient. As we have already indicated, the binding nature of these rules does not have a bearing on the increase in liability of the carrier, since they serve as the minimum necessary in order to protect the forwarder.

The Hamburg rules do not give rise to doubts when art 4.1 extends the carrier's liability for the merchandise to the whole of the period during which they are in its safekeeping at the loading port, during the transportation and while at the unloading port. The following section describes in detail what happens when it is considered that the merchandise is in the safekeeping of the carrier; from the time when it takes charge at the loading port till the time when it delivers it at the unloading port.

3.3.7.3 Reporting of the damage and deadline for the exercising of a claim for liability

(A) Reporting of the loss and/or damage to the merchandise.   The receipt of the merchandise by the recipient presumes an admission of proof to the contrary, that the merchandise was delivered in the form

recorded in the bill of lading. In order to avoid this presumption, the possibility is established for the recipient to make a written claim, brought against 'the carrier or its agent at the port of unloading, for the losses or damage suffered and for the general nature of these losses or damage'.

This report must be made, in the case of apparent loss or damage, 'before or at the time of the removal of the merchandise and when they are placed in the safekeeping of the individual that is entitled to the receipt thereof' and 'if the losses or damage are not apparent, the notice must be made in the three days following the delivery'.

This report can be made by recording the reservation in the particular bill of lading for the receipt of the merchandise that was transported and delivered at that time to the bearer.

Nonetheless, this report or written reservation will be rendered null if the condition of the merchandise was checked and seen to be contradictory at the time of the reception, that is to say by both parties at the same time, or by their experts, or by the expert who is judicially appointed. This legal provision makes sense if we observe that the report is designed to challenge the presumption of proper delivery of the merchandise, and the contradictory verification can constitute proof of the condition of the merchandise at the time of delivery.

The omission of this report does not prevent the possibility of exercising claims of liability against the carrier. It only determines the need for the forwarder or recipient to prove the existence of losses or damage to merchandise.

According to the Hamburg rules, it is presumed that merchandise is delivered to the recipient in the condition described in the bill of lading, and in good condition in case a report is not drawn up. This presumption can be broken by the report made by the recipient of the freight about the existence of the loss or damage, specifying its nature, within the first working day following the date on which the freight transported was placed at its disposal. If the damage or loss is not apparent, the period for such a claim will be 15 days. The report must be made directly to the carrier or to its employees; should there be one effective carrier and one contractual one, the report made to either of these will be valid. In the case of delay in delivery, the resulting damage must be reported in writing within 60 days following delivery of the merchandise (art. 19).

(B) Prescription period for the exercising of a claim for liability. A claim for contractual liability, based on The Hague-Visby rules, is subject to a

period of prescription. It must be exercised against the carrier and the vessel – it being understood the shipowner and the captain – in the period of one year from the time when the merchandise was delivered or, in the case of loss of the merchandise, from the date on which it should have been delivered.

From the start the case law has interpreted this period as being one of prescription. This can be brought by the party concerned or ex officio, and no interruption in its calculation is permitted.

Section 3.6 of the Brussels Convention, amended by the 1968 Protocol, allows the parties to make a mutual agreement to extend this period of prescription for the exercising of the claim for liability, provided that they do this after the fact that gave rise to the claim.

The Hamburg rules lay down a period of two years for the exercising of claims against the carrier. This is a prescription period and as such it cannot be interrupted, although it is possible for it to be extended by the party against which the claim is brought, if it makes a written declaration to the claimant. The action of repetition that lies with the person who has been declared liable can be exercised when the prescription period has passed, if this is done within the period set down by the law of the state in which proceedings are brought (art. 20).

3.3.7.4 Causes of exoneration from liability

As has just been indicated, in the case of loss and/or damage to the freight, the liability of the carrier is presumed. This presumption admits proof to the contrary, of the use of due care on the part of the carrier or – what is more important for practical purposes – the existence of any cause of exoneration.

The Hamburg rules omit this list of causes that exonerate the carrier from liability, which in many cases is irrelevant since they imply the absence of blame or negligence on the part of the carrier and its employees. But the judgment can be simplified in any case.

(A) Nautical errors.

(B) Cases of unforeseen events and of force majeure.

Unforeseen events and *force majeure* are typical causes of exemption from civil liability, and these extend to the factors causing the damage and/or loss that could not have been anticipated or, if they were anticipated, were unavoidable.

In addition, the causes of exemption classified in section 4.1 include other cases of unforeseen events:

- 'fire, unless this was caused by a fact or fault on the part of carrier'. In reality, a fire constitutes a presumption of lack of diligence by the carrier, which functions to reverse the burden of proof. The existence of a fire exempts the carrier from proving that it acted with due care, and the burden of proving a lack of due care in order to achieve the liability of the carrier lies with the forwarder.
- 'hazards, damage or accidents at sea or in other navigable waters'. In order for the carrier to be exempt from liability, it is necessary for the accident to go beyond what could be controlled by the captain.
- 'acts of war'.
- 'public enemy acts'.
- 'detention or seizure by sovereign bodies, authorities or peoples or (...) a judicial embargo'.
- 'quarantine restrictions'.
- 'strikes, lock-outs, or ... stoppages or ... work to rules wholly or partially imposed on the work, for whatever cause'.
- 'riots or civil disturbances'.

(C) Facts that can be attributed to the forwarder. Section 4.2 contains three cases in which the cause of damage can be attributed to negligent conduct on the part of the forwarder, and consequently the carrier is exempt from liability.

The first of these is generic, and makes it possible to include any atypical situation in which the cause of damage and/or loss can be attributed to a form of conduct (by act or omission) by the forwarder, the owner of the merchandise or its agents or representatives: (i) 'act or omission of the forwarder or owner of the merchandise of its agent or representative'.

The other two classify forms of conduct that entail a defective form of compliance with the forwarder's obligations:

- 'insufficient packing'.
- 'insufficiencies or imperfections of the markings'.

It is necessary to observe the role played by the declarations made in the bill of lading, at the time when these are issued when the merchandise is loaded. This is because there is a presumption that the merchandise was delivered in proper condition and that the packaging and the markings were correct, since if that was not the case, the carrier would have expressly recorded this.

(D) Concealed defects. This cause refers to 'the concealed defects that are not observed by reasonable diligence'. These concealed defects pertain to the vessel and have a bearing on the carrier's obligation of

seaworthiness. In so far as compliance with this obligation is subject to a duty of care, provided that the defects of the vessel could not have been observed by a diligent carrier – the shipowner – following an ordinary inspection prior to loading merchandise, it shall be exempt from liability.

(E) Salvage or attempted salvage. In those cases in which a salvaging of goods or saving of individuals is involved, the itinerary may be altered and damage and/or loss to the freight may be occasioned, and in principle this damage and/or loss would not be the carrier's responsibility. In the same way, exoneration from liability applies in cases of damage and/or loss caused on the grounds of 'saving or attempted saving of life or goods at sea'. This statement is excessively broad. While it is reasonable that it covers both saving and the attempt, since the justification does not lie in the success of the salvage operation, it does not seem fair that the salvaging of goods is included along with the saving of persons. The saving of persons can always be justified on humanitarian grounds and because of the value of human life, which is greater than that of the salvaging of transported freight. However, the justification is unclear in the case of salvaging of goods. Should this be successful it could lead to a right for compensation. In any event, it does not seem fair that the financial interests of the forwarder or recipient could be placed at risk for the benefit of the financial interests of a third party. Furthermore, this action provides exemption from risk coverage for damage to the freight, and could give rise to a right of compensation for the carrier.

3.3.7.5 Quantitative limitation of the compensatory debt

(A) Scope of this limitation. At the same time as a binding regime of liability is imposed on the carrier under The Hague-Visby rules, the compensatory debt for loss and/or damage to merchandise is limited. This limitation operates not only on the carrier's liability but also on the amount of compensation. Therefore not only the carrier and its employees or supervising representatives can benefit from this, but benefit can also be gained by those parties that insure the risk of compensation or guarantee the satisfaction thereof.

This quantitative limitation on the compensatory debt operates with respect to the damage and/or loss of merchandise, but it does not affect the compensation for other damage occasioned by a breach of its obligations by the carrier or its employees. And at the same time it is irrelevant that the compensatory debt derives from the exercising of a claim for contractual or extra-contractual liability.

Regardless of the appropriateness of applying a quantitative limit on the compensatory debt, this will in any event be calculated on the basis of the value of the merchandise at the place and on the date on which they have been unloaded under the contract – in the case of damage – or at the place and on the date on which they should have been unloaded – in the case of loss.

(B) Limits on liability. Generally speaking, The Hague-Visby rules limit the liability of the carrier for damage and/or loss of merchandise to the sum of 666.67 units of account per load or units, or two units of account per kilogram of gross tonnage of the merchandise loss, whichever is higher.

Any contractual agreement that seeks to reduce this limit on liability will be null and void. However, it is possible to increase the limit on liability by means of an agreement between the forwarder and the carrier or its agents, or the captain.

The Hamburg rules increase the quantitative limit of the compensatory debt by 25 per cent when damage and/or loss of merchandise is involved ('835 Units of account per load or 2.5 units of account per kilogramme in gross tonnage, if the quantity is greater' (art. 6.1a)). They also establish a limitation in the case of compensation for a delay in delivery (two and a half times the freight sum to be paid for merchandise that suffered a delay, without it being possible to exceed the total sum for freight payable by virtue of the contract (art. 6.1b)). However, under no circumstances can the sum of the two previous compensatory sums exceed the limit set out in 6.1a for the case of total loss of merchandise (art. 6.1c).

The unit of account is the Special Drawing Right defined by the International Monetary Fund, whose daily value or quotation is set in relation to a basket of currencies that are officially quoted (euro, pound sterling, Japanese yen and United States dollar). The conversion of this unit into euros will be made on the date set by the law of the competent court (section 4.5b of the 1924 Brussels Convention, amended by the Protocol of 1979). In our case, we must consider the compensatory obligation, which is a value debt whose determination is made in rulings. This is done in such a way that the conversion will be made by considering the corresponding quotation on the date of the ruling.

(C) Cases in which this limit on liability does not operate.

(a) Declaration of the value of the merchandise. The previous limit on liability does not operate when the forwarder has declared the nature and the value of the merchandise, prior to the shipment and this is recorded in the bill of lading.

In these cases, the compensatory debt will, in principle, be limited to the stated value. Naturally, if damages or losses are partial, the compensation will be proportional to the declared value.

Nevertheless, the carrier can establish that the value of the merchandise was less than that declared, and in this case reference will be made to the true value. This is established by section 4.5 of the Brussels Convention, modified by the 1979 Protocol, which states that the sum declared in the bill of lading 'will constitute a presumption unless there is evidence to the contrary, but this will not be binding on the carrier, who will be able to challenge this'.

In addition, this declaration of value made by the forwarder and contained in the bill of lading will not operate if the carrier stated its reservation about said declaration of value of the merchandise in its own bill at the time of making the shipment.

(b) Existence of misrepresentation or serious blame on the part of the carrier. 'Neither the carrier nor the vessel will be entitled to benefit from the limitation on liability, if it is demonstrated that the damage is due to an act or omission by the carrier that took place, whether with the intention of causing damage, or recklessly and with the knowledge that these would be likely to lead to damage'. It is necessary to prove that the carrier has acted either deceitfully – that is in a malicious manner with the intent to cause the damage – or with reckless imprudence, being aware of the damage that could probably be produced to the freight. The existence of misrepresentation and serious blame cannot therefore be presumed. This has to be substantiated, although use can be made of the proof of judicial presumption, on the basis of the evidence, for this purpose.

The Hamburg rules also prevent the carrier from making use of the limitation on liability if it can be proved that loss, damage or delay in delivery arose from an action or omission by the carrier carried out with the intention of causing this damage or recklessly or knowing that this would probably be occasioned (art. 8 Hamburg Convention).

3.4 Carriage of goods by rail

3.4.1 Introduction

The international carriage of merchandise by rail is regulated by means of international conventions, either of a bilateral or a multilateral nature. This latter group includes the Berne Convention of 9 May 1980, relating to the international carriage by rail (ICRC).

Appendix B of the Convention consists of the 'Standard rules relating to the contract of international carriage of merchandise by rail', and these are the rules that we are going to analyse below.

This Convention was amended by the Protocol of 20 December 1990.

3.4.2 Object and scope of the Convention

3.4.2.1 Scope of application

It shall apply to all of those shipments of merchandise that are transported with a direct bill of lading established for journeys that include the territories of at least two states and that exclusively cover lines inscribed in the list of the Central Office, the body that assumes the Secretaryship of the Organisation.

It shall not apply to those shipments whose place of origin and of destination are located in the territory of the same state, or – even though they may travel through another state – they do so in transit. They may travel in transit through a third country when there is neither loading nor unloading of any merchandise in the same.

The Convention will also not apply in the case where travel takes place by rail through two different states that have stipulated accords by virtue of which said carriage is not considered to be international.

The shipments may be transported:

(a) between stations of two adjacent states; or
(b) between stations of two states and in transit through the territory of a third,
(c) when the lines along which the carriage is effected are used by only one of these three states, they shall be subject to the internal trade regime applicable to said railway, when the shipper – on making use of the corresponding bill of lading – so requests and the laws or regulations of some of the states concerned are not contrary to this.

'Station' terminus covers railway stations, the ports of navigation services and all of the other establishments of transport companies open to the public for the undertaking of the contract of transport.

3.4.2.2 Objects accepted on condition or excluded from the carriage

The following merchandise shall be accepted for carriage under certain conditions:

(a) The materials and objects accepted for carriage on the conditions of the regulations relating to the international rail transport of hazardous merchandise (IHR).
(b) Funeral transportations.

(c) The railway vehicles that travel on their own wheels.

(d) Live animals must be accompanied by an escort designated by the shipper. In this case, the railway shall be exempt from any loss or damage resulting from a risk that the escort has the objective of avoiding. An escort shall not be necessary when this is so determined in the international tariffs or at the request of the shipper when the railways or animals that participate in the carriage do not require one.

(e) Those objects whose carriage presents special difficulties due to size, weight or structure shall not be admitted except under the conditions laid down individually in each case.

Without prejudice to all the matters stated above, the Convention leaves open the possibility of the contracting states reaching specific agreements about the carriage of certain merchandise.

On the other hand, we find that the following are excluded from carriage:

(a) All objects that can be transported by the mail authorities.

(b) Objects that, owing to their size, weight or structure cannot be adapted to the form of carriage requested.

(c) Objects whose carriage is prohibited.

(d) Materials and objects excluded from transport by virtue of the regulations relating to the international rail transport of hazardous merchandise (IHR).

3.4.2.3   Transportation obligation of the railway

The railway is obliged to effect any carriage of merchandise by complete freight cars, provided that the conditions laid down in the standard rules are met:

(a) That the shipper complies with the standard rules, complementary provisions and tariffs.

(b) That this is possible given the normal transport resources that make it possible to meet the ordinary traffic needs.

(c) That said carriage is not impeded by any circumstance that the railway cannot avoid, and whose redress does not depend on the latter.

However, it shall not be bound to undertake the carriage of that merchandise whose loading, transhipment and unloading necessitate certain special resources, but only when the stations have such resources available.

An obligation to undertake the service will exist when the carriage of merchandise can be effected without delay.

The cases where a service is suspended or eliminated or certain shipments are excluded or accepted on condition shall be reported to the public and to the railways without delay. They should also be reported to the railways of the other states so that they can be made public.

3.4.2.4 Tariffs

The price of carriage and the accessory costs are to be calculated in accordance with the terms of the tariffs that are legally in force, published in each state and valid at the time of the conclusion of the contract.

The tariffs must contain all the special conditions applicable to the carriage. The tariff conditions cannot modify the content of the standard rules, unless the latter expressly establish this. The tariffs must be applied to all under the same conditions.

The railways can conclude particular agreements in relation to the tariffs, provided that these are applicable to other users that find themselves in similar situations.

3.4.2.5 Special conditions concerning certain types of carriage

Special provisions exist for the transporting of private freight cars under the Regulations referring to the international carriage of private freight cars by rail (IHR).

There are special provisions in the regulations referring to the international rail carriage of containers (IRCo).

For the carriage of special packages, railways shall be able – by means of tariff clauses – to agree to special provisions in accordance with the regulations referring to the international carriage of express parcels by rail (IREx).

For the carriage of hazardous merchandise, there are special provisions under the regulations referring to the international carriage of hazardous merchandise (IRH).

3.4.3 The contract of transport

3.4.3.1 Form and terms of the contract

All international shipments must be accompanied by a bill of lading that will be presented and duly completed by the shipper. It shall establish a bill of lading for each shipment and this shall only be concerned with the freight of one single freight car.

Railways shall set out a specimen copy of a bill of lading for low speeds and another specimen copy for high speeds, which shall include a duplicate copy for the shipper. The specimen copy of the bill of lading selected by the shipper shall state whether the merchandise has to be transported at low or high speeds. A request for low speeds for one part of the journey and for high speeds for another part of it shall not be accepted, unless there is agreement between the railways concerned.

The bill of lading shall be printed in two languages, or possibly three, of which at least one shall be one of the work languages of the organisation and shall be drafted in Latin characters.

(1) Content of the bill of lading:

(a) Designation of the station of destination.
(b) Name and address of the recipient, who shall be a private individual or any person in law.
(c) Denomination of the merchandise.
(d) The weight of the merchandise or an analogous statement.
(e) For detailed shipments: the number of bulk cargoes and a description of the packing; for complete freight: cars that contain one or more elements of freight invoiced in combined rail and sea.
(f) For the shipments whose freight is the responsibility of the shipper, the freight car number and in addition, the tare for private freight cars.
(g) A detailed numbering of the documents required by the Customs authorities and the other administrative authorities that accompany the bill of lading or that mention that they are at the disposal of the railway at a specific station or at a Customs office or the office of any other authority.
(h) The name and address of the shipper together with the handwritten signature. The prescriptions in force at the departure station shall determine the concepts of 'full freight car' and 'detailed shipment' for the whole of the journey.

As appropriate, the bill of lading shall contain all of the other statements established by the standard rules. It shall only be possible to include other statements if these are imposed or accepted by the laws and regulations of a state.

It is prohibited to replace the bill of lading with other documents or to add others that are not accepted by the standard rules.

It shall be possible to use complementary sheets in the case in which the part reserved for the shipper is insufficient. These sheets shall become part of the bill of lading and shall have the same format.

The general order of things shall be that each shipment is to be accompanied by a bill of lading, but there are certain cases in which more than one bill of lading may be issued:

(a) When by its nature, the merchandise cannot be loaded as a whole.
(b) The merchandise that is partly the responsibility of the railway and partly the responsibility of the shipper.
(c) The merchandise that has to be loaded as a whole infringes the Customs provisions or those of other administrative authorities.
(d) That merchandise whose loading as a whole is prohibited.

It can be deduced, from all of the statements on the bill of lading, that there is a set of responsibilities for the shipper. The latter shall be liable for the accuracy of the declarations and statements written on the bill of lading.

(2) Verification.   For its part, the railway is entitled to verify the contents of the bill of lading. To such an end, it shall invite the shipper or the recipient to be in attendance at the checking. In the event of neither of the parties being present, it shall do the same in the presence of two witnesses that are not a part of the railway. This act shall have the same validity as if it had been effected in the presence of the former.

If it is recorded in the bill of lading that, as a result of the verification, it turns out that the shipment does not correspond to the data stated in the bill of lading, the costs that have been caused by the same shall be levied on the merchandise, increasing the price of the carriage.

(3) Verification of the weight, of the number of bulk cargoes and the true tare of the freight cars.   Each state shall determine in which cases the railway shall be obliged to carry out a check. The railway shall include the result of these checks in the bill of lading.

If a difference in weight is discovered, the shipper shall pay the price difference that exists between the price that related to the declared weight and the price that related to the checked weight. The weight that is checked at the station of departure, or that declared by the shipper, will continue to serve as a basis in order to calculate the price of the carriage.

(4) Overloading.   Once the excess loading of a freight car has been observed, it shall be possible to remove this from the freight car, requesting

that the shipper state the way in which it wishes this excess to be disposed of. The same shall be requested of the recipient of the freight.

If a legally entitled person shall be able to make use of the excess freight, forwarding it to:

(a) the station of destination of the main freight;
(b) another station of destination;
(c) or stating that it is to be returned to the station of departure; in any of these three cases, the excess freight shall be treated as being a different shipment.

(5) Excess rates. For the cases where a difference in weight is observed between that which is declared and that which is checked, or if there is excess freight, the difference between the price of carriage and a compensation for possible damage shall be paid. Furthermore, the railway shall be entitled to receive an excess rate for:

(a) Irregular, imprecise or incomplete designation of the materials and objects excluded from the carriage by virtue of the IRH.
(b) Irregular, imprecise or incomplete designation of the materials and objects accepted for carriage under certain conditions by virtue of the IRH, or a breach of said conditions.
(c) Irregular, imprecise or incomplete designation of the price that had to be paid and that was paid, when such a statement implies a more reduced tariff.
(d) Designation of a weight less than the true rate, which implies a lower price.

If there is a statement indicating a weight that is less than the true rate and of an excess load for one particular freight car, the excess rates corresponding to the two infringements shall be received in accumulate form. The amount of the excess rates and the reason why they are to be collected shall be included in the bill of lading.

It shall not be possible for any excess rate to be collected in the case of:

(a) An inaccurate statement of the weight when the weighing procedure is obligatory for the railway.
(b) An imprecise indication of the weight or, in the case of an excess load, if the shipper has requested that the weighing procedure be effected by the railway in the bill of lading.
(c) An excess load occasioned during the carriage due to atmospheric influence, when it is established that the freight did not exceed the limit at the time of the delivery of the merchandise.

(d) By excess load we consider this to be the excess of the weight of the freight car as a whole.

(e) An increase in weight of the merchandise that is produced during the carriage, without there being an excess load (that is to say, the weight of the freight car falls within its limits), if it is established that this took place due to atmospheric influences.

(f) An imprecise statement of the weight, when the difference between the weight stated in the bill of lading and that which is verified does not exceed 3 per cent of the declared weight.

(6) Itinerary. The shipper may establish the itinerary that is to be followed in the bill of lading, marking this out at cross-border points or frontier stations and, as appropriate, by transit stations between railways. There are a set of situations that need to be assimilated into the outline of an itinerary. These will be:

(a) The names of the stations at which the formalities required by the Customs authorities or other administrative authorities have to be carried out, or those at which a certain degree of care of the merchandise must be provided

(b) The designation of the applicable tariffs, when this is sufficient in order to determine the stations between which the tariffs requested must be applied.

(c) A statement of payment of the whole or part of the costs up to x.

The transport costs and the delivery periods are going to be calculated according to the itinerary set out by the shipper or, in the absence thereof, according to the itinerary that the railway sets out.

The shipper has the power to set the applicable tariffs down in the bill of lading. This entails the setting out of an itinerary. In such a case the railway will not be responsible for the damage that may result from such a choice, unless there has been misrepresentation or serious culpability on its part. The railway will be bound to comply with said itinerary, if the conditions necessary for the application thereof are met. Should this not be possible, the railway has the authority to select the itinerary or the tariffs that could be more advantageous for the shipper.

(7) Delivery periods.

(a) In principle, these are set down in the agreements concluded between the railways that take part in the carriage or by the international tariffs applicable between the station of departure and that of arrival. None of these periods can be longer than the following:

(i) For complete freight cars:
  • At high speeds:
    – Shipping period, 12 hours.
    – Carriage period, for an indivisible fraction of 400 km, 24 hours.
  • At low speeds:
    – Shipping period, 24 hours.
    – Carriage period, for an indivisible fraction of 300 km, 24 hours.
(ii) For detailed shipments:
  • At high speeds:
    – Shipping period, 12 hours.
    – Carriage period, for an indivisible fraction of 300 km, 24 hours.
  • At low speeds:
    – Shipping period, 24 hours.
    – Carriage period, for an indivisible fraction of 200 km, 24 hours.

The carriage distance shall be calculated as the total distance between the station of departure and the station of destination.

(b) Apart from the generally established terms relating to the periods set out in the rules, railways can establish supplementary periods in the following cases:

(i) For those shipments that are presented for carriage outside the stations or that are to be delivered outside them.
(ii) For those carriages that are undertaken:
  • By a line that is not fitted out for the fast handling of shipments.
  • By sea or by navigable inland waterways.
  • By a route that does not possess a railway.
  • By a secondary line.
  • By a line whose rails are not of the usual width.
(iii) Or due to a reason of extraordinary circumstances such as difficulties in operation or abnormal traffic.

(c) The deadlines can also be extended when:

(i) It is necessary to carry out a form of verification when differences related to the entries stated in the bill of lading appear.
(ii) This is required for compliance with the formalities demanded by the Customs authorities or by administrative authorities.
(iii) Variations in the contract of transport take place.
(iv) It is necessary to take special care with the shipments.

   (v) It is necessary to make transhipments or rectifications in a defective freight.
   (vi) An interruption in the traffic takes place.
(d) The delivery period shall be suspended:
   (i) High speeds: on Sundays and certain public holidays, when the laws and regulations establish this.
   (ii) Low speeds: Sundays and legal public holidays.
   (iii) High and low speeds: Saturdays, when the laws and regulations of a state establish this.
      These extensions and suspensions must always be mentioned in the bill of lading.
(e) It shall be considered that a piece of merchandise is delivered within the established deadline when:
   (i) The arrival of the merchandise is notified and is placed at the disposal of the recipient.
   (ii) The merchandise is at the disposal of the recipient when dealing with shipments that have to be delivered at the station and that are not the subject of an arrival notice.
   (iii) The merchandise shall also be at the disposal of the recipient when dealing with shipments that are to be delivered outside the station.

(8) Condition, packing and marking of the merchandise.   If the railway accepts merchandise for carriage that shows manifest signs of breakage, it shall be possible to require that the condition of said merchandise be stated on the bill of lading.

As regards packing, there will be certain merchandise which, by its nature, requires certain special care which the shipper must provide. It is to follow the measures that are available thereto for packing in terms of the appropriate railway tariffs and regulations. Should these rules not be followed, the railway can reject the carriage of merchandise or record the fact that the shipper did not comply with these in the bill of lading. In any event, the shipper shall be liable for the consequences that could arise due to a lack of proper packing.

In detailed shipments, the shipper is obliged to state the following in each load:

(a) The name and address of the recipient.
(b) The station of destination.

The following cannot be accepted for carriage, if not undertaken by a full freight car:

(a) Fragile objects.

(b) Those that could spill in the freight cars.

(c) Merchandise that could stain or cause deterioration of other loads.

This is the rule, unless said loads can be packed or attached together in such a way that they cannot break, be lost, stain or cause deterioration to other loads.

(9) Documents required by Customs or other administrative authorities. The obligation to attach the bill of lading and the documents that may be necessary to comply with the formalities required by Customs or other administrative authorities lies with the shipper.

If these documents are not attached to the bill of lading or made to be delivered by the recipient, the shipper must state the station, the Customs office or the office of any other authority at which said documents are at the disposal of the railway in the bill of lading.

Once the documents are received, the railway has no obligation to revise them or declare that they are sufficient. The shipper remains as the party liable for the damage that could arise as a consequence of the lack of the same, except in the case in which they are missing due to a fault that can be attributed to the railway. In such a case, the latter shall be the party liable and shall have to pay a sum in compensation that will never be greater than that which should be paid in the case of loss of merchandise.

The shipper must comply with the provisions that Customs or other administrative authorities establish with respect to packing and the tarpaulin covering of the merchandise. Should it fail to do so, the railway will take charge of this and the corresponding costs will be levied on the merchandise.

The railway shall be entitled to reject those shipments where the Customs facilities or those of other administrative authorities are deteriorated or are defective.

3.4.3.2 Fulfilling the terms of contract

(1) Delivery of carriage and loading of the merchandise. The merchandise delivery operations shall be governed by the rules in force at the station of departure. The job of loading these lies with the shipper or the railway, as this is set out at each station.

If the loading was carried out by the shipper, the latter shall be the party liable in the event of this proving defective. The burden of proving that the loading of the merchandise has been defective when it was done by the shipper lies with the railway.

(2) Formalities required by the Customs or other administrative author-ities. When the merchandise has been loaded, the railway is responsi-ble for complying with the same, being able to undertake it by itself or entrusting this work to an agent.

The shipper is empowered to request – by means of the bill of lading – attendance at these operations or it is to fulfil these formalities itself. In either of these two cases it is able to make payment of the Customs duties and other possible costs.

The situation may arise whereby the shipper indicates one particular station for compliance with these formalities where it is not possible to comply with them. In such a situation, the railway may proceed in the manner that it deems most advantageous for the shipper. Likewise, regardless of the fact that the station of arrival of the merchandise does not have a Customs office, it shall be possible for the recipient to comply with said formalities if this is accepted under the laws and regulations of the state for said station. The use of these rights by the shipper entails the payment of costs that are levied on the merchandise.

(3) Delivery of the merchandise. The railway has the obligation to deliver the bill of lading and the merchandise to the recipient at the station of destination, against payment of the sums due to the same from the shipping agent. The acceptance of the bill of lading by the shipping agent binds it to pay the sum of the credits that are its responsibility.

Situations assimilated into the delivery of the merchandise:

(a) The delivery of the latter to the Customs or consumption authorities.
(b) Storage by the railway or depositing in the possession of a trans-port agent or in a public storage place.

Once the merchandise has arrived at the station of destination, the shipping agent is entitled to request that the railway furnish the bill of lading and the merchandise.

Should any loss or damage to the merchandise take place, the ship-ping agent or recipient are entitled to reject acceptance of the same as soon as the damage or the loss alleged are verified.

(4) Payment of the costs. These must be paid by the shipper and form part of the price of the carriage. The shipper that assumes the payment of the whole or part of the costs has to record this in the bill of lading, mentioning one of the following elements:

(a) 'Free of carriage': if it solely takes responsibility for the price of the carriage.
(b) 'Free of carriage, covering the …': if it takes responsibility for other costs in addition to the price of carriage. It must specifically indicate the costs that are included.
(c) 'Free of carriage up to x': if it takes responsibility for the price of carriage up to x.
(d) 'Free of carriage, covered up to x': if it takes responsibility for other costs in addition to the price of carriage up to x.
(e) 'Free of all costs': if it takes responsibility for all costs.
(f) 'Free for …': if it takes responsibility for a specific sum.

All of those costs that the shipper does not take responsibility for shall be considered to be the responsibility of the recipient. However, the costs will always be met by the shipper when the shipping agent has not taken the bill of lading or exercised its rights.

With regard to accessory costs, such as the costs of docking, storage, weight, etc., whose collection results from a fact that can be attributed to the recipient or a request made by the latter, these shall always be paid by the same, except in those cases in which it is necessary for the shipper to take responsibility for them due to the fact that there are goods that are susceptible to deterioration.

Within these circumstances, there will be cases where it is not possible to determine the sum for the costs in advance. In such cases, the costs will be entered in a clearance report. They will subsequently be the subject of a settlement of account with the shipper, in a maximum period of 30 days after the expiry of the delivery deadline. The costs that are paid in advance must be recorded by the station of departure in both the bill of lading and in a duplicate copy.

(5) Rectification of the sums collected.   In the cases in which a tariff is applied in an irregular manner or that there is a mistake in the collection or the setting of the costs, the surplus amount shall be repaid, ex officio, by the railway. Alternatively, the latter could be paid the difference lacking that may exist, provided that this difference exceeds four account units per bill of lading.

Payment of the difference lacking that is owed to the railway shall be the responsibility of the shipper, provided the bill of lading was not withdrawn. This is because, if the bill of lading was withdrawn, the shipper shall be released from payment. The recipient shall pay the complementary sum of the difference lacking. The sums owed to the railway shall accrue interest at a 5 per cent annual rate from the day of the receipt of the notification to make payment or from the day of the claim or, should neither of these cases apply, from the day of the court proceedings.

(6) Repayments and disbursements. The shipper can levy a charge on its shipment up to the value of the merchandise. The railway is not bound to make the repayment until the sum thereof has been paid by the recipient, within a period of 30 days that is stated for this purpose.

If the merchandise, as a whole or in part, has been delivered to the recipient without having previously collected the repayment, the railway shall be bound to make payment of the sum of the damage to the shipper, covering up to the sum of the repayment, unless there is an appeal against the recipient.

Shipping against cash on delivery shall give rise to the collection of a rate established in the tariffs, and shall be paid even though the repayment has been annulled or reduced by a modification of the contract of transport.

Disbursements shall not be accepted unless they are made in accordance with the provisions in force at the station of origin. Both disbursements and repayments must be recorded in the bill of lading.

3.4.3.3 Modification of the contract

The shipper is entitled to modify the contract, instructing:

(a) That the merchandise be removed from the station of departure.
(b) That the merchandise be detailed on route.
(c) That the delivery of the merchandise be postponed.
(d) That the merchandise is delivered to a person other than the one designated in the bill of lading.
(e) That the merchandise be delivered at a different station or that it be returned to the station of departure.
(f) The setting of a repayment.
(g) An increase, decrease or cancelling of the repayment.
(h) The acceptance of the costs of a shipment that are not prepaid or an increase in the costs accepted.

The complementary provisions or the international tariffs in force between the states participating in the carriage shall allow for other instructions to be accepted in addition to those mentioned. These shall never involve a separating of the shipment.

These instructions must be reported by means of a written statement and have to be reproduced and signed by the shipper in a duplicate copy of the bill of lading. This will be presented to the railway at the station of departure, which shall stamp and return it to the shipper.

When the shipper requests an increase, reduction or cancellation of a repayment, it shall present the certificate that it has been issued with. The certificate is to be returned to the interested party after it has been rectified. In the case of cancellation, it shall not be returned.

If the railway carries out the instructions of the shipper without having demanded the presentation of a duplicate copy, when this has been passed on to the recipient, the railway shall be responsible to the latter for such damage as may result. In such a case, the compensation shall not exceed that established for the case of the loss of the merchandise.

The right to modify the contract of transport becomes extinguished when:

(a) The bill of lading has been withdrawn by the recipient.
(b) The recipient has accepted the merchandise.
(c) The recipient makes use of its right stemming from the contract.
(d) The recipient is authorised to give instructions once the shipment has entered the Customs territory of the country of destination.

From this time onwards, the railway must follow the instructions of the recipient.

The recipient is entitled to modify the contract.

The latter can exercise this right when the shipper has not taken responsibility for the costs corresponding to the carriage in the country of destination and neither has it recorded the following statement in the bill of lading, 'Recipient not entitled to give subsequent instructions'.

The instructions that the recipient gives shall only be valid when the shipment is in the Customs territory of the country of destination. In such circumstances, it is entitled to instruct:

(a) That the merchandise be detained on route.
(b) That the delivery of the merchandise be postponed.
(c) That the merchandise be delivered to a person other than the recipient recorded in the bill of lading.
(d) That the merchandise be delivered at a station other than the one recorded in the bill of lading, provided that this is in the same country of destination.
(e) That the shipment comply with the formalities demanded by the Customs or other authorities.

Similar to the instructions given by the shipper, those given by the recipient do not imply a separating of the shipment either.

All of these instructions must be reported by means of a written declaration in conformity with the specimen copy set down by the railway. Instructions issued in forms other than those prescribed will be considered null and void.

The right to modify the contract becomes extinguished:

(a) When the bill of lading is withdrawn.
(b) When the merchandise is accepted.
(c) When use is made of the rights stemming under the contract for the recipient.
(d) When the person designated by the recipient withdraws the bill of lading or makes use of its rights. This person is not entitled to modify the contract.

The railway shall only be able to refuse to carry out subsequent orders:

(a) When these are not possible.
(b) When carrying them out could disrupt regular service.
(c) When carrying them out is against the laws and regulations in force in any state.
(d) When the value of the merchandise – if a change in the station of destination is involved – does not cover the costs that could be levied thereon.

The party that gave the subsequent instructions shall be informed as soon as possible of the impediments that make it impossible to carry them out. Should the railway not be able to overcome such impediments, the person who gave the subsequent instructions shall be held responsible for the resulting delivery outcome.

In the event of it failing to carry out an instruction, the railway shall be responsible for the consequences of deficient or non-undertaking of an instruction. It shall not be possible for the compensation to exceed that which would apply in the case of a loss.

Other circumstances that allow the carrier to modify the contract are the occurrence of an impediment to the carriage, in those cases the railway shall decide whether it is preferable to transport the merchandise ex officio, modifying the itinerary or whether – in the interests of the shipper – it is appropriate to request instructions from the latter, providing it with the useful information that is available to the railway.

Should the continuation of the carriage not be possible, the railway shall be able to request instructions from the shipper. The latter shall be able to provide these to both the station of departure and the station at which the merchandise is located. A note of these instructions shall be made in the bill of lading. These instructions shall not be necessary in the case in which the impediments are temporary.

There is also a possibility that the shipper can provide preliminary instructions in the bill of lading in the case of impediments to the carriage appearing.

After a reasonable period has passed from the moment notice of impediment was given without any instructions from the shipper, the railway shall act in accordance with the rules relating to impediments to delivery in force at the place where merchandise is held up. Should the impediment cease prior to instructions being received from the shipper, the merchandise shall be sent on to its destination without awaiting further instructions.

Similar to the above, the railway shall report when there is any impediment to the delivery by the shipper and shall request instructions from the latter. Should the impediment cease before instructions arrive, the merchandise shall be delivered to the recipient, and notice of delivery shall be given to the shipper.

If the recipient rejects the merchandise, the shipper shall be able to give instructions – even when it cannot present the duplicate of the bill of lading.

The shipper can request that the merchandise be returned ex officio should some impediment to the delivery arise. The reasons shall be recorded on the bill of lading. In all other cases, the return of merchandise requires the shipper's express consent.

3.4.3.4 Conclusion of the contract of transport

The contract of transport is concluded from the time at which the railway shipper accepts the merchandise for carriage, accompanied by its bill of lading. The acceptance is demonstrated by the stamping of the seal of the station of departure on the bill of lading or a mark from a counting machine that includes the date of acceptance. All of the process stated must be carried out in the presence of the shipper, if the latter so requests.

Following the stamping of the seal or the marking by the counting machine, the bill of lading shall constitute proof of the conclusion and of the content of the contract of transport.

As regards the merchandise for which the shipper is responsible, the statements on the bill of lading relating to the weight of the merchandise or the number of bulk loads shall only constitute proof against the railway if the latter checked said weight or said number of bulk loads, and recorded these in the bill of lading.

The railway shall not be liable for either the weight of the merchandise or the number of bulk loads that appear in the statements in the bill of lading when it is clear that no effective lack corresponds to the difference in weight or the number of bulk loads. This shall especially be the case when the freight car is delivered to the recipient with the seal of origin intact.

The railway has the obligation to certify the receipt of the merchandise and the date of the acceptance for carriage in the duplicate of the bill of lading, prior to returning said duplicate to the shipper. This duplicate shall not have the value of a bill of lading that accompanies the shipment or of a waybill.

3.4.4 Liability and actions

3.4.4.1 Collective liability of the railways

That railway which accepts the carriage of the merchandise with the bill of lading shall be responsible for the whole of the journey up until delivery. The railways that may subsequently take responsibility for the merchandise shall assume the obligations that may stem from the contract.

Liability extends:

(a) To a delay in the delivery deadline.
(b) To the damage that results from the complete or partial loss of the merchandise.
(c) To the breakages that the merchandise may suffer.

It is to be exempt from this liability if these facts were caused by a lack of a legally entitled person, by an order by the same or due to a defect that is particular to the merchandise.

It is also liable for breakage or loss when:

(a) The carriage is carried out, in agreement with the shipper, in an uncovered freight car.
(b) There is a lack or absence of packing, though this is necessary.
(c) This takes place during the loading operations by the shipper or the unloading operations by the recipient.
(d) The nature of certain merchandise left exposed leads to loss or breakage.

(e) A shipment is made under an irregular, imprecise or incomplete denomination of objects excluded from carriage or accepted for this on a conditional basis.
(f) The carriage is a shipment of live animals.
(g) The carriage is a shipment that requires an escort.
(h) Defective freight, when the loading was carried out by the shipper.

The burden of proof in all of these circumstances lies with the railway.

3.4.4.2 Presumption in the case of reshipping

When the merchandise is reshipped and it is observed that it suffered damage or breakage, there is a presumption that this occurred during the latest contract of transport, provided the shipment had been in the safekeeping of the railway and that it had been reshipped in the same condition as it arrived at the reshipping station.

3.4.4.3 Presumption of loss of the merchandise

It is presumed that the merchandise was lost if it fails to be delivered or placed at the disposal of the recipient in the 30 days following the expiry of the delivery deadline.

The party entitled to compensation can also request that it be given notice if the merchandise is found within one year from the moment compensation is effectively paid. If found during this period, it will be able to demand that it be returned thereto within the 30 days following the receipt of the notice.

3.4.4.4 Amount of compensation in the case of loss of merchandise

This shall be calculated:

(a) With regard to the Stock Exchange listed price.
(b) Should this not exist, according to the current market value.
(c) In the absence of both of the above, according to the ordinary value of the merchandise of the same nature and quality, on the day and at the place where the merchandise was accepted for carriage.

It shall not be possible for the compensation to exceed 17 units per kilogram of missing gross tonnage. Compensation shall include the price of carriage, the Customs duties and other disbursed sums that result from the carriage of the lost merchandise.

3.4.4.5 Railway liability in the case of shrinkage

This is limited to those cases where, owing to the nature of the merchandise, shrinkage occurs with a certain frequency on route. In this situation, the railway is to be liable for the shrinkage on route that exceeds the tolerance levels stated below:

(a) 2 per cent of the weight for liquid merchandise or that delivered for carriage in a damp condition.
(b) 1 per cent for other merchandise subject to shrinkage on route.

It is not possible to maintain this limitation on the liability when the loss does not result from causes that justify the level of tolerance.

In the case of several bulk loads being transported with one single bill of lading, the shrinkage on route shall be calculated separately and this is to be stated in the bill of lading. If the whole of the merchandise is lost, no deduction resulting from the shrinkage on route shall be made in calculating the compensation.

3.4.4.6 *Amount of compensation in the case of breakage of the merchandise*

Should breakage take place, the railway is bound to pay the amount that reflects the loss of the value of the merchandise. The percentage of depreciation is determined at the station of destination.

The level of compensation cannot exceed:

(a) The sum that the same would have amounted to in the event of a total loss, if the whole of the shipment is depreciated due to breakage.
(b) The sum that it would have amounted to in the event of the loss of the depreciated part, if only one part of the shipment has been depreciated by the breakage.

3.4.4.7 *Amount of compensation in the case of a delay in delivery and an accumulation of sums of compensation*

Should damage, including breakage, result through exceeding the delivery deadline, the railway is bound to pay a sum of compensation that shall not exceed the quadruple amount of the price of carriage.

Should the entirety of the merchandise be lost, it shall not be possible for this sum of compensation to be added to the one established for cases of total loss of merchandise.

Should partial loss of merchandise take place, the stated sum of compensation for exceeding the delivery deadline shall not exceed the triple sum of the price of carriage of the part of the shipment that has not been lost.

Should breakage in merchandise take place that cannot be attributed to exceeding the delivery deadline, the sum of compensation stated for the case can be accumulated to that established for cases of breakage.

Under no circumstances can there be accumulation of sums of compensation established for cases of loss and breakage with that set out for the case of exceeding of the delivery deadline when this would exceed the sum that would be owed in the case of a total loss of merchandise.

There are other classes of restrictions set out in the tariffs. These are situations in which the railway grants particular carriage conditions, such as price reductions. As a consequence thereof, the amount of the sums of compensation is also limited. For this reason it is necessary that such a limitation be recorded in the tariff.

If, after a delay in the delivery has taken place, a breakage or a total or partial loss of the merchandise is proven to be due to misrepresentation or a possible type of misrepresentation that can be attributed to the railway, the latter must pay compensation for the whole of the damage proven.

These sums of compensation accrue interest, which may be requested by the party that suffers damage. These are set at 5 per cent annually, which shall be owed if the sum of compensation exceeds four account units for each bill of lading. This is to accrue from the day on which the administrative claim is made or, should this not be the case, from the day of the claim being filed in court.

The railway is likewise liable for the actions of its agents and the other individuals that it employs for undertaking the carriage. However, if the railway agents and other individuals issue bills of lading at the request of the interested party, or do translations or render any other kind of service, it shall be considered that they are acting on behalf of the individual to whom they render such services.

3.4.4.8 Liability in sea–railway traffic

For this type of carriage, each state shall be able to invoke the application of the causes of exoneration from liability set out for cases of loss, breakage or exceeding of delivery deadline when it is proven that these take place during the maritime journey, from the loading of the merchandise on board the vessel to the unloading thereof.

The causes of exoneration shall be as follows:

(a) Acts, negligence or omissions by a captain, seaman, pilot or the individuals employed by the transport company in the navigation or administration of the vessel.
(b) Non-navigability of the vessel.
(c) Fire, provided that it is proven that this did not take place due to an act or omission by the transport company, captain, seaman or pilot.

(d) Maritime hazards, risks or accidents.

(e) Salvage or the attempt to save lives or goods at sea.

(f) Loading of the merchandise on the bridge of the vessel on the condition that this was performed with the consent of the shipper recorded in the bill of lading, and that it is not on a freight car.

Even when the transport company invokes these causes of exoneration, it shall continue to be liable if the legally entitled person can prove that the loss, breakage or exceeding of the delivery deadline was caused by a fault on the part of the transport company, seaman or the employees thereof, other than those outlined in the first point.

If the same maritime journey was made by different companies, the liability regime shall be the same for all companies.

3.4.4.9 Liability in the case of a nuclear accident

The railway is exempt from liability when the damage is caused by a nuclear accident, or when the party operating a nuclear installation is established as the one liable.

3.4.5 Exercising of the rights

3.4.5.1 Verification of partial loss or breakage

When partial loss or breakage is discovered or presumed or when these are alleged by the legally entitled person, the railway is obliged to issue a document in which the condition of the merchandise, its weight, the extent of the damage, its cause and the time at which it took place are recorded. The legally entitled person shall be provided with a copy of the document and if it does not accept the content of the same, it shall be able to request that a check is made on the terms included in this document by an expert appointed by the parties.

3.4.5.2 Claims, legal actions: procedure and prescription

All claims against the railway must be made in writing.

The claim should be attached to the bill of lading, the duplicate and other documents that are deemed appropriate. These may be originals or legalised copies.

When the shipper makes a claim it has to attach a duplicate of the bill of lading thereto. Should the latter document be missing, it will require an authorisation from the recipient or prove that the latter rejected the shipment, in order to be able to file the claim.

If the recipient is the party that files the claim, it must present the bill of lading in the event that it has been furnished with the same.

The party liable to make the payment may appeal with the objective of seeking the refund of the sum paid. A legal action relating to repayments solely lies with the shipper.

The other legal actions that could arise as a consequence of the contract lie with:

(a) The shipper, up to the time prior to the recipient withdrawing the bill of lading, accepting the merchandise or exercising its rights.
(b) The recipient, until the time that the bill of lading is withdrawn, it accepts the merchandise or exercises its rights.

3.4.5.3 The parties against which a legal claim can be brought

(a) When this is the refund of a sum paid, the action can be exercised:
    (i) either against the railway that received said sum,
    (ii) or against the party that gained from an excess benefit.
(b) When this is an action relating to a repayment, it is possible to act against the railway of origin.
(c) The other legal claims stemming from the contract of transport shall be exercised against the railway of origin, the railway of destination or against such party on whose lines a liable action took place.

It shall be possible for a claim to be brought against the railway of destination, even when it received neither the merchandise nor the bill of lading.

When the plaintiff may claim against any of several railways, exercising its action against one of them extinguishes its right to act against the others.

3.4.5.4 Competence

The court of the state in which the defendant railway lies has competence to hear these types of claims.

3.4.5.5 Extinguishing of the action against the railway

The right to lodge claims against the railway concerning delays in the delivery, partial loss or breakage, becomes extinguished at the time the party entitled to do so accepts the merchandise. However, even given these circumstances, the action shall not be extinguished:

(a) If the party entitled to claim proves that the damage was caused by misrepresentation or a serious fault that can be attributed to the railway.

(b) In the first seven days, if the claim concerns a delay in the delivery period.
(c) If the claim is due to partial loss or breakdown:
  • If the loss or breakdown were detected prior to the merchandise being accepted.
  • If the necessary checks were omitted through the fault of the railway company.
(d) When there is damage that is not apparent and that can only be verified after the acceptance. In these cases, it is necessary to draw up a petition for verification immediately after the damage is discovered – and within the seven days following the acceptance – or establish that damage took place in the interval between acceptance and delivery.

When a piece of merchandise is reshipped, the sums of compensation for partial loss or breakage arising from one of the previous forms of transport become extinguished in such a way as if only one single contract was involved.

3.4.5.6 Prescription

As a general rule, these actions become time-barred for a period of one year. However, there are other cases in which time-barring takes place for two years when:

(a) It is an action for payment of a reimbursement collected by the railway from the recipient.
(b) It is an action for payment of the balance of a sale made by the railway.
(c) It is an action founded on damage caused by misrepresentation or possible misrepresentation.
(d) It is an action founded on a case of fraud.
(e) It is founded on one of the contracts of transport prior to reshipping.

The time-bar period starts to run:

(a) In cases of delay in delivery, partial loss or breakage, from the day delivery took place.
(b) In those for compensation for total loss, from the thirtieth day following the day of expiry of the delivery deadline.
(c) When these are actions for payment or for the restitution of the price of carriage, accessory costs, other costs or excess rates, or for actions of rectification, the application of tariffs or a calculation error:

- If by means of payment, from the day on which it was paid.
- If not, from the time the merchandise was accepted for carriage, if payment corresponds to the shipper – or from the time the recipient accepts the bill of lading, if it corresponds to the recipient.
- If this is for sums to be paid by means of a charges note, from the day on which the railway delivers the account of charges to the consignor.

(d) When the railway must return a payment made by the recipient at the place and time of the shipper, or the other way around, from the day on which the request for repayment is made.

(e) When it is a question of reimbursements, from the thirtieth day that follows the delivery expiry deadline.

(f) In other situations, from the day on which the right can be exercised.

In the case of a claim brought against the railway with the necessary substantiating documents, the prescription period shall be suspended until the day on which the railway rejects the complaint in writing and returns the documents. If the claim were partially accepted, the prescription period shall recommence for that part of the claim that remains in litigation. The burden of proof of the receipt of the claim or of the reply and that of the restitution of the documents shall lie with the party that invokes this fact.

Once an action has become prescribed, it cannot be exercised again. Both the suspension and the interruption of the prescription period are governed by the laws and regulations of the state in which the claim is exercised.

3.4.6 Relations between railways

3.4.6.1 Settlement of accounts between railways

Should a railway be entitled to collect the costs and other credits resulting from a contract of transport involving other participating railways, the latter should be paid the part that corresponds thereto.

The shipper railway shall be responsible for the price of the transport and for other costs that were not collected when the shipper accepted them as its responsibility and this was so stated in the bill of lading.

If, on the contrary, the railway of destination delivers the merchandise without collecting the costs or other credits that result from the contract of transport, it shall be liable to the other railways that participated in the transport and the other interested parties.

If the railway responsible for paying the other participating parties did not do so, it shall bear the consequences that may derive from the same, while maintaining the right of appeal.

3.4.6.2 Remedy in the case of loss or breakage

If a railway pays the whole of the sum of compensation in a case in which a loss or breakage of the merchandise took place, it shall have the right of redress against:

(a) The railway that caused the damage.
(b) The railways, should there be several, each one being liable for the damage it caused. If it is not possible to determine the part of the damage each caused, the burden of compensation shall be divided between all of them.
(c) If it is not possible to determine which railway caused the damage, the burden of compensation shall be divided between all of them.

There are also certain forms of redress similar to those set out for the case of loss or breakage for the case of not meeting delivery deadlines which specify the way in which the compensation payment is to be divided.

The railway that seeks to exercise its redress shall draw up its claim in one single and unique instance against all of the railways it failed to reach a settlement with. The jurisdiction the plaintiff selects or the jurisdiction corresponding to the defendant railway, if there are several defendants, shall have competence to hear these cases.

3.5 Carriage of goods by air

3.5.1 Introduction

Using weight as a criterion, carriage by air plays a small role in freight moved between EU countries (about 0.1 per cent) and in external trade (0.9 per cent of exports, 0.32 per cent of imports). If value is the criterion then the figures increase to 4.0 per cent, 24.5 per cent and 23.3 per cent, respectively.

While the international air cargo industry is rapidly changing and technologically driven, the same certainly cannot be said about the legal machinery which supports it. Indeed, there has not been, until recently, a change in the international air legislation since the Warsaw Convention was originally written in 1929.

The recent Montreal Convention (MC) makes important amendments to the Warsaw regime, adjusting the 70-year-old Convention to the technological developments and the reality of modern trends.

The MC is based on the 'Montreal Protocol 4' (MP4) which was the fourth Amendment of a protocol, in Treaty terms, to the Warsaw Convention of 1929 that was put forth in Montreal in 1975. Twenty-four years later the MP4 finally became an operational international law in most countries after being adopted by leading trading nations in 1999.

There are great similarities between the MP4 and the MC. Both represent a major change in the international cargo laws since the Warsaw Convention and introduced the same changes, long expected by the cargo industry. In fact, the MC adopted all of the cargo-related advances achieved under MP4. We will further discuss this later.

3.5.2 The Warsaw Convention

The Warsaw Convention of 1929 is the international treaty that has governed international air-related cargo and casualty claims in the aviation transportation industry for the past 70 years. It was the product of two international conferences, the first held in Paris in 1925 and the second in Warsaw in 1929, and four years of work by the interim Comité International Technique d'Experts Juridiques Aériens (CITEJA) formed at the Paris Conference.

Drafted at a time when aviation was a fledgling industry with a dubious safety record and in need of protection from excessive claims for compensation, the Warsaw Convention imposed a series of limits on the liability of air carriers for damages. By today's standards, these limits are now very low and even those laid down in the various amending agreements (protocols)[6] which comprise the so-called Warsaw system offer a largely inadequate liability system for modern transportation.

The Convention originally had two primary goals:

- To establish uniformity in the aviation industry among nations with different legal systems and philosophical points of view with regard to 'the procedure for dealing with claims arising out of international transportation and the substantive law applicable to such claims', as well as with regard to documentation such as tickets and waybills;
- To set fair limitations of liability for the encouragement of industry growth, promoting investment and the taking of financial risks. The clearly overriding purpose of the Warsaw Convention was to limit air carriers' potential liability in the event of accidents. The liability limit was believed necessary to allow airlines to raise the capital needed to expand operations and to provide a definite basis upon which their insurance rates could be calculated.

The nations drafting this provision had a direct interest in establishing liability limits, since nearly all existing airlines were either owned or heavily subsidised by the various contracting states. The drafters also believed that a liability limit would lessen litigation.

The Warsaw Convention rules encouraged shippers to either declare value or buy insurance for the protection of their goods and allow the industry to offer economical service and expand its capability by spreading the risk of loss among carriers and insurance companies. In this sense, without the Warsaw Convention rules, service rates would hardly be economical.

There are currently more than 135 parties to the Warsaw Convention either in its original form or one of its amended forms. Some states separately have adopted laws or regulations relating to international carrier liability. In addition, there are private voluntary agreements among carriers relating to liability. The result of these many instruments is a patchwork of liability regimes.

The Warsaw Convention principles are lofty, but needless to say, the aviation industry has changed since 1929. In the ensuing 70 years, there have been many calls for change. The Montreal Convention is designed to replace the Warsaw Convention and all of its related instruments and to eliminate the need for the patchwork of regulation and private voluntary agreements.

3.5.3 The Montreal Convention

The Montreal Convention[7] establishes a modernised and uniform legal framework to govern the liability of air carriers for damage to passengers, baggage and cargo incurred during international journeys. It represents a considerable improvement over the current international regime in this area, the system based on the Warsaw Convention of 1929, and it aims to completely replace that regime over time.

3.5.3.1 Legal status

On 5 September 2003, the United States became the thirtieth contracting state to ratify the Montreal Convention, thus complying with the minimum number of ratifications needed to replace the Warsaw Convention system. The Montreal Convention therefore entered into force 60 days following the deposit of the thirtieth ratification, on 4 November 2003.

3.5.3.2 Scope of application

The MC generally is limited by art. 1 to commercial international air carriage, including flights between two states party to the Convention or a round trip from a state party to the Convention with an agreed stopping point in another state, regardless of whether that state is party to the Convention. Article 2 notes that the Convention may cover air carriage provided by a state for compensation.

3.5.3.3 Policy goals

The public policy goals for MC are identical to those of the 1929 drafters. The major changes have been made to strengthen the law internally and halt legal attempts to circumvent the original purposes of the Warsaw Convention. The MC equipped the legal liability system with the ability to accurately forecast cargo claims outcomes, with an expected decrease in litigation and insurance costs.

These changes also reflect an attempt by the law to catch up with industry technology and get back to uniformity in claims handling from one country to another.

Inconsistent court rulings around the world and attempts by lawyers to avoid mandated damage limits based on technicalities have not merely led to change, but a new legal environment which will be far friendlier to air carriers, forwarders and shippers.

The drafters of MC sought four major policy goals:

(a) To re-establish standards of the original 1929 drafters; to set fair limitations of liability for the encouragement of industry growth, promoting investment and the taking of financial risks;
(b) To reflect 70 years of dramatic technological change in the air cargo industry;
(c) To re-establish international claims uniformity among nations with different legal systems and philosophical points of view; and
(d) To re-establish a definite basis upon which insurance rates could be calculated for the industry.

3.5.3.4 Major rules

Pursuit of these policy goals resulted in six major changes now found in MC:

(a) MC defines a new damage limitation in terms of 17 SDRs per kilogram of damaged freight. The damage limit is no longer based upon the value of gold or a national currency in an effort to re-establish international uniformity and to discourage forum shopping.
(b) MC recognises the common law doctrine of comparative fault, a principle which essentially compares the conduct of all parties to a dispute for the purpose of apportioning the percentages of culpability to each party.

(c) MC exonerates the carrier from damages caused by (a) inherent vice of the cargo; (b) defective packaging; or (c) government acts such as Customs examinations.

(d) MC changes the rules regarding the duty of a plaintiff to produce evidence. The new rules are technical, but far more equitable than in the past.

(e) MC in art. 4 allows for the use of electronic air waybills or shipments by 'any other means which preserves a record of the carriage'.

(f) MC abolishes the concept of 'wilful misconduct' as a basis for disregarding the Warsaw Convention damage limitation.

Although the MC affects personal injury and baggage claims of passengers, the summary set forth below specifically addresses those substantive changes which relate to claims for loss or damage to cargo.

3.5.3.4.1 *Intermodal reality.*

The MC takes a next step to acknowledge the truly intermodal nature of modern air carriage.

Under a new art. 18 of the MC, all modes of carriage would be deemed to have been by air and thus covered under the Montreal Convention if the contract of carriage reflects only intended movement in the air mode.

For example, if a carriage of goods by an air carrier is booked from Rotterdam to New York, any ocean or road links will be considered to have been air moves and thus covered under the MC.

All that will be required for this result is that the air waybill did not mention any road or ocean links. The specific language intended for art. 18 is as follows:

> If a carrier, without the consent of the consignor, substitutes carriage by another mode of transport for the whole or part of a carriage intended by the agreement between the parties to be carriage by air, such carriage by another mode of transport is deemed to be within the period of carriage by air.

The benefits of this art. 18 are obvious. Instead of wrangling and expensive legal debate over what local law or damage limitation might apply to a cargo damage during any particular part of an intermodal international air move the MC would streamline the process by making all aspects of the move subject to one law and a uniform damage limitation of 17 SDRs per kilogram.

3.5.3.4.2 Comparative fault concept to be universal.

'Comparative fault' or 'contributory negligence' happens where some act of the shipper combines with an act of the carrier to cause cargo damage or loss. A sliding scale is used to judge the conduct of (a) the shipper, (b) the air forwarder, and/or (c) the air carrier to determine the degree to which fault on the part of one party has contributed to the cargo loss. For example, imagine that the court has found that some typographical error on the shipper's label is 30 per cent responsible for cargo misdelivery which resulted in a €1000 loss. In such event, the carrier's liability would be reduced by 30 per cent to €700.

The Warsaw Convention originally acknowledged this concept of shared fault, providing that an air carrier could be exonerated wholly or partially from liability, if there were contributory negligence on the part of the shipper. However, under the Warsaw Convention the doctrine could be applied only if the court hearing the case recognised the 'contributory negligence' as a part of its national law. Indeed, many civil law nations do not recognise the concept of 'contributory negligence'. Thus, in violation of a central Warsaw Convention goal, results from one country to another have not been uniform where the doctrine of 'comparative fault' is concerned.

MC in art. 20 and the MP4 in art. 21 change this provision to provide carrier and air forwarders with a defence of 'contributory negligence' regardless of whether that legal doctrine is recognised in the different countries. It is now a matter of treaty that cannot be changed by a court.

3.5.3.4.3 The duty to provide evidence.

The Warsaw Convention set a level of liability that was limited in exchange for reversal of the burden of proof. That is, instead of the plaintiff having to prove fault on the part of the carrier, the carrier had to disprove fault in order to avoid paying compensation for loss or damage to baggage or cargo. The reason behind this internationally consistent regime was to provide certainty and reduce legal costs that were present when liability was unlimited but the plaintiff had to prove the carrier was at fault.

Following this logic, under the Warsaw Convention whenever an air waybill was issued automatically it was assumed that cargo had been received in good order and condition. The carriers were charged with the 'assumption' of cargo receipt in good order and condition even though the freight may have come off the roller bed truck in a sealed unit-loading device, with no opportunity for him to inspect contents.

Under these circumstances, it was the carrier's obligation to prove it did not damage the cargo.

Under MP4 and MC, the rule is reversed.

MC and MP4 both at art. 11 provide that statements in the air waybill 'relating to the weight, dimensions and packing of the cargo as well as those relating to the number of packages' may not be used as legal presumptions or assumptions against the carrier. The only exception to this rule is where the air waybill specifically says that the freight has been 'checked by the carrier in the presence of the consignor' or with regard to an outwardly apparent condition of the cargo.

This will mean that air carriers and forwarders who receive sealed containers 'said to contain' certain goods which then arrive damaged at destination without any obvious record of tampering will not automatically be their responsibility. However, the carrier will still be responsible for the stated weight and outwardly apparent condition of the cargo, but as to all other liabilities, it will be the obligation of the plaintiff to prove that the cargo was actually delivered to the carrier in good order and condition.

This is a significant change in reversing the legal obligation to provide primary evidence.

3.5.3.4.4 *Wilful misconduct.*

MC makes a major break with the legal tradition that a wrongdoer should be more severely punished depending upon the degree of his misconduct. The drafters of MC have completely eliminated the concept of 'wilful misconduct' where air cargo is concerned. Under the original Warsaw Convention, a carrier stood to lose its damage limitation if found responsible for such things as fraud, misrepresentation or intentional misconduct. The drafters of MC removed all such considerations.

Under art. 22 of the MC, proof of wilful misconduct does not deprive the carrier of the benefit of the liability limitation. Prior to this amendment, wilful misconduct provided cargo shippers with the ability to avoid the limitation.

However, a potential moral risk is arising from this change as there are no consequences whatsoever for intentional misconduct. To illustrate the point, it seems that even setting fire to cargo intentionally would not result in a loss of the damage limitation protection under the MC.

After years of seeing the damage limitation provisions of the Warsaw Convention eroded by clever legal arguments, the drafters at Montreal have sent a message. Shippers are well advised to buy cargo insurance because from now on the Warsaw Convention damage limitation as amended by MC will stand. There will be no exceptions. There will be no point making clever arguments.

However, one of the most important differences between the MP4 and the MC in this matter is that the MP4 is very clear on that the damage limitation is unassailable as: 'The limit may not be exceeded whatever the circumstances which gave rise to liability.'[8] This leaves no room for introducing other legal tools, such as an agreement, to the carrier liability regime. The MC, on the other hand, gives an opportunity to the shipper to increase the carrier's liability by an agreement. By doing this the shipper can *ex-ante* introduce the wilful misconduct of the carrier to the law governing the relationship between the shipper and the carrier.

3.5.3.4.5 Uniform damage limits.   The cargo damage limitations observed under the Warsaw Convention are based on weight. The damage limitation under the Warsaw Convention was based on the value of gold from 1929. Most countries such as the US established it at US$20 per kilogram. Unfortunately, other countries such as Australia have used the modern value of gold as the guide for determining a limit which came to around US$400 a kilogram. In direct violation of one of the original 1929 Treaty goals, recent years have seen the outcome of a particular claim dependent upon the country in which the lawsuit happened to be filed.

For example, if freight were damaged on a move from Sydney to Los Angeles, the plaintiff would always be well served to pursue recovery in Australia where a US$400 per kilogram limitation would yield recovery far in excess of that available to citizens in Los Angeles.

To correct this situation, art. 22 of MC and the MP4 change the maximum liability limitation to 17 SDRs per kilogram.

The MP4, in addition, commands that the official limits of liability be honoured, as it is specifically stipulated in art. 24 of the MP4 that: 'The damage limit may not be exceeded whatever the circumstances which gave rise to liability.' This statement from the MP4 makes it very clear that there is no possibility of increasing the carrier's liability. Such a legal feature, however, does not exist in the MC, as it is stated in art. 22 that: 'A carrier may stipulate that the contract of carriage shall be subject to higher limits of liability than those provided for in this Convention or to no limits of liability whatsoever.' In other words, it is possible by an agreement to increase the carrier liabilities in countries that are subject to the MC regime.

The MC in art. 18(4) and the MP4 in art. 18(5) also expand and clarify the damage presumption by stating that if 'For the purpose of loading, delivery or transhipment, any damage is presumed, subject to proof to the contrary, to have been the result of an event which took place during the carriage by air.'

3.5.3.4.6 Calculation of the liability limits.

One of the long dealt issues in carriers' liability has been the question of whether the weight of undamaged cargo in a particular shipment can be added to the damaged portion of the shipment for purposes of calculating the limitation.

The traditional rule was that only the damaged portion of a particular shipment may be used to calculate the value of a particular claim. Thus, if two of four boxes are damaged, only the two boxes can be used to calculate the claim. This said, subrogation lawyers have successfully argued that the weight of an entire shipment should be considered if injury to one component might have diminished the value or operability of an entire system being shipped. Thus, if only a 1 kilogram component to a 5000 kilogram computer system were damaged, there would be a €100 000 damage limitation for the single kilogram device, not €20 (or any equivalent value to the '65 milligrams gold of millesimal fineness 900' at that time) as would be the normal rule for damage to a single kilogram.

MC and MP4 adopt this same approach in art. 22. The exact language is:

> ... when the destruction, loss, damage or delay of a part of the cargo of an object contained therein, affects the value of other packages covered by the same waybill ... the total weight of such package or packages shall also be taken into consideration in determining the limit of liability.

In other words, if the damaged piece is an integral part of the entire shipment, then the carrier cannot limit its liability to the weight of the damaged piece.

3.5.3.4.7 Exceptions to carrier liability.

Article 18 of MC expressly adopts the traditional exceptions to carrier liability in the following cases:

(a) Inherent defect, quality or vice of that cargo;
(b) Defective packing of that cargo;
(c) An act of war or an armed conflict;

(d) An act of public authority with regard to the entry or exit of cargo such as where Customs may cause damage during the course of inspection.

Consistent with provisions of the Warsaw Convention and its related instruments, art. 20 of the MC details the conditions under which a carrier can exonerate itself, wholly or partly, from liability by showing, for example, that the person claiming compensation caused or contributed to the damage by negligence or a wrongful act or omission (see the subsection on comparative fault).

3.5.3.4.8 The written notice of claim requirements has not changed.   Just as in the original Warsaw Convention, written notice of claim must be given within specified periods, and a lawsuit filed within two years, or the claim for cargo damage of delay will be void.

3.5.3.4.9 Documentation.   Articles 3–11 of the MC discuss documentation requirements for international air carriage of passengers, baggage and cargo. Most significantly, they preserve the benefits to the cargo industry achieved under MP4.

By all accounts, the most awaited provision of MC is a revised art. 5 of the Warsaw Convention. Article 4 of the MC and art. 5 MP4 replace the statement requiring that the consignor 'make out' and 'hand over' an air waybill with the requirement that an 'air waybill shall be delivered' or that 'any other means which would preserve a record of the carriage to be performed may, with the consent of the consignor, be substituted for the delivery of an air waybill'. It is this change that clears the way for the use of electronic air waybills. Before MC it was clearly established that air carriers were required to issue a 'paper' air waybill. IATA[9] currently estimates the cost of each such paper air waybill to be US$5 or US$6 each. Thus, as a matter aside from the question of technology, the issue of electronic air waybills is economically significant.

3.5.3.4.10 Legal technicalities are dismissed – the waybill checklist.
Another feature of MC is to eliminate Warsaw Convention vulnerability to the effects of outdated, meaningless and often overused legal technicalities. To this aim, the MC addresses art. 8 of the Warsaw Convention.

Article 8 of the Warsaw Convention has required that the air waybill contain a virtual checklist of information which the 1929 drafters viewed as mandatory. This information included such things as the following:

(a) Names and addresses of shipper and consignee
(b) Number of packages
(c) Weight – dimensions
(d) Nature of goods being shipped
(e) Type of packaging
(f) Marks and numbers

If any of this required information was left off the air waybill, there was no damage limitation available to the carrier.

One particularly sacred requirement of art. 8 was that all stopping places for the flight be listed in addition to its origin and destination. In 1929, this information was believed important because it would allow shippers to track their cargo from one country to another over an extended period of time until final destination was reached. The listing of stopping places would also let a shipper know if its cargo might pass through some hostile enemy state.

Nowadays, freight is tracked by use of the master air waybill number. By phone or Internet, the process is both instant and electronic.

The entire concept of art. 8 became obsolete long ago. There is no commercial reality to the listing of 'stopping places' on an air waybill. There is only a very technical opportunity for lawyers to disregard the international intent of nations.

The industry has paid a high price for sloppy document preparation and art. 8 defects. Still, nothing could be done to correct this situation because the Warsaw Convention is a treaty which must be strictly interpreted. The Warsaw Convention could only be changed by an Act of Nations.

An example of how absurd things became in the past couple of decades is seen in the case of TAI PING. This case involved the movement of a high value shipment of aircraft parts from Chicago to Hong Kong via Anchorage and Narita. Unfortunately, a clerk failed to insert Anchorage and Narita as 'stopping places' on the air waybill. Then, as luck would have it, the shipment was lost.[10]

Perhaps the only sensible aspect of this entire case was foresight on the part of the shipper in obtaining cargo insurance which resulted in full payment of the claim by the Tai Ping Insurance Company. Following the payment, Tai Ping Insurance Company sought to recover its loss with a lawsuit against Northwest Airlines.[11] In the lawsuit, Northwest Airlines immediately offered compensation under the Warsaw Convention limit of US$1320. Tai Ping Insurance Company rejected the offer, claiming that Northwest Airlines should not have benefit of its damage limitation because Anchorage and Narita had been omitted as 'stopping places' on the bill of lading in violation of art. 8.

Northwest lost this case. It is very clear that the entire case was decided on the basis of legal technicality in the sense that neither the shipper nor the carrier had ever checked the 'stopping places' or even attempted to track the freight.

The failure to type airport codes for Anchorage and Narita in the air waybill was simply disastrous for Northwest. Instead of paying the Warsaw Convention damage limitation of US$1320, Northwest was hit with a judgment to the amount of US$231 000 plus interest. Calculating the revenue for this shipment on the basis of US$2.50 per kilogram for 66 kilograms, the result was shipment revenue for Northwest of US$165. If Northwest's cost for the shipment on a net/net basis is subtracted, the result would have been a profit for Northwest in the approximate amount of US$40.

Northwest would need to make 5803 identical shipments to get back its original US$40 in profit because of a typographic error on the air waybill that absolutely no one really cared about.

To correct this, MC and MP4 make the damage limitation uniform as failure to issue a waybill or list certain particulars on the waybill (place of departure, destination, etc.) does not prevent the carrier from benefiting from the Convention's liability limitation (art. 9).

Article 5 of the MC replaces language requiring that 'the air waybill shall contain the following particulars ...' or the carrier loses the ability to limit his/her liability. Under MC, the air waybill needs only to have 'an indication of the places of departure and destination and an indication of the weight of the consignment' and if the departure and destination are within the territory of a single contracting party but stopping in another country, then and only then does the stopping place within the territory of another state need to be included.

Under MC, non-compliance with the provisions of art. 5 does not appear to result in a loss of liability limits.

It is important to bear in mind that MC and MP4 only apply where both the origin and destination countries have adopted it. Thus, on a claim involving cargo from Spain to Andorra, the old Warsaw Convention would apply because Spain has adopted MC, but Andorra has not. In that circumstance, a failure by the air carrier to issue a paper air waybill, complete with listed 'stopping places', would result in loss of the damage limitation.

3.5.3.4.11 Jurisdiction. Article 33(1) of the MC, like the Warsaw Convention, allows a suit to be brought against a carrier in the country:[12]

(a) Of its incorporation; or
(b) Of its principal place of business; or
(c) Where the ticket was purchased; or
(d) Of destination of the cargo.

3.5.3.4.12 Actual carrier which is not party to the waybill. Articles 39–48 of the MC define the rights of passengers and consignors in operations where all or part of the carriage is provided by a carrier that is not party to the contract of carriage (e.g. code-share operations, freight consolidators). The provisions follow the precedent set by the Guadalajara Convention. Pursuant to art. 40, when a claim arises under the Convention, a claimant may bring suit against the carrier from which the carriage was purchased or against the code-sharing carrier operating the aircraft at the time of the accident.

3.5.3.4.13 Countries' reservation. To accomplish its fundamental purpose of establishing uniformity in the context of international carriage by air, the MC limits reservations available to states party to it. Article 57 describes the only two possible reservations that states may make. These reservations allow states to be exempt from application of the Convention: (a) the operations of state aircraft and (b) the operations of aircraft chartered by the military. These limited reservations are generally consistent with the reservations available under the Warsaw Convention and its related instruments. The reservation relating to state aircraft operations was revisited to clarify that the reservation is available only for non-commercial operations related to the functions and duties of a sovereign state.

3.5.3.4.14 Shippers' liability. Article 10 of the MC is expanded, giving greater protection to the carrier by making the shipper responsible for the correctness of the particulars relating to the cargo and make the latter responsible for any loss or damage which an irregularity, incorrectness or incompleteness of those particulars causes to the air carrier or to any third party to whom the carrier is liable.

3.5.3.4.15 Conclusion. The provisions described above reflect the many benefits that accrue under the MC to the air transportation industry and its consumers. One key benefit not reflected in the provisions themselves is the benefit of uniformity.

3.6 Multimodal transport

The world of transport has changed considerably over the last few decades as international transportation of goods is increasingly carried out on a door-to-door basis, involving more than one mode of transportation. Transport users require seamless reliable and cost-effective containerised[13] door-to-door transport and consider the transport mode(s) by which their shipments are carried as less important provided delivery is on time.

Goods stowed in a container could be transported by different means of transport, such as ships, railway wagons, road vehicles or aircraft, from the point of origin to the final place of destination, without being unpacked for sorting or verification when being transferred from one means of transport to another. Gradually, more and more logistics operators have taken responsibility for the whole transport chain under one single transport contract. Shippers needed to pursue one single operator (multimodal transport operator, MTO), in the event of loss of, or damage to, the goods involved in multimodal transport, who would be responsible for the overall transport. Cargo liability arrangements, however, remain modally oriented and do not provide shippers with a transparent and uniform liability regime. This may result in uncertainty where time and place of cargo loss or damage cannot be established and in higher costs due to claims handling and litigation. Overall, there was a need for an international legal framework for multimodal transport of goods.

3.6.1 Definition and legal regime

Multimodal transportation means

> the carriage of goods by at least two different modes of transport on the basis of a multimodal transport contract from a place in one country at which the goods are taken in charge by the multimodal transport operator to a place designated for delivery situated in a different country.[14]

Another important term in the multimodal landscape is that of the 'multimodal transport operator' (MTO) which means

> any person who on his own behalf or through another person acting on his behalf concludes a multimodal transport contract and who acts as a principal, not as an agent or on behalf of the consignor or of the carriers participating in the multimodal transport operations, and who assumes responsibility for the performance of the contract.[15]

A multimodal operation is made up of a number of unimodal stages of transport, such as sea, road, rail or air. Each of these is subject to a mandatory international convention or national law.

In spite of various attempts to establish a uniform legal framework governing multimodal transport no such international regime is in force. The United Nations Convention on International Multimodal Transport of Goods 1980 (MT Convention) has failed to attract sufficient ratifications to enter into force. The UNCTAD/ICC Rules for Multimodal Transport Documents, which came into force in January 1992, do not have the force of law. They are standard contract terms for incorporation into multimodal transport documents. The rules, being contractual in nature, will have no effect in the event of conflict with mandatory law.

The lack of a widely acceptable international legal framework on the subject has resulted in individual governments and regional/subregional intergovernmental bodies taking the initiative of enacting legislation in order to overcome the uncertainties and problems which presently exist. Concerns have been expressed regarding the proliferation of individual and possibly divergent legal approaches which would add to already existing confusion and uncertainties pertaining to the legal regime of multimodal transport.

Unimodal transportation – applicable international conventions

The following is a list of the various international conventions applicable to unimodal transportation:

(a) Transport by sea:
   - International Convention for the Unification of Certain Rules of Law Relating to Bills of Lading, 1924 (The Hague rules);
   - Protocol to Amend the International Convention for the Unification of Certain Rules Relating to Bills of Lading 1924, 1968 (The Hague-Visby rules);
   - Protocol Amending the International Convention for the Unification of Certain Rules of Law Relating to Bills of Lading, 1924, as Amended by the Protocol of 1968, 1979;
   - United Nations Convention on the Carriage of Goods by Sea, 1978 (Hamburg rules).

(b) Transport by road:
   - Convention on the Contract for the International Carriage of Goods by Road (CMR), 1956.

(c) Transport by rail:
  - Uniform Rules Concerning the Contract for International Carriage of Goods by Rail (CIM), Appendix B to the Convention Concerning International Carriage by Rail (COTIF), May 1980;
  - Protocol to amend CIM-COTIF, 1999.

(d) Transport by air:
  - Convention for the Unification of Certain Rules Relating to International Carriage by Air (Warsaw Convention), 1929;
  - The Hague Protocol, 1955;
  - Montreal Protocol No. 4, 1975;
  - The Montreal Convention, 1999.

In the absence of a uniform liability system for multimodal transport, the liability for each stage of transport is determined by the relevant unimodal convention or national laws, which adopt varying approaches to issues such as the liability questions. For example, all transport law conventions currently in force provide for monetary limitation of liability, but the relevant levels vary considerably. For a better appreciation of the issue, an overview of the relevant amounts is provided in Table 3.1.[16]

Table 3.1   Simplified overview over limits of liability according to mode of transport under international unimodal conventions in force

	Sea		Road	Rail	Air
The Hague rules: £100/kg (approx. 114 SDR/kg)	H/V rules: 2 SDR/kg or 666.67 SDR/load	Hamburg rules: 2.5 SDR/kg or 835 SDR/load	CMR: 8.33 SDR/kg	COTIF/CIM: 17 SDR/kg	Warsaw Convention 17 SDR/kg

Another problem is the extent to which these mandatory conventions applicable to unimodal transportation would also influence contracts where more than one mode of transport is involved, bearing in mind that some of these unimodal conventions also extend their scope into multimodal transport. For example, the CMR (art. 2), CIM (art. 2) and Montreal Conventions specifically include provisions dealing with transport of goods by more than one mode.

Where goods are carried in sealed containers, it is often difficult to identify the stage/mode of transport where a loss, damage or delay in delivery occurs. Under the present regulatory framework, however, both the incidence and the extent of a carrier's liability may depend crucially on:

(a) whether a loss can be localised to a particular stage and mode of transport;
(b) which of a considerable number of potentially applicable rules and/or regulations is considered to be relevant by a court or arbitral tribunal in a given forum.

Thus, the greatest shortcomings of transport law are considered to be:

> the vast differences between the rules governing the different transport modes. Different grounds of liability, different limitations of liability, different documents with a different legal value, different time limits to submission of the lawsuit. Where it may perhaps be said that this particularism did not constitute such a formidable problem when unimodal transport was still predominant, its drawbacks become glaringly obvious when attempts are made to combine different transport modes, and, inevitably, their different legal regimes into a single transport operation governed by a single contract. (De Wit, 1995)

The establishment of a widely acceptable legal framework for multimodal transport has proved to be a difficult task. Over the years, there have been several attempts to solve the problem by a uniform law text of some kind, but none of these has provided a satisfactory result.[17] The 1980 UN Convention on Multimodal Transportation of Goods (the S Convention), which operates a modified uniform system of liability for claims arising out of multimodal transport contracts, has failed to attract sufficient signatures and ratifications to enter into force. The UNCTAD/ICC Model Rules for Multimodal Transport Documents which came into effect in 1992 have no status of mandatory law, but will override any conflicting contractual provisions if they are incorporated into a contract. Both the MT Convention and the UNCTAD/ICC rules give precedence to mandatory law.

These two legal tools, however, have the largest influence on the current legal regime governing multimodal transportation since they are widely adopted in multimodal transportation contracts and their provisions and rules are part of some regional and national multimodal laws. We dedicate the following two subsections to describe their scope and content.

3.6.2 United Nations Convention on International Multimodal Transport of Goods 1980

3.6.2.1 Legal status

Although the MT Convention has not succeeded in attracting sufficient ratifications to enter into force and thus does not have any obligatory effect itself, its provisions have significantly influenced the type of legislation enacted in a number of countries/regions.

3.6.2.2 Scope of application

The MT Convention applies to all contracts of multimodal transport between places in two states, if the place of taking in charge or delivery of the goods as provided for in the multimodal transport contract is located in a contracting state (art. 2). While the MT Convention recognises the right of the consignee to choose between multimodal and segmented transport, its provisions are mandatory for all contracts of multimodal transport falling within the provisions of the MT Convention (art. 3).

3.6.2.3 Documentation

The MT Convention includes extensive provisions on documentation covering negotiable and non-negotiable multimodal transport documents, their contents, reservations and evidentiary effect (art. 5–10).

3.6.2.4 Liability

The liability of the multimodal transport operator (MTO) for loss of, or damage to, goods as well as delay in delivery is based on the principle of 'presumed fault or neglect'. That is to say that the MTO is liable if the occurrence which caused the loss, damage or delay in delivery took place while the goods were in his charge, unless the MTO proves that he, his servants or agents or any other person of whose services he makes use for the performance of the contract, took all measures that could reasonably be required to avoid the occurrence and its consequences.

The MT Convention adopts a uniform system of liability of the MTO for both localised and non-localised damage which means that the same liability regime is applied to the entire multimodal transport, irrespective of the stage at which the loss or damage occurred (art. 16 (1)), except that in cases of localised damage the limits of liability are to be determined by reference to the applicable international convention or mandatory national law which provide a higher limit of liability than that of the MT Convention (art. 19).

The period of responsibility of the MTO includes the entire period during which it is in charge of the goods, that is from the time it takes the goods in its charge to the time of the delivery (art. 14). The MTO is also liable for the acts and omissions of his servants or agents or any other person of whose services he makes use for the performance of the contract (art. 15).

The MTO's liability for loss of, or damage to, goods is limited to 920 SDR[18] per package or other shipping unit, or 2.75 SDR per kilogram of gross weight of the goods lost or damaged, whichever is higher. If, however, the multimodal transport does not, according to the contract, include carriage by sea or by inland waterway, the limitation amount is raised to a higher level of 8.33 SDR per kilogram of gross weight of the goods lost or damaged, without alternative package limitation (arts. 18 (1) and (3)).

The limitation of liability of the MTO for loss resulting from delay in delivery is calculated by reference to the rate of freight, that is an amount equivalent to two and a half times the freight payable for the goods delayed, but without exceeding the total freight payable under the multimodal transport contract (art. 18 (4)).

The MTO, however, is not entitled to limit its liability if it is proved that the loss, damage or delay in delivery resulted from an act or omission of the MTO done with the intent to cause such loss, damage or delay or recklessly and with knowledge that such loss, damage or delay would probably result (art. 21).

3.6.2.5 Time limit

The MT Convention provides for a period of two years within which legal proceedings relating to international multimodal transport have to be instituted in order to prevent the claim from being time-barred. A recourse action by the MTO for indemnity against subcontractors, however, is possible even after the expiry of limitation period, provided that it is permitted under the law of the state where proceedings are instituted and that it is not contrary to the provisions of another applicable international MT Convention (art. 25).

3.6.2.6 Jurisdiction

Concerning jurisdiction, the MT Convention gives a wide option to the claimant to institute an action for claims relating to international multimodal transport. It clearly provides that the plaintiff may sue in one of the following places:

(a) The principal place of business or residence of the defendant;
(b) The place where the multimodal transportation contract was made;
(c) The place of taking the goods in charge or the place of delivery; or
(d) Any other place agreed upon and evidenced in the multimodal transportation document (art. 26).

3.6.2.7 Arbitration

Following the growing trend in international commercial disputes, the MT Convention also recognises arbitration as an alternative to judicial proceedings. It provides that the parties may agree, in writing, to submit their disputes under the MT Convention to arbitration. Regarding the place of arbitration, the same options are available to the claimant as would be available for jurisdiction (art. 27).

3.6.3   UNCTAD/ICC Rules for multimodal transport documents

3.6.3.1 Legal status

The Rules do not have the force of law but are of purely contractual nature and apply only if they are incorporated into a contract of carriage, without any formal requirement for 'writing' and irrespective of whether it is a contract for unimodal or multimodal transport involving one or several modes of transport, or whether or not a document has been issued (Rule 1).

3.6.3.2 Scope of application

Once the Rules are incorporated into a contract, they override any conflicting contractual provisions, except in so far as they increase the responsibility or obligations of the MTO. The Rules, however, can only apply to the extent that they are not contrary to the mandatory provisions of international conventions or national law applicable to the multimodal transport contract (art. 13).

3.6.3.3 Documentation

The Rules envisage the possibility of issuing both 'negotiable' and 'non-negotiable' multimodal transport documents, including evidentiary effect of information contained in the document (Rules 2.6 and 3). However, since the Rules are of purely contractual nature, it is doubtful whether their incorporation into multimodal transportation documents would have the effect of creating a negotiable document in all jurisdictions. Rule 3, concerning evidentiary effect of the information contained in the multimodal transport document, provides that such information shall be prima facie evidence of the taking in charge by the MTO of the goods as described in the document unless contrary indications, such as 'shipper's weight, load and count', 'shipper-packed container' or similar expressions, have been included in the printed text or superimposed on the document. This would mean that such pre-printed clauses would destroy the evidentiary value of the document which is clearly undesirable. The Rule further provides that proof to the contrary shall not be admissible when the multimodal transportation document has been transferred to the consignee, who in good faith has relied and acted on such information.

3.6.3.4 Liability

Similar to the MT Convention, the liability of the MTO under the Rules is based on the principle of presumed fault or neglect. That is to say that the MTO is liable for loss of, or damage to the goods and for delay in delivery, if the occurrence which caused the loss, damage or delay in delivery took place while the goods were in his charge, unless he can prove that no fault or neglect of his own, his servants or agents or any other person of whose services he made use for the performance of the contract, caused or contributed to the loss or delay in delivery (Rule 5.1). Although the basis of liability of the MTO under the Rules is similar to that under the MT Convention, there are significant differences between them. First, unlike the MT Convention, under Rule 5.1, the MTO is not liable for loss following delay in delivery unless the consignor has made a declaration of interest in timely delivery which has been accepted by the MTO. Second, if the multimodal transport involves carriage by sea or inland waterways, the MTO will not be liable for

> loss, damage or delay in delivery with respect to goods carried by sea or inland waterways when such loss, damage or delay during such carriage has been caused by:
>
> (a) act, neglect or default of the master, mariner, pilot or the servants of the carrier in the navigation or in the management of the ship;
> (b) fire, unless caused by the actual fault or privity of the carrier. (Rule 5.4)

These defences, however, are made subject to an overriding requirement that whenever loss or damage resulted from a lack of seaworthiness of the vessel, the MTO must prove that due diligence was exercised to make the ship seaworthy at the beginning of the voyage

(Rule 5.4). The provisions of Rule 5.4 are intended to make the liability of the MTO compatible with the The Hague-Visby rules for carriage by sea or inland waterways.

Similar to the MT Convention, the period of responsibility of the MTO includes the period from the time it takes the goods in its charge until the time of their delivery.

Furthermore the MTO is also liable for the acts and omissions of its servants, agents or any other person of whose services it makes use in order to fulfil the contract (Rule 4.2).

The limitation amounts established by the Rules for loss of, or damage to, goods are clearly lower than those of the MT Convention. Thus, according to Rule 6.1, unless the nature and value of the goods are declared by the consignor and inserted in the MT document, the MTO shall not be liable for any loss of, or damage to, the goods in an amount exceeding the equivalent of 666.67 SDR per package or unit, or 2 SDR per kilogram of gross weight of the goods lost or damaged, whichever is the higher. In the same way as the MT Convention, a higher limit is provided for cases where the multimodal transport does not, according to the contract, include carriage by sea or inland navigation. In such a case the liability of the MTO is limited to an amount not exceeding 8.33 SDR per kilogram of gross weight of the goods lost or damaged (Rule 6.3), without any reference to package limitation which is more appropriate for sea transport.

Similar to the MT Convention, specific provisions on limitation of liability of the MTO are made for cases of localised damage. Under Rule 6.4, when the loss or damage occurs during one stage of transport, in respect of which an applicable international convention or mandatory national law would have provided another limit of liability (and not a higher limit as provided by the MT Convention), if a separate contract had been made for that particular stage of transport, then the limit of liability of the MTO for such loss or damage should be determined by reference to the provisions of such convention or mandatory national law.

The liability of the MTO for delay in delivery of the goods or consequential loss or damage is limited to an amount not exceeding the equivalent of the freight under the multimodal transport contract (Rule 6.5).

The MTO is not entitled to limit his liability if it is proved that the loss, damage or delay resulted from a personal act or omission of the MTO done with the intent to cause such loss, damage or delay, or recklessly and with knowledge that such loss, damage or delay would probably result (Rule 7).

3.6.3.5 Time limit

Rule 10 sets the time-barred period at nine months. Thus, the MTO will be relieved from liability unless the suit is brought within nine months after delivery of the cargo, or of the date when the cargo should have been delivered. This is to allow the MTO the possibility of instituting recourse action against the performing carrier, as most uni-modal conventions such as The Hague-Visby rules set the time-barred period at one year. The MT Convention provides for a period of two years.

3.6.3.6 Jurisdiction and arbitration

Unlike the MT Convention, the Rules do not include any provisions dealing with jurisdiction and arbitration. Multimodal transport documents currently used in practice usually provide for any dispute to be determined by the courts in accordance with the law at the place where the MTO has its principal place of business.

4
Contract to Provide Logistics Services: Warehousing and Resources

4.1 Introduction

As we have already explained, 3PL providers nowadays provide more than just transport services. Market demands have led 3PL providers to be considered as 'solution providers', offering and developing capabilities that exceed the traditional domain of transport; in other words, 3PL providers must offer value-added services.

This chapter will focus on those aspects of logistics contracts that do not concern transportation and that are usually seen as offering no added value because they are related to the administration of the services as opposed to the services themselves. However, in our view, if parties approach these issues in a constructive way they can cut costs and therefore provide better service.

We will first consider warehousing: the main obligations of the 3PL provider and the liability and other common contract clauses related to warehousing activities.

Secondly, the chapter will address issues concerning personnel. Outsourcing has become a major issue in labour relations since it often results in job losses. Increasingly, worker representatives are insisting they be given information and consulted prior to any possible outsourcing; at times they are even suggesting that joint management–union committees be set up to study outsourcing proposals. We will focus on the following main questions: what are the legal obligations in an outsourcing situation, in the case of both labour force outsourcing and any other business activity? When do temporary employment agency workers become 'de facto' employees of the client? And lastly, what are the special obligations imposed by European directives and conventions in outsourcing scenarios?

Finally, this chapter will cover the insurance issues arising from a logistics contract through a concise and comprehensive study of the general principles and a description of the related risks, practices, rights and obligations.

4.2 Warehousing

4.2.1 Obligations of the warehouse owner

4.2.1.1 The obligation of warehousing

The essence of a 'deposit' type of contract consists in the depositary accepting the obligation to store the property of another party, through taking possession of this property, when so requested by the depositor. A priori, it is not possible to determine the specific obligations concerning warehousing that are incumbent on the professional depositary, i.e. to identify the specific measures that may need to be taken with respect to the property deposited. However, in general terms, this type of contractual agreement will contain the following aspects:

- The depositary is responsible for the necessary surveillance to prevent any loss or theft of the property deposited.
- The depositary must preserve the property deposited in accordance with the nature thereof.
- In compliance with the obligations relating to storing the property, the depositary can employ and use any auxiliary staff and employees that they consider necessary.
- In principle, the depositary is not obliged to insure the property deposited.

However, the obligations of the depositary in respect of the storage of the property deposited do not merely consist of complying with a fairly broad range of appropriate forms of conduct, but in addition, they include the obligation to observe a certain degree of care in undertaking the former. This is referred to as an obligation of diligent activity. In this section, we will discuss ways of determining of the level of care that can be required from a professional depositary, and analyse the functions that the care satisfies within the warehousing obligation regime.

4.2.1.2 The obligation to maintain the establishment in the condition it was in prior to delivery

The property is delivered on the assumption that the depositary's obligations concerning the storage and return thereof are exigible. However, in the case of a professional deposit, the depositary will be bound, starting from the moment that they first enter into a contractual relationship, to maintain the conditions and security measures necessary in order to ensure the fulfilment of their warehousing obligations – even if the property has not yet been delivered – and likewise to ensure the correct function and operation thereof.

The obligation that we are examining here does not, strictly speaking, constitute an aspect of the warehousing obligation in itself, but rather forms an independent obligation that is imposed on the depositary by virtue of their status as a professional entity and as the owner of an establishment.

4.2.1.3 The duty of supervision

The obligation to warehouse the property can be demanded from the moment at which the depositary first takes receipt of the property. Although the specific content of this obligation may differ in each case, depending on the circumstances, there are certain minimum aspects which can never be missing. For example, it is inconceivable to have a contract of deposit in which the depositary is not bound to fulfil their supervisory duties with the necessary alacrity in order to detect any new development that could have a bearing on the security of the property deposited. The supervisory activity is appropriate in itself, in order to guarantee a high degree of security for the property, with respect to the dangers represented by loss, damage or theft. Furthermore, the supervisory duty also presumes that the depositary is complying appropriately and properly with the other duties that may be incumbent on them through the terms of the warehousing obligation. These, for example, include setting up a proper supervisory system that will enable preservation measures to be adopted as necessary in each case, should the depositary be obliged to undertake this, or to provide due notice to the depositor regarding the necessity or convenience of such measures, as applicable.

The importance of assuming the supervisory activity imposes an obligation on the depositary to notify the depositor of any shrinkage and damage that the property deposited may suffer 'immediately when they appear'.

Accordingly, the depositary must provide the supervisory mechanisms considered necessary and sufficient, taking into account the particular circumstances, the professional nature of the activity undertaken, and the nature of the property deposited. Within these parameters, the depositary should enjoy a certain degree of autonomy when it comes to selecting the material resources (alarms, fire detectors, television cameras, etc.) and/or the staff that they consider appropriate. However, in all events, they will provide such resources as are legally imposed on them, and also those that could have been contained in the express or implied bid made to their clients.

Accordingly, the absence of the surveillance mechanisms that could be considered to be required on the basis of what has been mentioned above, could constitute a case of a breach of the warehousing obligation, with any resulting consequences, without it being necessary to expect that this may be attributed to the effective loss, theft or deterioration of the property deposited.

4.2.1.4 The obligation of preservation

In principle, the depositary is bound to preserve the property in accordance with its nature, and with respect to any internal or external prejudicial agents that may be likely to cause any detriment to it. This is a means of guaranteeing not only that the property deposited remains within the depositary's sphere of control, but also the physical and economic integrity of the property for the period of time it is in storage.

In the case of an ordinary deposit, the depositary is obliged to undertake all such preservation measures that are appropriate to the circumstances. However, for ordinary deposits, the content of the preservation obligation is usually determined in a stricter manner. This may take the form of a relatively broad range of operations that have to be carried out on the property, in compliance with the standard guidelines determined by the technical and collective nature of the activity.

At the same time, on some occasions the preservation obligation of a professional depositary is more limited in content than that of an occasional depositary. This is not incompatible with the fact that the depositary may be required, within the scope of their obligation, to provide a particularly qualified level of care, specifically on the basis of their own professionalism.

In effect, the depositary usually undertakes to provide the resources necessary in order, in so far as may be possible, to avoid any deterioration of the property deposited due to the influence of external agents (for example, maintaining a specific temperature or degree of humidity, or implementing mechanisms to prevent or fight the danger of fires or floods). In exchange, in so far as any damage or shrinkage that could arise from the particular nature of the property deposited is concerned, it is common for the scope of the obligations, as well as the faculties for action with respect to the particular property, to be wholly restricted for the depositary.

In principle, however, the scope of the depositary's obligations and associated faculties in view of preserving the integrity of the property, with respect to the risks deriving from its particular nature, will be determined, in each case, by the particular characteristics of the objects deposited for storage, the conditions of the establishment in question, and the uses and the express or implied agreements of the parties. Thus, in the case of a contract for a garage or a supervised car parking area, the company is bound to undertake a surveillance activity and to protect the vehicles parked at its establishment from any damage that could be suffered by the influence of external agents. However, as a rule, and unless there is agreement to the contrary, the company is not obliged to provide the maintenance and preservation of the vehicles in respect to any form of damage that could arise from their particular nature, even in the case that there is a material possibility of having known of the condition of each vehicle and of acting accordingly. In other cases (e.g. the storage of fur coats, carpets, furniture), the activity that the depositary has to undertake is restricted to maintaining the objects deposited in the conditions of cleanliness, packaging, etc. that may be required for their subsequent preservation, by means of maintaining the static environmental conditions.

In the context of this discussion, the depositary is responsible for making the plea and proving all data and circumstances that could contribute towards setting limits on the scope of their warehousing obligation, in terms of the preservation of the objects deposited, for the event in which these may have suffered damage or shrinkage. In the absence of such evidence, the depositary will be considered to have assumed the obligation to carry out all preservation activities necessary to avoid damage, and that the damage specifically took place due to a breach of this obligation.

On the other hand, there is no doubt that any activity carried out by the depositary must in any event conform to the requirements of good faith, and that these same requirements could be imposed on the depositary under certain circumstances, requiring them to observe a form of conduct in relation to the object deposited outside of the scope of its ordinary activity. However, as a general rule, some restrictive criterion must be applied when it comes to determining the room for manoeuvre that the depositary must acknowledge in view of complying with their obligations. The basic principle, in view of any unexpected event, is that of providing due notice to the depositor, so that the latter can adopt the measures that it considers to be most appropriate. Only in the absence of this possibility will the depositary have the duty, and even the obligation, to take measures that go beyond the scope of its normal undertakings.

4.2.2 Liabilities

It is common knowledge that the liability regime established for transportation (exonerations, limitation of liability, time-barred periods, etc.) does not apply in the case of damage that occurs in a warehouse.

Therefore, if an item of merchandise that has been entrusted in storage to a 3PL provider suffers any form of damage, the applicable liability regime for him can be summed up as follows:

(a) *System of liability:* as a general rule, there is assumption of guilt on the part of the 3PL provider for any damage to merchandise that occurs when in it is their safekeeping.

(b) *Facts leading to the liability of the 3PL provider:* the operator is answerable for any partial or total loss, and for any partial or total breakage or damage, to the merchandise they have been entrusted with.

(c) *Extent of liability:* the 3PL provider is liable from the moment at which the merchandise is delivered into storage and safekeeping, until such time as that same merchandise is delivered to the client, or to a third party following instructions of the client.

(d) *Amount of liability:* the 3PL provider is liable not only for the value of the merchandise, but also for the sum that may be demanded thereof. He is responsible for any damage caused, due to the fact that he has liability, without any limit on the degree of liability. In summary, the 3PL provider is answerable for all damages (without limitation).

(e) *Exoneration of liability:* the 3PL provider is liable in the event of misrepresentation, blame or negligence, with the exception of cases where the loss or damage comes about as a consequence of:
   - An unexpected circumstance or *force majeure*;
   - A fault on the part of the depositing party;
   - The nature and particular defect of the merchandise, but only provided that:
     - Everything necessary was done to prevent the damage and,
     - The client was immediately notified.

Responsibility for all the above lies with the depositing party.

Hence, the storage company could allege the concurrence of circumstances beyond the scope of its business activity as an exonerating cause. In view of this, it is not bound by contract to take special preventative measures; furthermore, there are certain circumstances which – while being foreseeable – could not specifically have been avoided, even by adopting the measures necessary, given the circumstances and the characteristics of the particular activity.

This must be viewed in connection with the duty of informing the client: the duty to report on measures that could be adopted and the risks against which there are no specific measures; the duty of informing the client of any option of taking out insurance, at the client's expense, that may cover such eventualities, etc.

(f) *Time-barring:* the time-barred period during which action can be taken to bring a claim against the storage company in the event of loss or damage is, unlike the period allowed for any damage or loss to the merchandise in transport, determined in ordinary legislation and can, normally, be interrupted.

In summary, the most fundamental aspects relating to the liability of the depositing party are as follows (see also Table 4.1):

- Liability extends not only to damage, but also includes any consequential detriment caused.
- There is no limited liability.
- There are no specific reasons for exoneration from liability other than unexpected circumstances and *force majeure*.
- It is not necessary to make a protest within a given time period in order to make a claim.

Table 4.1

	Liability regime: deposit/storage of merchandise
System	Liability for presumed culpability
Generating facts	Total loss Partial loss Damage or breakage
Scope	From the receipt of the merchandise until its delivery to the recipient
Amount	Damages

Exoneration	Unexpected circumstances
	Force majeure
	Culpability of the depositing party
	• In principle, the recipient is not liable for any damages that arise as a result of the nature and particular defect of the merchandise, provided:
	  – The necessary steps to prevent or remedy the damage were taken
	  – The depositary party was notified of the damage

4.3 Personnel

4.3.1 Introduction

Outsourcing has become a major issue in labour relations, since it often results in the loss of jobs. Increasingly, workers' representatives are insisting upon prior information and consultation on possible outsourcing, or even joint management–union committees to study outsourcing proposals. In some countries, opposition on the part of workers' representatives has made it very difficult for some companies to take advantage of important opportunities to reduce costs through outsourcing.

4.3.2 Legal framework

The first legal framework for outsourcing business activities was drawn up in 1977 when the EU adopted a Directive entitled 'On Approximation of the Laws of the Member States Relating to the Safeguarding of Employees' Rights in event of Transfers of Undertakings, Business or Parts of Businesses' (77/187/EEC). This became known as the 'Acquired Rights' or 'Transfer of Undertakings' Directive.

This Directive had been regulated in order to protect the rights of workers who were transferred from one employer to another as a result of privatisation, contracting out, compulsory competitive tendering, private finance initiative, or a merger.

As with all European directives, it had to be transposed into the law of the member states. These laws soon acquired the acronym TUPE.

If workers were transferred due to one of the changes mentioned above, the rights and obligations of the transferor organisation arising from a contract of employment are transferred to the transferee. Trade unions used these regulations creatively to ameliorate any injury to conditions and pay. Not surprisingly, there were plenty of disputes about when the Directive-based national regulations applied and what exactly they said.

In the light of the many difficulties that the original Directive encountered (such as the UK government refusal to acknowledge government privatisation as part of the TUPE regulations), in 1994 the European Commission proposed a new directive (98/50/EC). The 98 Directive expanded the definitions of a 'transfer' and confirmed its application to public, private and non-profit organisations. It also required member states to protect the pension rights, and required the consultation of employees, including unrepresented workers, and specified what information must be supplied to them. Possibly less helpful to the employees were the provisions of the new Directive, that excluded insolvent businesses from its scope of application and allowed agreements to change contracts to 'help business survival'. This was changed, when the 98 Directive was amended in 2001 (Directive No. 2001/23/EC). This last version of the Directive introduced some changes; the most important changes pertain to the transfer of pension schemes and transfers after bankruptcy.

Both the Directive and the corresponding national laws have been the subject of a great deal of frequently inconsistent judicial analysis, with some discrepancies between the European Court of Justice rulings and the national ones. We will try, however, to present in this section facts that are less questionable, as well as the different approaches to some of the issues when needed.

It is essential to emphasise first that any provision of any agreement (whether a contract of employment or not) is void so far as it would exclude or limit the rights granted under the Directive, and as the survey had demonstrated it has significant influence on any outsourcing activity.

The following is a list of the major principles of the Directive:

(a) Employees employed by the previous employer when the under-taking changes hands automatically become employees of the new employer on the same terms and conditions. It is as if their contracts of employment had originally been made with the new employer. Thus, employees' continuity of employment is pre-served, as are their terms and conditions of employment under their contracts of employment.

(b) Employees have the right to be informed and consulted about the transfer through elected representatives or a recognised trade union.

(c) Employees are protected against dismissal for any reason relating to the transfer unless the dismissal was for an economic, technical, or organisational reason entailing changes in the workforce.

4.3.2.1 Scope of the Directive

4.3.2.1.1 Application of the Directive. The issue of when the Directive and the adopted national laws apply has been the most complex aspect of the regulation and the court rulings dealing with it. There is no specific definition of an undertaking contained in the Directive. Decisions made by European and UK courts, as well as employment tribunals, determine the interpretation of a transferred undertaking and include such things as the sale of a business by sale of assets, a merger, a change of licensee or franchise and the transfer of a particular function to a contractor (i.e. outsourcing).

For the Directive to apply, the transfer does not have to be a commercial transaction; therefore, the Directive covers organisations in the public sector as well as non-commercial organisations such as charities. The chief criterion, which determines whether the Directive applies, is the degree to which the undertaking retains its identity after it is transferred to the new employer. Factors which are considered in examining this include whether capital, employees, intangible assets such as customer goodwill and work procedures, transfer with the undertaking. One European Court of Justice decision cast doubt on whether the Directive would apply to some labour-intensive transfers in which neither a majority of the workforce nor assets transferred. Another European Court of Justice decision created uncertainty about whether the Directive would be applicable to transfers between two public organisations. However, in several cases in Spain and in Germany, it was established that the Directive covers the determination of a contracting-out arrangement by a public body, and a switch from one contractor to another, even if the only tangible assets to be transferred were the workers themselves. We will return to this point and describe the important recent developments and their practical implication later on in this section.

The first question that should be posed when examining the notion of 'undertaking' is what the 'entity' that constitutes the undertaking actually is.

The UK Employment Appeal Tribunal[1] came out with the following guidelines for establishing the 'entity':

- There needs to be a stable economic entity not limited to one specific works contract, and an organised grouping of people and assets enabling the exercise of the activity pursuing a specific objective;
- The entity must be sufficiently structured and autonomous, but does not necessarily include significant assets;
- In certain sectors, including cleaning and surveillance, the entity could be reduced to its manpower;
- An organised group of workers performing a common task may amount to an economic entity; and
- An activity is not in itself an entity – this requires for its identity its workforce, management staff, the way in which the work is organised and, where appropriate, the operational resources available to it.

After establishing the 'entity' part of the 'undertaking' definition, we should establish a definition of when an 'undertaking' is 'transferred' from one employer to another.

The following are the guidelines of the UK Employment Appeal Tribunal for establishing a 'transfer':

- The decisive criterion is whether or not the entity in question retains its identity, which is likely to be indicated by whether its operation is continued or resumed;
- In labour-intensive situations, an entity can retain its identity after transfer where the new employer does not merely pursue the activity in question, but also takes over a major part of the workforce previously employed to perform that task;
- It is necessary to consider all the factors characterising the transaction, but each is a single factor and none should be considered in isolation;
- It is, therefore, relevant to consider whether tangible assets have been transferred, the value of intangible assets at the time of transfer, whether the majority of employees are taken on by the new employer, whether the customers are transferred, the degree of similarity of the activities pre- and post-transfer and the period, if any, during which they are suspended;
- The type of business or undertaking is relevant and this may affect the degree of importance to be attached to each of the criteria;
- If the entity can function without a significant transfer of assets, the maintenance of its identity cannot logically depend on the transfer of such assets;
- Even if assets are owned and required to run the entity, their absence does not preclude a transfer;
- Similarity between the service provided by the old and new undertaking providing a contracted-out service, or the old and new contract holder, is not in itself enough to establish a relevant transfer;
- The absence of a contractual link between the old and new undertaking may indicate no relevant transfer but it is not conclusive since it is not in itself necessary;
- If no employees are transferred, the reason for this can be relevant in determining whether or not there has been a relevant transfer.

The reader of these guidelines can get the correct impression that the rules of implementing the Directive are over-complicated and vague.

However, for the purpose of simplification, the following is a list of examples of recognised 'transfers':

- Where a contract to provide goods or services is transferred in circumstances which amount to the transfer of a business or undertaking to a new employer;

- Where all or part of a sole trader's business or partnership is sold or otherwise transferred;
- Where a company, or part of it, is bought or acquired by another, provided this is done by the second company buying or acquiring the assets and then running the business, and not by acquiring the shares only;
- Where two companies cease to exist and combine to form a third;
- A transfer between two companies at the same group.[2]

The regulations can apply regardless of the size of the transferred undertaking. Thus, the regulations equally apply to the transfer of a large business with many thousand employees and to that of a very small one (such as a shop, pub or garage) and apply equally to the public and private sector.

Following is a list of common activities that are not considered to be a 'transfer' of undertaking and as a result, not governed by the Directive:

- Transfers by share takeover because, when a company's shares are sold to new shareholders, there is no transfer of the business – the same company continues to be the employer;
- Transfers of assets only (for example, the sale of equipment alone would not be covered, but the sale of a going concern including equipment would be covered);
- Transfers of a contract to provide goods or services where this does not involve the transfer of a business or part of a business (more details on this option are given later in this section in the discussion of the Süzen case);
- A hiving off of profitable sections of a company in liquidation.

In this context, it is important to mention that the last amended Directive specifically excludes operations involving seagoing vessels. This was decided in view of the special nature of seagoing employment and designed to provide a greater flexibility for the marine navigation sector.

4.3.2.1.2 The definition of an 'employee'.   In general, the Directive will apply to any person:

- Working under a contract of employment or employment relationship as defined by the national laws of each member state;
- Employed through an employment agency; or
- Holding office under, or in the service of the state.

In the case of agency workers, the party who is liable to pay the wages (the employment agency or client company) is the employer for the purposes of the Directive.

4.3.2.1.3   *The employer's position in a transfer.*   Under the Directive, when an undertaking is transferred, the position of the previous employer and the new employer is as follows:

• The new employer takes over the contracts of employment of all employees who were employed in the undertaking immediately before the transfer, or who would have been so employed if they had not been unfairly dismissed for a reason connected with the transfer. An employer cannot just pick and choose which employees to take on.

• The new employer takes over all rights and obligations arising from those contracts of employment, except criminal liabilities and rights and obligations relating to provisions about benefits for old age, invalidity or survivors in employees' occupational pension schemes.

• The new employer takes over any collective agreements made on behalf of the employees and in force immediately before the transfer. The transferee is obliged to observe the terms and conditions of the collective agreements until the date of termination or expiry of the collective agreement, or the entry into force or application of another collective agreement.

• Neither the new employer nor the previous one may fairly dismiss an employee because of the transfer or a reason connected with it, unless the reason for the dismissal is an economic, technical or organisational (ETO) reason entailing changes in the workforce. If there is no such reason, the dismissal will be unfair. If there is such a reason, and it is the cause or main cause of the dismissal, the dismissal will be fair provided an employment tribunal decides that the employer acted reasonably, in the circumstances, in treating that reason as sufficient to justify dismissal. If, in this case, there is a situation of redundancy, the usual redundancy procedures still will apply. It is important to emphasise, however, that the various courts usually only allowed the defence a very narrow definition of an ETO reason. In order to fall within the scope of an ETO reason, the employer must be able to show that the dismissal was a necessity, and that the objective of their plan was to achieve changes in the workforce. An employer may not claim ETO if, for example the dismissal was carried out solely in order that the business realise a higher value.

- The new employer may not, unless the contract of employment so provides, unilaterally worsen the terms and conditions of employment of any transferred employee.
- The previous and new employers must inform and consult representatives of the employees.

4.3.2.1.4 *The employees' position in a transfer.*   When an undertaking is transferred the position of the employees of the previous or new employers is as follows:

- Employees employed in the undertaking immediately before the transfer (or who would have been so employed had they not been unfairly dismissed for a reason connected with the transfer) automatically become employees of the new employer, unless they inform either the new or the previous employer that they object to being transferred.
- An employee's period of continuous employment is not broken by a transfer, and, for the purposes of calculating entitlement to statutory employment rights, the date on which the period of continuous employment started is the date on which the employee started work with the old employer. This should be stated in the employee's written statement of terms and conditions; if it is not, or if there is a dispute over the date on which the period of continuous employment started, the matter can be referred to an employment tribunal.
- Transferred employees retain all the rights and obligations existing under their contracts of employment with the previous employer, and these are transferred to the new employer, with the exception that the previous employer's rights and obligations relating to benefits for old age, invalidity or survivors under any employees' occupational pension schemes are not transferred. If the new employer does not provide comparable overall terms and conditions, including pension arrangements, an employee may have a claim for unfair dismissal.
- An employee claiming to have been unfairly dismissed because of a transfer has the right to complain to an employment tribunal.
- Transferred employees who find that there has been a fundamental change for the worse in their terms and conditions of employment as a result of the transfer generally have the right to terminate their contract and claim unfair dismissal before an employment tribunal, on the grounds that actions of the employer have forced them to resign. Employees may not make this type of claim solely on the

grounds that the identity of their employer has changed, unless the circumstances of an individual case change, and that change is significant and to the employee's detriment.

In both the above cases, dismissal because of a relevant transfer will be unfair unless an employment tribunal decides that an economic, technical or organisational reason entailing changes in the workforce was the main cause of the dismissal, and that the employer acted reasonably in the circumstances in treating that reason as sufficient to justify dismissal. Even if the dismissal is considered fair, employees may still be entitled to a redundancy payment.

4.3.2.1.5 *The right and obligation of consultation and information.*
Employers are obliged to consult with either the recognised trade union or elected employee representatives. These requirements apply in respect of any employees who may be affected by the transfer, whether employed by the new or previous employers. An employer is required to inform and, if appropriate, consult either representatives of an appropriate recognised trade union or elected representatives of the employees. If there are no existing employee representatives the employer must allow employees to elect representatives before the transfer occurs. Consultation should be undertaken by the employer with a view to seeking the agreement of employee representatives to the proposed measures.

Employee representatives are entitled to the following information from both the original employer and the new employer:

- The fact that the relevant transfer is to take place;
- The reasons for the transfer;
- The date, or approximate date of when the transfer is to occur;
- The legal, economic and social implications of the transfer for the employees;
- The measures that are proposed by the old or new employer in connection with the transfer.

It can be assumed that failing to comply with obligations in terms of employee participation will not diminish the validity of the transfer. However, it may result in a complaint being brought against the employer by any of the following people:

- An employee who has been dismissed or who has resigned in circumstances in which they consider they were entitled to resign because of the consequences of the transfer. It may be unclear whether claims should be made against the previous or the new employer. Certain categories of employees are not entitled to claim unfair dismissal;

- An elected or trade union representative, if the employer does not comply with the information or consultation requirements;
- A representative or candidate for election who has been dismissed, or suffered detriment short of dismissal;
- A representative who has been unreasonably refused time off by an employer, or whose employer has refused to make the appropriate payment for time off, may also complain to an employment tribunal;
- An affected employee where the employer has not complied with the information or consultation requirements other than in relation to a recognised trade union or an elected representative;
- An employee who wishes to claim a redundancy payment.

Representatives need not be elected specifically for this purpose; an employer may inform and/or consult through an existing consultative body whose membership is elected, for example a staff council, provided that it is appropriate to inform and/or consult this body on this issue.

National legislation does not usually specify how many representatives must be elected or the process by which they are to be chosen. An employment tribunal may wish to consider, in determining a claim that the employer has not informed or consulted in accordance with the requirements, whether the arrangements were such that the purpose of the legislation could not be met.

An employer will therefore need to consider such matters as whether:

- The arrangements adequately cover all the categories of employees who may be affected by the transfer, and provide a reasonable balance between the interests of the different groups;
- The employees have sufficient time to nominate and consider candidates;
- The employees (including any who are absent from work for any reason) can freely choose who to vote for;
- There is any normal company custom and practice for similar elections and, if so, whether there are good reasons for departing from it.

The dismissal of an elected representative will be automatically unfair if the reason, or the main reason, is related to the employee's status or activities as a representative. An elected representative also has the right not to suffer any detriment short of dismissal on the grounds of their status or activities. Candidates for election enjoy the same protection. Where an employment tribunal finds that a dismissal was unfair, it may order the employer to reinstate or re-engage the employee or make an appropriate award of compensation.

Employees who are not consulted about a transfer of a business which has the effect of transferring their employment to another employer, as mentioned above, are entitled to claim compensation based on the failure to consult.

There has been some confusion concerning who is liable to pay the employees in such circumstances, the transferring employer or the employer to whom the employment contracts are transferred. In general, liability for claims arising in connection with transfers governed by the Directive are the responsibility of the transferee (also see subsection 4.3.2.1.6 'Liabilities transferred in undertaking deals under the Directive' below). However, on the question of compensation for failure to consult, there have been conflicting decisions by the UK Employment Appeal Tribunal. In the case of the TGWU[3] it was ruled that the liability to consult should stay with the transferor. The reasoning for this was that if it did not, there would be no incentive for a transferor to comply with the regulations of consulting and informing the employees and hence go contrary to the Undertaking Directive aims. However, in another case[4] it was concluded that the responsibility for such compensation rests with the transferee.

4.3.2.1.6 *Liabilities transferred in undertaking deals under the Directive.*

The courts in the past have not always consistently answered the question of what exactly is transferred by the transferor to the transferee by the Directive. Some recent UK Court of Appeal decisions[5] have at last clarified the law.

The UK Court of Appeal dealt with two cases in which employees suffered injuries prior to the transfer of an undertaking to which TUPE applies. The legal and practical question was, is the liability of the transferor for those injuries, which accrued before the transfer, transferred by TUPE to the transferee?

A subsequent issue in these cases was whether the benefit of the employers' liability insurance policy was capable of being transferred by TUPE.

The ruling was that the Directive's purpose was to safeguard employ-ees' rights. Therefore, the rights were not limited to those under the contract but also included those 'in connection with' contracts. Accordingly, any tortuous liabilities transferred with the contractual obligations.

Turning to the further issue of whether the transferor's rights under its employers' liability insurance are capable of being transferred by TUPE, the judge considered it important that TUPE be construed 'in such a way as to ensure that on the transfer the employee is not deprived of rights against his employer'.

While the transferee would have taken out insurance,[6] this was unlikely to cover liability before the employee was transferred to the transferee. The transferor, however, had 'a vested or contingent right to recover from his insurers under the employers' liability policy in respect of his liability to the employee'. The transferor's insurers had received a premium in respect of such liability and there was no reason why TUPE should be construed to enable those insurers to keep the premium but avoid the liability. It was ruled, therefore, that the com-pensation be paid from the insurer of the transferor.

The last amended Directive established joint liability of the trans-feror and the transferee in respect of obligations which arose before the date of transfer from a contract of employment or an employment rela-tionship existing on the date of the transfer. We still have to wait for new European Court of Justice rulings to see how this new Directive is interpreted in cases similar to the ones mentioned above.

The new Directive also established that the transferor is obliged to notify the transferee of all the rights and obligations which will be transferred, to the extent that they are known to the transferor at that time. However, failure on the part of the transferor to notify will not affect the transfer of the right, or the obligation and the rights of any employee in respect of the transferee and/or the transferor.

4.3.2.1.7 Transfer of undertakings under suspension of payments and bankruptcy.

A question that arose frequently in many of the Directive-related cases in the European Court of Justice was that of the extent to which employees also enjoyed protection in cases concerning the transfer of an undertaking in a situation where a company was facing a suspension of payment or bankruptcy. The European Court rulings on these matters were that in all cases concerning suspension of payment the Directive applies but, regarding bankruptcy, the member states are at liberty to reach their own decision. The idea underlying this approach was to allow enough flexibility to enhance the survival opportunities for these troubled businesses.

This distinction has been abused in a number of circumstances. A familiar example in the Netherlands is the case concerning Ammerlaan, where the employer attempted to circumvent the labour regulation governing compensation for dismissal, by having the company declared bankrupt. Although the Dutch court ruled that the law relating to bankruptcy had been abused, the Dutch law provided no recourse in terms of compelling the employer to re-employ the employees dismissed by the trustee in bankruptcy.

The last amended Directive referred to this issue for the first time. It maintained the common former European Court of Justice rulings that the contractual rights of the employees do not transfer where the original employer is subject to proceedings whereby he may be adjudicated bankrupt, or wound up for reasons of insolvency, by order of court.

However, in order to limit such cases of abused bankruptcy processes, the Directive emphasises that if the sole or main reason for the institution of bankruptcy or insolvency proceedings is the evasion of an employer's legal obligations under the Undertaking Directive, then the Directive applies to a transfer effected by that employer.

4.3.3 Outsourcing and TUPE: the Süzen case

The Süzen court ruling gave a coherent framework to distinguish between cases of contracted-out service transfers from one provider to another in which the Directive automatically applies, and other cases in which it does not. But while it is thought that some employers are likely to make the best of this ruling, competing fiercely for contracts in the service sector because winning them would enable them to keep costs down by not having to honour existing employee rights, both unions and employers feel that in the majority of cases it will make little difference.

The decision in the Süzen case led to immediate calls in the UK for the Department of Trade and Industry to clarify exactly what the ruling would mean under the TUPE arrangements. It had become widely accepted that TUPE applied very broadly to transfers of undertakings, and even businesses opposed to the broad interpretation had become used to tendering for contracts on that basis. Interested parties did not have to wait long for clarification, as following the European ruling in Süzen the UK Court of Appeal[7] applied the new ruling.

In the Süzen case it was held that a changeover of contracts to provide services to a customer is not of itself a transfer. According to this ruling, to count as a transfer it has to comply with the following:

- The transfer from one undertaking to another of significant tangible or intangible assets or,
- The taking on by the new employer of a major part of the workforce in terms of number or skills, as assigned by the predecessor, to fulfil the terms of the contract.

No fewer than five further European Court decisions concerning outsourcing approved the ruling in the Süzen case.[8]

4.3.3.1 The implication of the ruling for labour-intensive outsourcing contracts

In practical terms, the ruling in the Süzen case means that in the type of outsourcing situations where no assets transfer, as often happens in labour-intensive functions, commonly cleaning, security, maintenance, etc., whether a transfer occurs will depend on whether a major part of the workforce is taken on.

Since employment tribunals are expected to follow the Süzen case, it will be material, therefore, for those who wish to avoid the application of the Directive in a labour-intensive function, not to take on a major part of the workforce, in terms of numbers or skills. But first, as a word of warning, the fact that employees are not taken on will not of itself prevent the Directive from applying. There may be certain cases where no assets or employees are transferred, where there may be still a Directive transfer such as in the UK Court of Appeal ruling in the Unison case.[9] In this case RCO won a contract to provide specialist cleaning services at a new hospital to which an NHS Trust was transferring its operation. It offered jobs to employees of the outgoing contractor, but only on a non-TUPE basis. The employees rejected the terms and therefore no employee transferred and no assets transferred. The Court of Appeal held nonetheless that TUPE applied.

This will occur when the courts take into account the motive of the new employer in wishing to avoid the Directive, the nature of the job transferred (specialist as opposed to non-specialist jobs), or when other factors other than employees and assets will point towards the transfer.

When the UK courts found that the reason for not taking over the employees in labour-intensive contracts had a legitimate cause the Süzen case applied, and it was concluded that the transfer is not governed by the Directive. The following are two recent cases demonstrating this approach:

- The Williams case[10] dealt with a changeover of security services. The customer requiring the security service stipulated that the new contractor should not hire any of the previous contractor's staff and therefore, no staff were transferred. Furthermore, no asset transferred between the outgoing and the incoming contractors.
- The Ministry of Defence[11] took back in-house from its contractor the function of guarding services at an army camp. No assets were taken over and no staff taken on by the Ministry of Defence. The reason for not employing staff was that for strategic reasons armed guards were required for the camp in the future and the contractor's guards were not licensed to carry arms. Because the Ministry of Defence therefore had a legitimate economic reason for not taking on the staff of the contractor, there was no TUPE transfer.

4.3.3.2 The implication of the ruling for asset-reliant outsourcing contracts

Where the economic entity is an asset-reliant function, a different approach must be adopted in the enquiry. Unlike for a labour-intensive function, here the transfer of staff is less determinative of whether there is a TUPE transfer. The transfer of asset and other matters become much more important. Thus held the European Court of Justice in the case of Oy.[12] This case dealt with a change of bus operators on a number of bus routes in Helsinki. Of 45 employees employed by the outgoing contractor, 33 were taken on by the new operator, albeit on less favourable terms and conditions. No vehicles or other assets connected with the operation of the bus routes concerned were transferred. Two bus drivers who had been re-employed by the new operator brought the case to the Finnish courts, arguing that a transfer of an undertaking had taken place and that they were entitled to be employed on the same terms and conditions that they had previously enjoyed with the outgoing bus operator. Here the European Court concluded that the Directive did not apply. In labour-intensive operations there might be a transfer even though no assets are transferred, but if the undertaking depends on the use of substantial assets such as a plant and equipment, the provision of the service could not fairly be regarded as an activity based essentially on manpower alone, and other factors had to be taken into account. In this case it was possible to run the bus routes without buses. It was an asset-reliant service and as the buses were not transferred, there was no transfer in the eyes of the Directive, even though most of the employees were taken on.

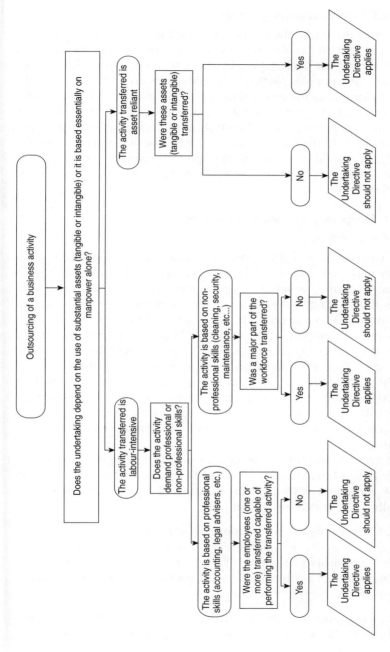

Figure 4.1 Applying the Undertaking Directive

4.3.3.3 Service outsourcing contracts

It is possible to take the European Court cases of Süzen and Oy literally and rely on the absence of employees or assets to maintain the position that the Undertaking Directive does not apply. This position allows, for example, parties to consider non-Undertaking Directive bids in tendering for services. However, adopting a non-TUPE stance in the UK courts carries with it considerable risks, since those courts tend to look behind the surface facts and apply other criteria as well. However, since the recent ruling of the European Court of Justice will apply, or at least will serve as an important reference point for most future cases, it is important to understand the fundamentals as outlined in Figure 4.1.

4.3.4 Temporary employment agencies

4.3.4.1 Introduction

The complexity and the creativity needed in business management today make the simplicity of the labour market as represented by the employer–employee relationship seem irrelevant and ancient. Nowadays, it is no longer surprising to see workers working side by side and performing the same task, while only some of them belong legally to the firm as employees. At the same time, it is not uncommon to see the employees of a supplier working on-site at the client firm, assembling the final adjustments to the just-in-time operation system.

The legal world has been following the real world and has been trying to regulate what is actually happening for quite some time. New rules have had to be established for these forms of employment that no longer had the critical factor of an employer–employee relationship.

In general, and for the purpose of our discussion, we can identify three types of individual (as opposed to company) workers, who could work for a firm without being considered legally, and as a result, fiscally, to be employees of that firm:

- A freelancer who renders his professional services to the company;
- Employees of a temporary employment agency working on the firm's premises performing a variety of tasks;
- Employees of a company that was contracted to perform a specific task in the client firm business.

For the purposes of this discussion we will focus on the two latter types of workers who are not the firm's employees.

Temporary employment agencies specialise in hiring workers and 'leasing' them out temporarily to other firms. Their business is carefully regulated, in order to ensure that the workers' rights are not abused or simply 'forgotten'. Therefore, there are specific regulations that govern the activities of temporary employment agencies, both nationally and internationally. In this section we will describe these regulations and their practical implications for the client firm.

Another group of employees, to be set apart from temporary employees, are the employees of the 3PL provider working on the client's premises. They form a separate group as they typically constitute an entire work unit of activity in the user's firm (such as the administration of benefits, clerical support services, part of the assembly process of the supplier), remain in these jobs for an indefinite length of time (and, thus, are probably not temporary), and are likely to be former employees of the firm where they continue to work, in spite of having been transferred to the payroll of the staffing company.

The work of employees of a company that is performing part of the business of a user firm under a work or services contract is, as mentioned above, governed by a different set of regulations. These regulations have been supplemented by court decisions, which call for drawing a clear distinction between an activity of subcontracted services done by another company using its workers, and a mere assignment of employees, which, unless it complies with the applicable rules, is considered in most cases as an unlawful activity.

The adoption of the ILO (International Labour Organisation) Convention No. 181 concerning private employment agencies (PREAs) and temporary working agencies (TWAs) on 19 June 1997, recognises these developments and at the same time underlines the important role private intermediaries may and already do play in supplying a temporary and flexible workforce.

There are two main categories of temporary workers: (1) the employees of staffing companies or temporary employment agencies who take short-term assignments at other user firms where they actually carry out the work, and (2) direct-hire employees of the company itself who may have fixed-term contracts or form part of an in-house labour pool, i.e. they are on call indefinitely and change jobs within the company as needed.

In the following section we will describe the recent developments in the regulation of temporary employment, concentrating mainly on the former type of temporary employment.

4.3.4.2 Definitions of temporary employment agency and temporary worker

4.3.4.2.1 The definition of a temporary employment agency.   The ILO defines a temporary work agency (TWA) as follows:

> any natural or legal person who, under national legislation, is qualified to recruit workers who then become its legal employees, with the view of making these workers available to a third party user who supervises this work and with whom the agency has signed an agreement contract. (ILO Convention 1996)

Originally, temporary workers were hired to replace female workers who were on maternity leave, or any workers on sick leave. During that period the temporary employment sector was completely oriented towards administrative functions, but later on, increasing numbers of firms started using temporary workers to deal with sudden and short changes in production demands.

It is the growing need for firms to be flexible which explains much of the spectacular growth of this sector in several European countries in the 1980s and the 1990s.

In most European countries and in the US, regular firms have the legal possibility to hire out workers to other employers; however, in countries with licence requirements (such as Spain), these firms also require a licence.

4.3.4.2.2 The definition of a temporary worker.   The definition of a temporary worker varies according to different national law. In French law, for example, fixed-term contracts of employment are limited to a maximum of an uninterrupted duration of 18 months. If a contract is extended beyond that period, then it will immediately be reclassified as a permanent contract of employment, with all the consequences that entails. Temporary work is very strictly regulated in France, and there are only certain very specific reasons for an employer to hire a temporary worker:

- To replace a regular employee, in case of absence or permanent leave of that employee;
- To provide staff in the case of a temporary increase in activity of the enterprise;
- In the case of seasonal employment.

The main consequence is that if the user firm does not respect these strict regulations, the courts will immediately consider the contract of employment to be a permanent contract of employment.

What is the relationship between the user firm and the temporary employment agency? This question will be discussed in the section below.

In France, within the first two days of taking on the services of a temporary employee, a contract must be drawn up between the user and the temporary employment agency. This contract must outline the purpose for which the employee is hired, the type of work that employee is going to be engaged in, the duration of the assignment and sometimes the possibility of renewing that assignment, the remuneration, which has to be equivalent to the salary earned by any employee working in the company in the same position, and the main characteristics of the position to be filled. There is also a second contract, to be signed between the user and the temporary employee, which has to contain more or less the same clauses.

The user is responsible for all the working conditions of the temporary employee in his company, as stipulated by law and the collective bargaining agreements. Temporary workers in France enjoy exactly the same rights as all other employees of the user in respect of working hours, night work, weekly days of rest, and security. The user is also obliged to provide the temporary employee with access to all the facilities which are available to the other employees of the company.

If these rules are not respected in full then the temporary employee can demand the reclassification of the contract of employment, and criminal liabilities can be imposed on the user. In any case, after 18 months a temporary worker in France will be automatically considered to be a permanent employee.

4.3.4.3 Temporary employment in some EU countries

4.3.4.3.1 United Kingdom. During the 1980s and the 1990s the UK was at the forefront of countries advocating flexibility as a response to increasingly turbulent and competitive conditions in product markets.

Traditionally, the British system of industrial relations had relied upon collective bargaining rather than legislation as a source of minimum terms and conditions of employment. Thus, in contrast to many European legal systems, there was no legislation of general application regulating minimum wages and working hours. In the 1970s several individual employment rights were finally legislated, but the majority of these individual rights were partial in their coverage, being restricted to those categories of dependent labour which satisfied the criteria of being 'employees'. Many casual workers were excluded from these rights by virtue of lacking the necessary 'mutual obligation', a concept which has been interpreted as requiring mutual obligations to maintain the employment relationship in being over a period of time.

English law distinguishes between the temporary worker who is directly employed by the enterprise, and the temporary worker who is employed through an agency. A temporary worker who is employed directly by the company will have access to employment protection, depending on the duration of the employment. However, if a temporary employee is working for an agency and is supplied as part of the triangular relationship, then what will count is the classification of the employer in that contract.

The only restriction in the UK on supplying temporary workers is when it occurs as a direct replacement for employees who are involved in an industrial dispute with the user.

As far as the direct obligations of the user are concerned, there are a few isolated provisions that extend obligations to the user. The sex and race discrimination legislation specifically applies to contract workers, so the user in that situation who discriminates on the grounds of gender could be liable in the same way as an employer could. The way that the health and safety legislation is framed in the UK also means that the user would be liable, in practice, for any sort of accident or breach of the health and safety regulations on the premises. Beyond that, most of the protective legislation applies only to employees.

4.3.4.3.2 Spain.   Up until late 1993, Spain was one of a several countries that prohibited any private mediation in the labour market. This prohibition was almost absolute. The activity of temporary employment agencies was considered to be a form of labour force traffic, and, therefore, unlawful. This situation was transformed during the period between late 1993 and the middle of 1994. There were several reasons for this transformation: an acute economic recession, a high rate of unemployment, a rather poor performance by the public employment sector in its attempts to manage the demand and supply of labour, rapid changes in the production process and in the way of organising work, the rise of new production activities, new professions and new skills, the pressures of diversified labour demand and, finally the general context of the introduction of broad reforms of labour legislation which aimed at increasing the economy's capacity to create jobs.

In December 1993, in an attempt to respond to the critical situation caused by economic recession and the considerable loss of jobs, the Spanish government introduced Royal Decree Law No. 18/93, which contained emergency measures for promoting employment. This new regulation lifted the ban on non-profit employment agencies, as well as making it legal to hire employees by temporarily assigning them to another company. This was followed by Act No. 14/94 of 1 June 1994, that was concerned with temporary employment firms. The following year, the Spanish government introduced the regulations to deal both with employment agencies and integrated services for employment, as well as temporary employment firms.

Spain also ratified ILO Convention No. 181 of 1997 on private employment agencies.

Act No. 14/94 defines TWAs as firms 'whose business consists of making available to a user firm, on a temporary basis, the employees hired by that firm'.

Hiring employees with the aim of assigning them temporarily to another enterprise had therefore been accepted as a lawful activity in Spain.

However, only duly authorised temporary work agencies may hire employees in order to assign them temporarily to other enterprises. Any act of assigning employees outside of the scope of a TWA is still considered to be illegal traffic with labour, with the consequent liabilities.

TWAs are real employers, in contract to employment agencies, whose purpose is merely to put the employee in touch with an employer who needs to fill a vacancy, which under normal circumstances is their only task.

As real employers, TWAs are responsible for organising and managing the labour of the workers, nor do they assume the obligation to make themselves a certain work or service as the object of a commercial agreement.

Temporarily assigning employees outside the legal scope of a TWA is considered a case of illegal traffic with labour, and involves serious liabilities or responsibilities for employers who commit such an offence. The 'Infractions and Sanctions in the Social Order Law' [*Ley sobre infracciones y sanciones en el orden social*] imposes harsh economic sanctions on acts involving the illegal transfer of workers. As far as the criminal aspect is concerned, the Spanish Penal Code establishes a punishment of between two and five years' imprisonment and a 6–12 month fine[13] for entities which illegally traffic with workers. Furthermore, the employees concerned are legally entitled to become permanent employees of either the enterprise that assigned them or the enterprise to which they were assigned, according to their own choice, and their new work conditions should be the same as those of an employee in the same or a similar position in that enterprise. According to Spanish court rulings, this right exists, as long as the contract is in force or as long as there remains a situation of transfer. Given the possibility of such, it is clearly important that any contracting firm must exercise caution, and must ensure that the enterprise providing the temporary workers is in a regular legal situation, i.e. that it has obtained appropriate official permission, to avoid situations in which the agency workers will be considered de facto as employees of the user. Meanwhile, this is the only activity that a TWA may engage in, and they are not permitted to engage in any other form of mediation in the labour market.

TWAs are only allowed to operate once they have obtained prior administrative authorisation. Administrative authorisation is granted for an initial term of one year, and may be extended for two further periods of one year each. After that, the TWAs may be granted authorisation to remain indefinitely in operation.

In Spain, temporary contracts of employment are 'causal' contracts, i.e. they are only permitted in certain circumstances, and to fulfil certain temporary needs, i.e. needs of the user firm which are clearly of a restricted time frame. Following the legalisation of the TWA, these contracts continue to be of a 'causal' nature, and the TWA can only enter into this type of contract. Thus, the TWA may not assign employees to perform any kind of work in a user firm, even though the work may be temporary.

There are four cases in which contracts may be concluded between the TWA and the user firm to temporarily assign employees to the latter:

- To perform given work or services, for an unspecified, yet in all cases limited, period of time;
- To meet circumstantial market requirements, a work backlog or an excess volume of orders;
- To replace employees of the user firm whose positions must be reserved for them;
- To temporarily fill a position that is normally held as a permanent position during the process of selecting or promoting the person who is to hold it permanently.

There are no other circumstances under which employees may be temporarily assigned to a user firm. Furthermore, the law explicitly forbids a TWA and a user firm to conclude any contracts in four particular cases:

- To replace employees of the user firm who are on strike;
- To carry out such activities or work as may be singled out by means of regulations as being particularly dangerous in respect to the health or safety of the worker. The list of activities which are ruled out has not yet been drawn up;
- To fill a position that was held previously by a permanent member of staff, who was dismissed by the user firm during the preceding 12 months on the basis that the position no longer needed to be filled;
- If the contract involves assigning employees to another temporary work agency.

Any contract between the TWA and the user firm must be in writing.

The powers of managing and controlling the work of an employee working on a contract between a TWA and a user firm are exercised by the latter, for as long as the employee works at the user firm.

The TWA holds the power to impose penalties, and therefore, the user firm must report to the TWA any manifestation of behaviour on the part of the employee that the user firm considers to constitute a breach of contract.

The employees of a TWA working under contract with a user firm are represented by the employees' representatives of that user firm, for as long as they continue to work there, in the case of any complaint they wish to make in respect of the working conditions.

Consequently, workers employed on a contract between a TWA and a user firm may file a complaint against the user firm, through the employees' representatives, concerning the conditions under which they carry out their work.

These representatives, however, do not represent employees in any complaints they make against the temporary work firm.

Finally, the user firm must inform the employees' representatives of every contract concluded between the temporary work firm and the user firm, and of the reason for doing so, within 10 days of entering into the contract.

4.4 Insurance

4.4.1 Insurance classes and applicable legislation

Most human activities are subject to an element of uncertainty and any consequences that may arise. These consequences may be very diverse in nature and are, above all, of an economic nature.

From olden times man has sought to protect himself from these unexpected and accidental occurrences in very diverse ways. One of the means that he has made use of has been to safeguard himself against damage and loss through insurance contracts. The purpose of these is for one contracting party to redress any negative financial detriment that has arisen for the other contracting party due to an accidental or unforeseen event.

It is, therefore, understandable that the differing nature of the events that a contracting party may be exposed to, has resulted in the existence of several different types of insurance. Our analysis of these types of insurance will concentrate on two main criteria:

(a) With regard to the means of redressing the damage, the insurance may be:

    1. *Objective compensation insurance*. This form of insurance determines the cover for any damage on the basis of a specific evaluation, which has been agreed upon beforehand, based on the true value of the object. This category includes all forms of insurance in which the harmful event affects the interest on capital assets (fire, transport, theft and automobile insurance, reinsurance, etc.).

    2. *Subjective compensation insurance*. In this case, since it is impossible to provide a specific evaluation of the damage, the value is calculated subjectively and in advance by the party that seeks to cover the financial risk. This category exclusively covers insurance on human life, in three respects: death, survival and mixed.

(b) With regard to the objective of the insurance, we can distinguish between:

    1. *Insurance on objects*. With this type of insurance the interest directly falls on specific and determined objects. This category covers insurance against theft, of livestock, against fire, and of issues related to land transport.

    2. *Insurance on capital*. The interest that is insured affects the whole of the capital or one part of the insured party (public liability insurance, automobile insurance and reinsurance).

    3. *Insurance on persons*. This form of insurance covers any financial risks deriving from a harmful event suffered by a person (life insurance, insurance against sickness and accidents).

4.4.2 The concept and legal nature of the insurance contract

An insurance contract may be defined as that by which the insurer is bound, by means of the collection of a premium and for the case in which the event whose risk is the object of coverage takes place, to pay compensation with the agreed limits, for the damage that is occasioned to the insured party, or to meet a level of capital, income or other agreed provisions.

In accordance with this definition, an insurance contract would appear to be a formal contract, since the policy that the law requires is obligatory for the existence of the contract, bilateral and synallagmatic. The reason for this is that obligations for the two contracting parties arise from the contracts. These can be onerous, where both parties seek economic advantages; they can also be random, in which case it is fate that decides whether the insurer has to pay out the compensation agreed, when it has to do this, and the amount of compensation; of a successive nature, if the content does not terminate with one single compensation payment but rather there are successive compensation payments; of compliance, in which case the insured party, in general terms, subjects it to the general conditions of the policy arranged in advance by the insurer; corporate or professional, in which case it is only possible for the insurer to insure the specific party prior to the insurance contract.

4.4.3 Elements of insurance contracts

4.4.3.1 Personal elements

Two persons necessarily act in all insurance relations: the insurer and the insured.

(a) Insurer   This is the person who is obliged to compensate for any damage, in exchange for receiving a premium. The insurer must necessarily be an authorised insuring entity, entered in the register of the Ministry of the Economy and Revenue, and the capacity to be an insurer is restricted to public limited companies, mutual assurance companies and insurance cooperatives.

Insurers require the assistance of two other corporate bodies in order to carry out their activities. These are private insurance intermediaries, and they may belong to two types: insurance agents, connected to the insurer by means of an agency contract, that act with powers of representation, and insurance brokers that carry out their intermediary activity without any association with the insurer, their task being exclusively advisory.

(b) Insured   This is the person who concludes and signs the contract with the insurer, and pays the premium. In general terms, an insured concludes the contract in his own name, thus assuming the legal position of an insured party. But he can also contract the insurance

on behalf of someone else, in which case these two legal positions – insured and insured party – constitute different entities. In this case, the figure of the insured takes on particular significance, since this is the person directly liable to the insurer, and who is bound to the obligations stemming from the contract and even for the payment of the premium. However, in the case of a claim, it will be the insured party that collects the compensation. The insured cannot seek to exercise their contractual rights, as they lack the status of being the insured party.

(c) Beneficiary   This is the person who benefits from the rights acquired by the insured.

4.4.3.2   Pecuniary elements

There are two pecuniary elements: the premium and the interest insured.

(a) The premium   This is the consideration for the risk that is assumed by the insurer. It constitutes an essential element of the insurance, and there can be no contract without the parties reaching an agreement concerning the premium.

The premium is not determined solely by the insurer. Its calculation is subject to control by the public authorities, in accordance with the established applicable regulations.

Insurance law recognises a double system with regard to premiums, these being the single premium and the periodic premium. In the first system, the amount of the premium is singular for the whole of the duration of the insurance, and is paid on only one occasion. In the second it is paid over regular periods of time.

The premium is payable in advance and is indivisible, in the sense that once it is paid, the insurer can assume it, even though the risk coverage may end and the contract cease to be effective.

(b) The interest insured   In this case what is insured is not an asset in itself, but rather the interest that the insured party has in the asset exposed to the risk.

The interest has to be lawful, since if it is against the law, morality or public order, it cannot be insured. The absence of any interest entails the nullification of the contract.

The interest insured must be quantified in economic terms, or there must at least be the possibility of assessing it a posteriori.

There should be no confusion between the value of the interest insured and the insured sum which can be used in order to calculate the premium. This also represents the maximum limit of the provision by the insurer (the compensation). This helps us when it comes to distinguishing between:

- Full insurance: when the value of the insured interest coincides with the insured sum that was agreed some time previously.
- Over-insurance: when the insured sum is greater than the interest insured.
- Infra-insurance: when the sum insured is less than the interest insured.

In practice, cases of full insurance are rare, except in cases of life insurance, since the value of the asset on which the interest lies usually varies over time. Therefore, the final value will be less than the sum insured.

The most common occurrence in practice is infra-insurance. This results from the desire of the insured party to pay a lower premium. However, it involves running the risk that the insurer will not compensate for the effective damage suffered in the event of a claim.

Finally, we will briefly discuss double insurance, multiple insurance and co-assurance.

Double insurance exists in situations where the insured party contracts different contracts to insure the same interest with several insurers. In these cases the insured party is bound to inform each insurer of the other contracts concluded. Failure to meet this obligation leads to a penalty for the insured party, consisting of the insurers no longer being obliged to pay compensation in the event of a claim.

Multiple insurance is considered to exist when an insured party contracts policies with several different insurers, with each policy partially covering the damages caused by an accident.

Finally, co-assurance is considered to exist when, by means of one or several contracts, the insured party concludes contracts with different insurers that have previously reached an agreement with regard to the risk participation that each one of them bears.

4.4.3.3 Formal elements

4.4.3.3.1 The policy. As a general rule, most legislative codes establish that the contract is to be recorded in writing, but they do not explicitly require the contract to be in writing in order for it to be valid. This circumstance ensures that the position can be sustained whereby the policy meets a mere evidentiary function, rather than the existence of the contract. Nevertheless, the contract does not take effect until the policy is signed. We can conclude that insurance contracts are formal in nature, because they do not actually exist as such, and no obligations can arise for either party, until the policy is drafted.

The policies in which insurance contracts are documented do not require prior approval by the public authorities, except when authorisation is requested to initiate the insuring activity or to extend it to new areas.

The usual practice is for a separate policy to be issued for every specific insurance operation. However, in certain areas (e.g. transport), the insurer covers all interests of the insured party that can be insured, in as far as it sets out the risks over an agreed period of time. This type of policy is known as a payment or floating policy.

Apart from the policy itself, this form of insurance involves issuing a complementary document – for each one of the interests – that can be referred to as any of the following: a declaration of payment, a notice, a coupon, or insurance certificate.

4.4.3.3.2 Other documents.   In addition to the policy, there are other documents that play a special role at certain times in the life of some contracts:

(a) The *insurance proposal*: a document in which the future contracting party sets out its intention to complete the contract. Only the insurer can issue this document, and it then binds the insurer for 15 days, in such a manner that it can be considered to be an irrevocable offer of a contract. Thus, once the applicant has signed this document, it can be stated that the contract has been completed. It follows from this that insurance companies prefer to apply simple insurance;

(b) The *provisional cover note*: the document that provides coverage prior to the issuing of the policy;

(c) The *appendix or supplement*: a document that modifies some terms of the policy; and

(d) The *insurance certificate*.

4.4.3.4 Causal element: risk

The reason for the obligation assumed by the insured party is the provision made by the insurer. The insurance is stipulated in such a way that one party compensates the other (or a person designated by the latter) for the consequences of a harmful event. It follows from this that the risk, i.e. the possibility that a certain event may occur, constitutes a presupposition of the contractual cause, and is an essential element of the contract. In the absence of the possibility of a harmful event occurring, there can be no damage that can be compensated for and the contract would lack a cause. Moreover, it is necessary that the risk is individually featured in each contract, as insurance that considers any risk is invalid.

Furthermore, it is required that the nature of the risk covered be recorded in the policy, except in the case of maritime insurance which – owing to its special circumstances – can have the universality of the risk as the cause. In relation to cause, events can result from natural facts (e.g. death, illness), from voluntary human acts (e.g. theft, war), involuntary ones (accidents), material ones (homicide), or legal ones (acquisition of debts).

In all cases, the risk must be real, and effectively exist at the time the contract is concluded and throughout the term thereof.

A contract may cover one or several risks, but there are risks that cannot be covered. These are the risks that are unlawful, either because they are against the law or morality, or because they are caused by the insured party itself (legal uninsurability). However, legal uninsurability can also be technical in nature, for example in certain events that are difficult to quantify, due to their significance or their exceptional nature (risks of war, revolutions, volcanoes, earthquakes, etc.).

Given the importance that the element of risk has in all forms of insurance, legislators impose on insured parties a duty of collaboration with the insurers. This enables the risk to be determined in such a way that everything that the insured party knows that could affect the element of risk is declared, and that all declarations must be of a precise nature. Any failure by the insured party to fulfil the first of these requirements shall place them in a position of withholding; any failure to fulfil the second shall place them in a position of inaccuracy. In both cases, the consequence shall be the same, namely the possible rescission of the contract by the insurer.

However, not all cases involving withholding or inaccuracy result in the rescission of the contract. For this to occur, the withholding or inaccuracy must concern circumstances that could have a bearing on the ability to assess the risk. Therefore, instances of withholding or falsehood related to circumstances that are already known to the insurer cannot be taken into consideration, because in this case the risk could have been properly assessed. Determining a breach of this obligation would involve a question of fact that is submitted to the courts for consideration.

4.4.4 Content of the contract

4.4.4.1 The obligations of the insured

4.4.4.1.1 The duty to declare the risk.
Prior to concluding the contract, the insured has the duty to declare all known circumstances that could have a bearing on the assessment of the risk by the insurer and its subsequent aggravation. Given that the maxim of good faith is a characteristic of insurance contracts, the insured is obliged to provide precise and accurate information about the situation of the insured party, without any omission or withholding.

In the case of a reservation or inaccuracy, the insurer shall have a period of one month of becoming aware of this fact, during which to rescind the contract. The insurer will retain the premiums, unless they themselves have committed a serious error.

4.4.4.1.2 Reporting the aggravation of the risk.
The insured or the insured party are obliged to report, as early as possible, all circumstances that aggravate the risk and are a nature such that, had they been known to the insurer, would have resulted in the latter concluding the contract in circumstances that were more onerous for the insured party.

The insured or the insured party holds the same right in circumstances in which a lessening of the risk takes place. In such instances, the insurer must reduce the premium for the following period. Otherwise, the insured can opt to terminate the contract and demand the difference of the resulting premium.

4.4.4.1.3 Payment of the premium.
Unless there is agreement to the contrary, the single premium or the first of the periodic premiums can be demanded any time from the moment the contract is signed, and at the domicile of the insured. In this instance the principle prevails of payment in advance, and the indivisibility of the premium for the whole of the period that has already commenced.

In the case of non-payment of the premium, the insurer can opt between terminating the contract or demanding payment through legal proceedings, on the basis of the policy. Unless there is agreement to the contrary, cover through the insurance policy is suspended. If the insurer does not claim payment during certain legally established periods of time, the contract automatically expires after a prudential period of time has elapsed.

Should the contract not terminate or expire, payment of the premium will re-establish cover, 24 hours from the moment payment is made.

4.4.4.1.4   Notification in the event of a claim and the duty of information.
Reporting a claim is not an obligation in itself, but is rather the duty or
burden of the insured or the insured party, as can be set out in the
policy itself.

Any delay in complying with this does not result in the expiry or
loss of the rights of the insured party. The insurer remains bound by
contract to pay the compensation, and has the right to claim for
damages that may have been occasioned to it, which must be demonstrated in a separate procedure. Naturally, this right lapses when,
through any means, the insurer had direct knowledge of the claim.

Should an event occur that leads to claim, the insured party or the
insured will have to provide the insurer with various information
about the circumstances and the consequences of this event. A breach
of this duty does not render invalid the right to receive compensation,
except in the cases of misrepresentation or a serious fault on the part of
the insured party.

4.4.4.1.5 The duty to minimise the consequences of a claim event.
This duty applies only in cases of insurance for damage. It consists
primarily of the duty to salvage or use the means possible, within the
scope of the insured or insured party, to minimise the consequences
of the event leading to the claim. A breach of this duty entitles the
insurer to reduce its compensation payment in proportion with the
extent of the damage and the degree of fault on the part of the
insured party.

Even if the outcome is not positive, the salvage costs are to be met by
the insurer, provided that these are neither inappropriate nor disproportionate. They can extend up to the limit laid down in the contract
and, in the absence of an agreement, they are the costs effectively
caused, up to the limit of the sum insured.

4.4.4.2 Obligations of the insurer

The insurer has the following obligations with respect to the insurer
and the insured party:

(a) The obligation of documentation, as mentioned above, with
    respect to the compensation payment of the policy, and the
    recording thereof in its policies record book.
(b) Obligation to provide cover during the term of the contract.
(c) The obligation to pay compensation when the claim event has
    occurred, within the agreed limits, provided that the event has not
    come about due to bad faith on the part of the insured party.

4.4.5 Insurance for damage

4.4.5.1 Concept and classes

There are two different types of contract that fall into this category:

- The insurance of objects: this is a contract in which the insurer makes a commitment, in exchange for a premium, to compensate for the damage suffered to a specific object or objects, that have previously been designated by the insured, by an uncertain or unexpected event; and
- Economic insurance: this is a form of insurance whereby the insurer makes a commitment, in exchange for a premium, to compensate for the damage caused by the insured party to third persons, by the fact or facts laid down in the contract for which it may have public liability, or for unexpected damage to the particular patrimony of the insured party, as a consequence of certain financial transactions set out in the contract.

Economic insurance encompasses insurance for: public liability, loss of profit, seizure, credit and security or legal assistance.

4.4.5.2 Insurance of objects

4.4.5.2.1 Fire insurance.   Under this form of insurance, the insurer is obliged to compensate for the damage occasioned to the insured object by fire.

The contract extends to all damage that is suffered by the objects described in the contract, at the place described in the policy, by a fire that is caused by unexpected circumstances. This does not cover damage caused to commercial goods or objects of value that were at the site of the event leading to the claim, but it does cover damage brought about as a consequence of efforts to extinguish the fire.

4.4.5.2.2 Theft insurance.   This form of insurance covers the damage arising from the illegal removal (theft or robbery) by third parties, of the objects insured and damage caused as a consequence of the act of committing the offence. It does not cover acts of robbery or theft resulting as a consequence of a serious lack of prudence on the part of the insured party, or those perpetrated by family members or cohabiters.

4.4.5.2.3 Transport insurance.   This form of insurance obliges the insurer to compensate for the material damage that transported merchandise may suffer, on the occasion, or as a consequence, of transport. This includes the means of transport used and other insured objects, both during times of movement and at the preparatory stage, as well as during times of rest.

When compensation is paid, it should cover the salvage costs for the objects transported and the costs of reshipping the merchandise.

The compensation will cover the value of the merchandise at the site of loading plus the costs paid to the transport company for delivering it, and the insurance costs if these are to be paid by the insured party. If the transported merchandise was to be sold, the compensation is calculated according to the value of the same at the place of destination.

Appendix 1   Proposed Model of Letter of Intent

Letter of Intent between 'AAA' and 'BBB'

The companies 'AAA' (hereinafter, the 'CUSTOMER') and 'BBB' (hereinafter, the 'OPERATOR') (hereinafter, collectively referred as the 'Parties') have recently held conversation regarding the execution of a logistics contract (hereinafter, the 'Contract').

This document intends to establish the basis of the agreements the Parties have reached and to set out in writing the principles that will govern the negotiations that are going to be held in order to execute the Contract in the shortest possible term. These principles are as follows:

1. The Parties will negotiate a Contract to be signed [*scheduled date for the signature of the Contract*], incorporating the terms and conditions considered in this letter, and by means of which the OPERATOR will provide services [*include the services*].
2. The initial duration of the Contract will be [*include term of duration of the Contract*] years from the date it is signed. Either Party may terminate the Contract before the end of its term on [*include date of termination*] by notifying the other in writing [*include term decided*] months in advance of its intention not to renew the Contract. If either of the Parties exercises this right within the term agreed, the Contract will be automatically renewed for additional [*include term decided*] year terms.
3. Attached as Annex 1 is the price list for the services to be provided by the OPERATOR up to the termination of this Letter of Intent.
4. The activity forecast on which this price list is based is attached as Annex 2.
5. The operation in which the tariff is based is attached as Annex 3.
6. The price list will be reviewed in the event there are significant variations in the activity and/or the volume of business. The Contract will set forth the limits within which these variations shall be considered to be acceptable as agreed by the Parties, as well as the conditions for their review.
7. In any case, the price list will be reviewed at least once a year to take into account inflation.
8. The OPERATOR does not assume any liability vis-à-vis the CUSTOMER should it become impossible to perform the services as a result of variations in the activity and/or the volume of business that have not been previously notified and agreed in writing by the OPERATOR.
9. The invoices for the services provided to the CUSTOMER will be paid by the latter in a term of [*include term of payment*] from the date of the invoice.

The effectiveness of the agreements of principle reached between the Parties and contained in this document is subject to negotiation and, if applicable, the execution of the Contract. The terms of the Contract must, in any case, correspond to the terms of this letter and be satisfactory to both Parties. The rights and obligations that each Party will assume will be those derived from the Contract.

[Place and date]

'AAA'   'BBB'

_____   _____
Mr [   ]   Mr [   ]

Appendix 2   Proposed Model Contract

Logistics Services Agreement between 'AAA' and 'BBB'

In [   ] on [   ] [   ]

B E T W E E N

I.   Mr [   ], holder of National ID Document No. [   ] and address at [   ], of the first part, and
II.   Mr [   ], holder of National ID Document No. [   ] and address at [   ], of the second part.

THEY ACT AS FOLLOWS:

The former in name and on behalf of AAA (hereinafter referred to as 'THE CUSTOMER') with address at [   ] no. [   ] in [   ], Tax Code No. [   ], whose representation is evidenced in his capacity as [   ] pursuant to a deed executed before the Notary [   ] on [   ], number [   ] of his official record, and

The latter in name and on behalf of BBB (hereinafter referred to as 'THE OPERATOR'), with address at [   ] no. [   ] in [   ], Tax Code No. [   ], whose representation is evidenced in his capacity as [   ] pursuant to a deed executed before the Notary [   ] on [   ], number [   ] of his official record.

As they act, both parties hereby acknowledge their mutual capacity to contract in the terms of this Agreement and now therefore

W I T N E S S E T H
I.

That THE OPERATOR is a transport operator providing logistic services to third parties and so with the resources to pursue the activities of warehousing, transport and distribution of merchandise.

II.

THE CUSTOMER is a company dedicated to [   ] for which it requires an efficient chain for their logistic distribution.

III.

THE CUSTOMER is interested in hiring the services provided by THE OPERATOR, and both companies now therefore conclude this **LOGISTICS SERVICES AGREEMENT** to implement THE OPERATOR's warehousing, transport and distribution services, on the basis of the following

CLAUSES

ONE – DEFINITIONS

1.1   *Assets:* those assets, including the contracts (particularly the financial leasing contracts) to be acquired or subscribed by THE OPERATOR in order to provide the *services* contained herein and which, on termination hereof, shall be acquired by or assigned to THE CUSTOMER.

1.2   *Delivery note:* the transport document issued by THE OPERATOR stating at least the name of the addressee, destination and delivery point, delivery date, and the *products* loaded on board the vehicle, duly identified.

1.3   *Operating year:* the date of commencement of the first operating year shall be that on which the *platform* becomes operational, and concludes at the end of the calendar year following such date. Commencement of subsequent operating years shall coincide with the date of termination of the immediately preceding one.

1.4   *Central costs:* indirect costs incurred by THE OPERATOR in providing the *services* promised.

1.5   *Operating costs:* all costs of any type incurred by THE OPERATOR in providing the *services*, excluding *central costs* and *management remuneration*.

1.6   *Management accounts:* any costs, disbursements and costs forecast or made, which are established for each commercial period, according to the operating budgets.

1.7   *Fees:* management payment to THE OPERATOR by THE CUSTOMER.

1.8   *Packets, crates and/or pallets:* units of various *products* by which such *products* are usually delivered to THE OPERATOR for distribution to the delivery points, in which THE CUSTOMER dispatches its *products*.

1.9   *Commercial period:* a period of time of one month or, if applicable, that according to THE CUSTOMER's accounts calendar.

1.10   *Central Platform:* the distribution centre belonging to [   ] which will be built in [   ] and managed by THE OPERATOR.

1.11   *Platform:* refers to the Central Platform.

1.12   *Plant and equipment:* assets of an economic nature, acquired, rented or leased under contract for a period exceeding three months, and whose acquisition or contracting was approved by THE CUSTOMER in those cases where the parties agreed to the effect.

1.13   *Operating budget:* to be drawn up annually as of the date on which the *platform* becomes operational, setting out the costs, investments, divestments expenses and provisions necessary to provide the *services*.

1.14   *Initial period budget:* to be drawn up by the parties on signing this agreement for the period hereof and on the date on which the *platform* becomes operational, setting out the costs, investments, divestments expenses and provisions necessary to provide the *services*.

1.15   *Start-up budget:* the budget for the initial period.

1.16   *Delivery point:* the place where THE OPERATOR must provide the distribution and final delivery of the *products*.

1.17   *Stocks:* the *products* or merchandise duly stored at the Central *Platform*.

1.18   *Book value:* the historic value of the assets following deduction for depreciation.

TWO – PURPOSE OF THE AGREEMENT

2.1　The purpose of this Agreement is the provision to THE CUSTOMER by THE OPERATOR of the *services* defined in Clause Six in respect of the *products* mentioned in Clause Four, within the geographical field defined in Clause Three. In return for said *services*, THE CUSTOMER shall pay THE OPERATOR the charges and fees established in Clause Seven of this Agreement.

THREE – SCOPE OF THE AGREEMENT

3.1　THE OPERATOR hereby undertakes to render the services described herein below in [　　] territory.

3.2　The *services* defined herein below will be provided from the central *platform*, hereinafter referred to as the *platform*, in [　　], to the delivery points. On the signing hereof, said delivery points comprise the regional platforms and the various [　　] of THE CUSTOMER.

3.3　Exhibit no. [　　] hereto comprises an open list of the centres to be included within the scope of the Agreement, henceforth referred to as the *delivery points*. In addition, Exhibit No.[　　] is a description of the *platform* where THE OPERATOR will receive the *products* defined below. Said Exhibits may be enlarged in documents signed by both parties.

FOUR – PRODUCTS

4.1　The *products* which are the subject hereof are [　　] *products*.

4.2　Notwithstanding the foregoing, the parties may define any other *products*.

4.3　THE OPERATOR shall, without limitation on weight, size or any other characteristic, store, handle, transport and distribute the *products* defined in the previous point which are delivered to it for the provision of the *services* which are the subject hereof.

FIVE – EFFECTIVE DATE AND TERM

5.1　This Agreement comes into effect on the date of its signing.

5.2　However, it shall be for a term of [　　] years as of the date on which the *platform* becomes operational, planned for [　　]. In order to record the start-up of the *platform*, both parties shall sign a document to be attached to this Agreement as Exhibit No. [　　].

5.3　The Agreement is deemed to be automatically renewed for further one-year terms if neither party notifies the other in writing at least [　　]months in advance of the termination of the initial [　　]-year period or each successive renewal of its intention to end the Agreement.

SIX – THE OPERATOR'S SERVICES AND OBLIGATIONS

6.1　For the volumes indicated in the forecast to be provided by THE CUSTOMER, THE OPERATOR shall store, handle, transport and distribute the *products* delivered to it for their storage and distribution.

6.2　THE OPERATOR shall provide its warehousing *services* at the *platform* for the *products* delivered to it for their onward distribution to the designated delivery points. Said storage *services* will include the following:

6.2.1　Reception and unloading of the *products* at the *platform*.

6.2.2　On reception, verification of the *products* delivered to THE OPERATOR for storage and distribution, to ensure as follows according to the procedures agreed by the parties:

      6.2.2.1   Identification of the *products* and that they are in line with the documentation delivered:

      6.2.2.2   The absence of visible damage, so that the *products* require no further inspection to determine this.

   6.2.3   THE OPERATOR shall supervise deliveries of *products* to it in terms of their correct condition and quantities, including identification, classification and counting of the *products*: any which are apparently in poor condition, such damage being easily visible, will be rejected for distribution, with notification to THE CUSTOMER immediately. The same procedure shall be followed whenever flawed *products* are received at the *platform*.

   6.2.4   THE OPERATOR shall place and store the *products* within the physical parameters available at the *platform,* optimising space.

   6.2.5   THE OPERATOR shall prepare the *products* for dispatch and distribution, placing them in packets, cases or pallets, supervising the state and placement of said *products* in such packaging according to delivery orders received from THE CUSTOMER.

6.3   THE OPERATOR hereby undertakes to provide the distribution *services* to THE CUSTOMER in respect of the *products* delivered to it by THE CUSTOMER at the *platform*, and which must be supplied to the delivery points. Said distribution *services* shall include the following:

   6.3.1   Loading and transport of *products* supplied to them from the *platform* to the various delivery points indicated by THE CUSTOMER.

   6.3.2   Supply of the *products* at the delivery points indicated to it, with unloading at the entry dock or door provided for these purposes at each such delivery point.

   6.3.3   Control of the *products* delivered at their destination, against signature of the pertinent delivery note.

   6.3.4   Formalities in claims made concerning flawed *products* delivered to destination.

6.4   In providing the *services,* THE OPERATOR is responsible for compliance with all the legislation in place which may affect the provision of such services, particularly that concerning transport and warehousing of merchandise. However, THE CUSTOMER shall, on request from THE OPERATOR, provide any documents needed in order to comply with such legislation.

6.5   THE OPERATOR hereby specifically acknowledges that the *products* are the property of THE CUSTOMER and shall so state to any authorities or third parties in the hypothetical case of any attempt to exercise some right thereupon.

6.6   To provide the *services* listed above, THE OPERATOR shall, with THE CUSTOMER's prior approval, hire a staff of specialised employees. In order to establish a balance between the policy of permanent job-creation and the response capacity to THE CUSTOMER's needs as they alter with market conditions, THE OPERATOR shall select the personnel which will enable THE CUSTOMER to contribute to the creation of a suitable social frame. For these purposes, THE OPERATOR shall, with THE CUSTOMER's approval, seek the creation of stable employment opening up opportunities for all social sectors, notably those with priority requirements such as the unemployed, the disabled, women, young people, etc.

SEVEN – FINANCIAL TERMS
7.1   *Costs*
      7.1.1   THE CUSTOMER shall reimburse THE OPERATOR for all costs incurred by THE OPERATOR in the provision of the *services* described in Clause Six, including the cost of insurance and those charges excluded from the budgets but approved by THE CUSTOMER and which may be incurred by THE OPERATOR. Such costs shall be reimbursed in the terms established in this Clause.
7.2   *Budgets*
      7.2.1   THE OPERATOR shall, jointly with THE CUSTOMER, prepare and draft a start-up budget for the period between the effective date of this Agreement and the moment when the *platform* becomes operative, referred to henceforth as the initial period budget, and a detailed annual operating budget for the one-year term counted from that moment when the *platform* becomes operative, in accordance with the terms of Clause Five, for the provision of the logistic *services*, referred to henceforth as the operating budget.
      7.2.2   THE OPERATOR's budgets will be prepared in line with the planned volumes notified and approved by THE CUSTOMER according to item 7.2.5 of this Clause. There will be only one annual operating budget; annual operating budgets must be approved by both parties.
      7.2.3   Each year, THE OPERATOR shall submit the operating budget for the following year to THE CUSTOMER for its approval, two months in advance of the start of such operating year. The date of commencement of the first operating year shall be fixed according to Clause Five. Commencement of further operating years shall coincide with the end of that immediately preceding. The parties shall do everything possible in good faith to ensure that each operating budget is agreed to within the month following the date on which THE OPERATOR submits its proposal for the following year.
      7.2.4   The operating budgets must detail all the costs foreseen for the provision of the *services* by THE OPERATOR and the remuneration for the management, providing the basis for THE OPERATOR's invoicing in each commercial period. For these purposes, THE CUSTOMER hereby undertakes to provide all the information needed to prepare the budgets, detailed above and, in particular, to do so three months in advance of the operating year commencement date.
      7.2.5   Should the parties fail to reach an understanding on the operating budget for any year, the one in place at that time shall remain in effect until they are able to do so or the matter is settled as provided for in Clause Twenty.
      7.2.6   The parties shall do all in their powers to secure an understanding on the start-up budget. At all events, should that not be possible, THE CUSTOMER shall assume the costs incurred by THE OPERATOR for the start-up of the purpose of this Agreement.

7.3   *Accounting and invoices*

    7.3.1   THE OPERATOR shall prepare management accounts for each one-month commercial period or, as applicable, according to THE CUSTOMER's accounting calendar.

    7.3.2   THE OPERATOR shall bill THE CUSTOMER before the commencement of each commercial period according to the costs budgeted for such period. Payment will be as provided for in this Clause.

    7.3.3   THE OPERATOR shall deliver the following to THE CUSTOMER for each commercial period, within the [   ] days following the end thereof:

        7.3.3.1   The management accounts.

        7.3.3.2   A report on and analysis and explanation of any difference between the management accounts submitted and those budgeted.

        7.3.3.3   An invoice or credit note for the difference between the costs budgeted and those actually met by THE OPERATOR. Such credit note must be discounted from the total invoice to be submitted for the following commercial period.

7.4   *Management remuneration*

    7.4.1   The management remuneration, also called fee, is that received by THE OPERATOR for the provision of the *services* provided for herein.

    7.4.2   Said remuneration is calculated as a percentage of [   ]% of all *services* rendered, except for transport to which the figure of [   ]% applies. Remuneration for management shall, notwithstanding the foregoing, comprise a minimum of [   ] EUROS for the first operating year, understood as that defined according to Clause Five.

    7.4.3   Management remuneration may vary by [   ]% above or below the sum arising from the implementation of point 7.4.2 above. Such variation is determined on the basis of 50% for cost controls and 50% for the attainment of the agreed level of *service*.

7.5   *Long-term obligations*

    7.5.1   THE OPERATOR hereby undertakes not to commit to long-term contracts or capital investments involving outlay exceeding [   ] EUROS without prior consent from THE CUSTOMER.

    7.5.2   Following prior agreement between the parties, THE OPERATOR may assume unbudgeted costs provided that they are essential to providing the *services* hereunder. Notwithstanding the foregoing, THE CUSTOMER may at any time ask THE OPERATOR to refrain from assuming such charges. In such case, THE OPERATOR shall report to THE CUSTOMER on the adverse consequences to the *services* should it not assume such costs: at all events, THE OPERATOR is released from any liability in this respect.

    7.5.3   THE CUSTOMER shall compensate THE OPERATOR for costs incurred by THE OPERATOR arising from any requests from THE CUSTOMER for the provision of the *services*.

7.5.4   In addition, THE CUSTOMER shall compensate THE OPERATOR for employee dismissals previously accepted by THE CUSTOMER.

7.6   *Payments*

7.6.1   Invoices filed according to this Clause must be paid within the [   ] days following the commencement of each commercial period to which such invoices refer. Remaining invoices will be paid by THE CUSTOMER within the [   ] days following their presentation. All invoices will be paid by THE CUSTOMER without compensations or deductions of any sort.

7.6.2   All sums referred to herein or which must be paid hereunder are deemed not to include VAT, which shall be calculated at the rate applying to the sums established in this document.

7.6.3   Sums owed and due shall accrue interest at the [   ] plus three percentage points.

7.7   *Separate accounts*

7.7.1   THE OPERATOR shall keep separate accounts for all the activities and operations carried on to provide the *services* pursuant hereto.

7.8   *Suspension of the service due to non-payment*

7.8.1   Failure to pay any sum due means that THE OPERATOR will claim against THE CUSTOMER. After a period of seven days following such claim, THE OPERATOR shall be entitled to suspend part or all of the *services* until paid the sums claimed in full, without prejudice of any other legal actions which it may undertake to defend its rights hereunder.

7.8.2   During the period of partial or total suspension of the services, THE CUSTOMER continues to be liable for payment of the operating costs and management fee.

EIGHT – THE PARTIES' LIABILITIES

8.1   The parties shall strive to collaborate jointly as closely as possible, with the due diligence to be expected under such contracts, to ensure harmonious and effective implementation throughout the term hereof.

8.2   THE OPERATOR is liable for damage and loss to stock or merchandise caused by its negligence or that of its employees, subcontractors or agents. However, THE CUSTOMER hereby accepts and assumes a level of loss or damage to the stock of merchandise, to be established in each annual budget, based on experience before the implementation of this Agreement and THE CUSTOMER's experience prior hereto.

8.3   THE OPERATOR is not under any circumstances liable for breach or inadequate performance of the *services* committed hereunder, or for any other liability assumed pursuant hereto which may arise from any of the following circumstances:

8.3.1   Limitations or restrictions on THE OPERATOR's access to the merchandise destination delivery points, unless THE OPERATOR fails to comply with the procedures in place.

8.3.2   Limitations or restrictions on the possibilities for collecting the merchandise for distribution and any other flaw in the availability of *products* not attributable to THE OPERATOR.

8.3.3 Operational or organisational changes by THE OPERATOR to the personnel or other working resources or procedures adopted on instructions from THE CUSTOMER or accepted by it even though aware of the risk such changes may cause to the provision of the *services* by THE OPERATOR.

8.3.4 Act of God or *force majeure*, in the terms set forth in Clause Ten.

8.3.5 Breakdown or malfunction of THE CUSTOMER's computer system for a period exceeding four business hours.

8.3.6 Variations in the application of resources and *services* requested by THE CUSTOMER to meet unscheduled requirements.

8.3.7 Delivery delays due to rejection or hold-up of their reception by the recipient, if the service was provided correctly by THE OPERATOR.

8.3.8 Imposition by THE CUSTOMER of a new destination not notified reasonably in advance to THE OPERATOR.

8.3.9 The transport conditions, such as volume, dimensions or time-tables which are substantially different from those assumed and used as the basis for the preparation of the budget.

8.3.10 Imports or exports not originating in or destined to the territory referred to in Clause Three.

8.3.11 Damage to the *products* due to flawed packing or wrapping, when this was not caused by THE OPERATOR.

8.3.12 Errors or omissions in the information or instructions given by THE CUSTOMER to THE OPERATOR.

8.4 THE OPERATOR is not liable for the following:

8.4.1 Loss or damage to the merchandise unless such merchandise was in perfect condition for sale when delivered to THE OPERATOR for distribution. THE OPERATOR shall examine the condition of all stock on delivery and will issue delivery notes detailing the existence of any problem.

8.4.2 Any claim, unless such claim is notified to THE OPERATOR in writing within the 24 hours following handover at the delivery point. Both parties hereby undertake to require the recipients to notify any damage or loss at the moment of delivery with the pertinent indication in the delivery notes.

8.4.3 The content of any recipient, package or sealed container which has not apparently been opened, provided that this is not attributable to THE OPERATOR for the storage or transport *services*.

8.4.4 Losses arising from lapse or obsolescence of the *products* when not due to THE OPERATOR's negligence.

8.4.5 Any damage or loss to stock or merchandise due to unsuitable or insufficient packaging, unless such damage or loss could have been avoided had THE OPERATOR applied due diligence.

8.4.6 In case of supplies to delivery points due to cancellations or delivery orders given erroneously by THE OPERATOR.

8.4.7 For missing *product* on the opening of any pallet not apparently damaged at the time of reception.

8.5 Pursuant to the provisions of point two of this Clause, THE CUSTOMER accepts a given level of losses and damage to stock or merchandise including in the best conditions of management in the storage and distribution operations. THE OPERATOR is therefore liable for the aforementioned damage and losses in so far as the value thereof exceeds the admitted level of such losses and damages.

8.6 THE OPERATOR's liability for damage and loss to stock or merchandise extends from the moment when it takes such merchandise into its custody until it is handed over at the delivery points.

8.7 The monetary value of damage or loss to stock or merchandise shall be as follows:

    8.7.1 In case of loss, the replacement cost.

    8.7.2 In case of damage, the replacement cost or the cost of repair to THE CUSTOMER if the latter is less, following deduction of that part of the merchandise which could be recovered or used.

8.8 THE CUSTOMER hereby guarantees THE OPERATOR as follows:

    8.8.1 That the merchandise delivered to THE OPERATOR is suitable for storage and handling by THE OPERATOR in order for it to provide the *services* undertaken in this Agreement.

    8.8.2 The merchandise delivered to it is not illegal, hazardous or harmful.

    8.8.3 THE CUSTOMER will provide details as to the procedure for the storage of the merchandise and its expiration dates.

    In accordance with the terms of this section, THE CUSTOMER shall indemnify and hold THE OPERATOR harmless from any liability which may arise from breach of these guarantees and in respect of any claim which may be brought against THE OPERATOR as a result of damage or loss caused by the *products* distributed by THE OPERATOR.

8.9 Should THE OPERATOR not be in agreement with the content of any delivery or part thereof handed over to it for its custody, it shall be entitled to separate it, delay its delivery and condition such delivery upon a joint inspection by THE CUSTOMER and THE OPERATOR.

8.10 In general, within a period of [   ] month following the end of each year, THE OPERATOR shall pay THE CUSTOMER for damage and losses caused to the merchandise in excess of the permitted tolerance of such loss and damage. Notwithstanding the foregoing, THE OPERATOR shall pay any damage or loss which proves to be manifest and significant in relation to the amount fixed in each annual budget, within a period of [   ] month as of the moment when such damage or loss became known.

8.11 THE OPERATOR may, from one year to another, compensate increased stock with losses thereto: it shall not however receive any compensation in cases where profits exceed losses, without prejudice to the possibility of compensating them with future losses.

8.12 *Consequential losses.* Neither party is liable to the other for loss of profits or any other consequential and indirect losses which may be caused, except where such losses arise from death or personal injury caused negligently by the party in breach or its employees or agents.

8.13 *Limitation of liability*. In general, and despite what has been stated in this Clause, provided that THE OPERATOR has the insurance cover required under this Agreement, it shall not under any circumstances be liable for any loss and/or consequential damage of any type, cause or source beyond the monetary consequences covered by the associated policies.

NINE – INSURANCE

9.1 THE OPERATOR hereby undertakes throughout the term of the Agreement to contract and retain in effect the covers indicated herein below, with a leading national or international insurance company accepted and/or proposed by THE CUSTOMER. Similarly, all policies, premiums and any other possible costs involved in the contracting of the following insurance must be approved by THE CUSTOMER.

   9.1.1 THE OPERATOR hereby undertakes to contract 'all-risk' storage insurance guaranteeing any claim which may arise concerning the merchandise stored, in which THE CUSTOMER is designated as the insured and beneficiary of indemnification thereunder.

   The excess established in the policy will be for the account of THE CUSTOMER. Any amendment to such excess by the policy-holder or insured will be notified to THE CUSTOMER, which shall continue to meet it.

   THE OPERATOR hereby undertakes to keep the Policy referred to in this paragraph in effect in the conditions indicated throughout the effective term of the Agreement and any extensions hereto, and to notify THE CUSTOMER of any change or alteration which may affect the cover in place.

   9.1.2 THE OPERATOR shall take an 'all-risk' goods transport insurance policy covering the transport of the *products* from the *platform* to their delivery point, in which THE CUSTOMER is designated as the insured and beneficiary of indemnification thereunder.

   The excess established in the policy will be for the account of THE CUSTOMER. Any amendment to such excess by the policy-holder or insured will be notified to THE CUSTOMER, which shall continue to meet it.

   THE OPERATOR hereby undertakes to keep the Policy referred to in this paragraph in effect in the conditions indicated throughout the effective term of the Agreement and any extensions hereto, and to notify THE CUSTOMER of any change or alteration which may affect the cover in place.

   9.1.3 'All-risk' damage, theft and fire insurance covering the value of the machinery, computer system, furnishings, installations and other assets of the *platform* or which are necessary to the provision of the *service*.

   9.1.4 Civil liability insurance covering any risks which may arise from conduct for which THE OPERATOR's employees and personnel are responsible.

9.2 The premiums for the above-mentioned insurance are, with the exception of that for the civil liability insurance, considered to be costs and so will be reimbursed by THE OPERATOR to THE CUSTOMER.

9.3   Any indemnifications which the insurance company may be bound to pay for claims concerning the *products* delivered to THE OPERATOR shall be received directly by it; THE OPERATOR shall not be required to advance or pay any sum as a result of claims the insurance company may have agreed to meet.

9.4   The points of the previous paragraphs are understood notwithstanding any civil liability which may be incurred by THE OPERATOR, its employees or subcontractors as a result of fraud in the fulfilment of its obligations.

9.5   For its part, THE CUSTOMER shall take civil liability insurance in the same terms as THE OPERATOR for faulty *products*.

9.6   THE CUSTOMER shall notify THE OPERATOR of the current value of the *products* handed over and any changes to such value, along with the average per-kilogram value of its *product* in order to contract appropriate insurance cover. THE CUSTOMER alone is responsible for any fault, error or irregularity in such valuation and its notification.

THE OPERATOR hereby undertakes to maintain the valuation of the *products* up to date in accordance with the notifications received from THE CUSTOMER in this respect. THE OPERATOR shall be liable to the insurance company and to THE CUSTOMER for maintaining such updating as notified by THE CUSTOMER.

TEN – *FORCE MAJEURE*

10.1   Neither party shall be liable for breach of the Agreement caused by circumstances or conditions which each party could not have foreseen, or which were foreseen but were unavoidable.

10.2   Notwithstanding the terms of the previous paragraph, each party must make all reasonable effort to meet the obligations arising from this Agreement and, at all events, to ensure that the financial effects to the parties arising from such event are a minimum to each.

10.3   Following the occurrence of an event of *force majeure,* and throughout the duration thereof, THE OPERATOR shall adopt all reasonable resolutions and measures to ensure the continuity of the service, provided that THE CUSTOMER pays not just the costs referred to herein but any further cost associated with the adoption of such measures or resolutions. Should THE OPERATOR incur such additional costs, it shall notify THE CUSTOMER accordingly as soon as possible and shall come to an understanding thereon. THE CUSTOMER may, at any time, instruct THE OPERATOR to stop incurring such additional costs, in which case THE OPERATOR shall advise THE CUSTOMER of the adverse consequences to the *services* of such cessation and, at all events, THE OPERATOR shall not under any circumstances be liable therefor.

10.4   For the purposes of this Clause, strikes and riots are considered causes of *force majeure.*

10.5   The party which suffers delays or hold-ups or is prevented from meeting its contractual obligations for any of the causes in this Clause shall notify the other forthwith of its situation, with an estimate of the scope of such situation in respect of the impossibility of meeting its obligations, and indicating the forecast delay.

10.6 As soon as such cause of delay or non-performance ends, the party suffering said delay or prevented from performing, in full or in part, shall notify the other accordingly forthwith, setting out any repercussions of such developments.

10.7 Should non-performance of obligations of one party due to causes of *force majeure* cause the other any detrimental physical effect for its business, persisting more than [   ] days following notification, the party affected shall be entitled to terminate this Agreement, with 30 days' notice, provided that, on the date of such advance notice, the termination of the Agreement will result in a reduction of said detrimental physical effects.

ELEVEN – INSPECTION AND CONTROL

11.1 THE OPERATOR shall allow THE CUSTOMER and its duly authorised representatives to enter and remain on the *platform* in order to check the stocks of *products* and their operating and administrative conditions. To these ends, THE CUSTOMER shall notify THE OPERATOR of its intention to make such any inspection at least 24 hours in advance.

Any such inspection must be performed during working hours and may not under any circumstances disrupt THE OPERATOR's normal activity. For these purposes, those concerned shall be accompanied by THE OPERATOR's representative at all times.

11.2 THE CUSTOMER's managers, authorised representatives and auditors shall be entitled to examine and secure copies of the accounts and other files related to THE OPERATOR's provision of the *services*.

TWELVE – CONFIDENTIALITY

12.1 Each party shall provide the other with all the information deemed necessary and essential to the performance of this Agreement.

12.2 Both parties hereby undertake to keep secret any information they may obtain on the other's operations and activities, adopting all reasonable measures to prevent its disclosure and to ensure that it does not become known to anyone other than the person cleared to access such information.

12.3 The obligations established here must be complied with even after the termination of this Agreement, for a period of five years.

THIRTEEN – ASSIGNMENT, TRANSFER AND/OR SUBROGATION

13.1 This Agreement may not be assigned and/or transferred, and/or neither party may subrogate in its rights and obligations to the benefit of a third party without the such other party's prior written approval.

13.2 However, either party may assign or transfer it or subrogate its rights and obligations in favour of any company in the same group: the party assigning, transferring or subrogated remains liable to the other for the specific performance of each and every one of the obligations arising hereunder.

13.3 Notwithstanding the foregoing, THE OPERATOR may at any time use or subcontract the *services* of third parties to perform all or part of its obligations, while remaining liable for the correct performance of the *services* which are the subject of this Agreement.

FOURTEEN – TERMINATION

14.1 This Agreement may not be terminated by either party except in those cases where a serious and reiterated obstructive and intentionally wilful attitude is declared concerning the performance of any of the obligations considered essential.

14.2 Should either party be in breach, the party which met its obligations shall deliver to the party in breach a detailed description of what is claimed, together with any damages and losses which may have arisen from such breach. On the basis of said description, the parties undertake to reach a friendly solution endorsed by both.

14.3 Notwithstanding the provisions of the first paragraph of this Clause, both parties hereby agree that cancellation shall be extraordinary, demanded as the ultimate and only solution as against any other legal measures designed to fulfil the obligations, so that the claim for performance shall at all events be preferred.

14.4 In case of breach, the parties shall, in the settling of conflicts, abide by Clause Twenty of this Agreement.

14.5 Cancellation hereof in the absence of express written conformity by both parties may only be agreed according to Clause Twenty of this Agreement. The date of written notification of the wish to cancel the Agreement shall be the one actually taken into account should the date of the award granting cancellation become final following the contractual period hereof due to the expiration of its effective term so that, even during the time between said date and that of the award, should rescission lead to the termination of the Agreement pursuant to Clause Five, such contractual termination shall, having been notified prior to said date, have full legal effect.

In the period between application for cancellation hereof and the declaration of such cancellation by the arbitration body, the parties continue to be bound to perform this Agreement. However, the terms of this paragraph do not apply to breaches of points 7.1 and 7.4 of Clause Seven hereinabove, and the party affected may file for cancellation and is bound only to perform the services for which it was paid.

14.6 The Agreement ends if a party files for temporary receivership, is declared bankrupt or commences insolvency procedures.

14.7 It may also end in case of merger of one of the parties or a change of ownership of a majority of its shares, or a change to the existing shareholding structure of either company or their parent (provided that this is not the upshot of a reorganisation within the group itself) which involves loss of control of the company management: in such case, the other party may choose to continue with the Agreement or to deem it to have terminated and must notify the other of its decision within the 15 calendar days following the notification given by the company merged or sold.

14.8 Similarly, this Agreement terminates at the end of its contractual term as provided for in Clause Five, without prejudice of any extensions the parties may agree.

14.9 Notification to terminate this Agreement must be given in writing in line with Clause Seventeen on notifications, and must state the date as of which the party concerned will deem it to have ended.

FIFTEEN – CONSEQUENCES OF TERMINATION

15.1 In case of termination hereof, whether due to cancellation, the end of the established term, the impossibility of continuing herewith or any other circumstance implying the extinction hereof, the parties shall, within the week following the date of termination, in a single session, complete the final settlement of pending balances.

15.2 Within the [   ] months following notification of the termination of the Agreement in the circumstances provided for in Clause Five or, at the latest, on the Agreement termination date, whatever the cause of such termination, either party may notify the other in writing to demand that the plant, equipment and other assets acquired for the provision of the *services* be transferred to THE CUSTOMER on payment of their net book value (if more than zero) on the Agreement termination date. If, pursuant to this Clause, the plant and equipment are transferred to THE CUSTOMER, it shall also accept any assignment, subrogation or renewal of any contracts or loans concluded by THE OPERATOR (other than the contracts concerning the *platform* referred to in point 15.3 of this Clause) for the account of THE CUSTOMER and with its approval.

As of the notification mentioned in the previous paragraph, THE CUSTOMER shall indemnify THE OPERATOR and hold it harmless in relation to any such contracts and loans since the Agreement termination date, until they are assigned or renewed. The physical handover to THE CUSTOMER of all plant, equipment and assets must take place as soon as practically possible following the payment of such plant, equipment and assets.

Notwithstanding the terms of this Agreement and without prejudice of any other legal measures which may prove pertinent, THE OPERATOR is entitled to recover the plant and equipment assigned or leased should THE CUSTOMER breach its obligation to indemnify THE OPERATOR in accordance with the terms of the previous paragraph.

15.3 The following rules shall be observed concerning the *platform*:

15.3.1 THE CUSTOMER shall indemnify THE OPERATOR and hold it harmless in relation to any cost, liability, loss, procedure, demand and/or claim of any type which may have been incurred by THE OPERATOR at any time in relation with the *platform*.

15.3.2 In a written requirement, the parties shall be authorised for the [leases, licences, etc.] for the *platform* to be assigned by THE OPERATOR to THE CUSTOMER, the price for such assignment being [   ].

15.4 At all events, THE CUSTOMER takes over all personnel employed on the *platform*, maintaining them in the same terms as on the termination date.

15.5 By the deadline set, there may not be any of THE CUSTOMER's *product* in THE OPERATOR's hands and such *product* must, therefore, be withdrawn from THE OPERATOR's warehouses by THE CUSTOMER. For its part, THE CUSTOMER must pay all pending invoices even though such payment may represent an advance on the due dates initially agreed or established.

In the case of any *products* which may be in transit, THE CUSTOMER must pay the *service* in cash, without prejudice of THE OPERATOR's obligation to complete such service.

SIXTEEN – THE PARTIES' REPRESENTATIVES

16.1 THE CUSTOMER and THE OPERATOR shall each appoint a representative of the company with sufficient powers to represent it and act on its
behalf with a view to complying with each and every one of the obligations arising from this Agreement. Such representatives' decisions and
negotiations shall be binding on THE CUSTOMER and THE OPERATOR.

16.2 Through their representatives, the parties shall agree on procedures for
all relevant day-to-day aspects linking THE OPERATOR, THE CUSTOMER
and their suppliers, concerning at least the system of administration,
warehouse claims, stocktaking and responsibilities at delivery points.

SEVENTEEN – NOTIFICATIONS

17.1 Any notification made hereunder must, in order to be valid and have the
foreseen effects, be given by registered mail or through a Notary to the
address and for the attention of the following person or department:

AAA:
Attn. Mr [   ]
[   ]

BBB:
Attn. Mr [   ]
[   ]

17.2 The deadlines established herein for notifications are counted from the
evidenced date of sending of the registered letter or notarial communication.

17.3 However, all commercial notifications or those affecting the normal
implementation and performance of the Agreement may be given by the
means and in the form agreed by the parties.

EIGHTEEN – AMENDMENTS

18.1 This Agreement may be amended in part or in full only in a written
understanding signed by the parties' representatives.

NINETEEN – INTERPRETATION

19.1 The parties hereby undertake to provide all necessary collaboration in
settling any difference which may arise from the interpretation of the
Clauses hereof.

19.2 The Exhibits hereto form a part hereof and shall be construed jointly
with the Agreement.

TWENTY – SETTLEMENT OF DISPUTES, ARBITRATION AND APPLICABLE LAW

20.1 Any difference arising as to the interpretation and performance hereof
shall be settled in an agreement between the General Manager of THE
OPERATOR and the General Manager of THE CUSTOMER, within a
maximum term of one month.

20.2 On a subsidiary basis, in the absence of any solution pursuant to the previous point, both parties hereby expressly relinquish any venue which

may be available to them and agree that any litigation, divergence, question or claim arising from the interpretation and/or implementation of this Agreement or directly or indirectly related hereto, will be permanently settled in arbitration in the framework of the Arbitration Court of the Chamber of Commerce of [   ] which shall be entrusted with the administration of the arbitration and the appointment of the arbitrators in accordance with its Regulations and Bylaws. The parties likewise hereby specifically state their commitment to implement any arbitration award handed down.

20.3 This Agreement is subject to the [   ] legislation.

In witness whereof, the parties hereby sign this Agreement in duplicate and to a sole effect on the date and in the place set out in the heading.

Mr [   ]   Mr [   ]

_____   _____
in name and on behalf of   in name and on behalf of
AAA   BBB

Appendix 3 Tables of Carriage of Goods

Table A.1 Scope of application

	Road	Rail	Air	Sea
Object	Merchandise	Merchandise	• Persons • Equipment • Merchandise	Merchandise
Requirements	• Contract • Merchandise • Vehicles (automobiles, articulated vehicles, towage vehicles and semi-towage vehicles) • Remuneration • International – Result of the domicile and nationalities of the parties to the contract, irrespective of the application of the Convention	• International carriage • Lines inscribed in the list of the Central Office	• International carriage • Passengers, equipment or freight • Remuneration • Aircraft • Free carriage is subject to the Warsaw Convention if it is carried out by an air carriage company	• International carriage
Internationality	When the point of origin or delivery of the merchandise to the carrier – designated in the contract – and the place of destination or delivery of the merchandise to the recipient – designated in the contract – are located in different states, of which at least one is a Contracting Party of the CMR	All of those shipments of merchandise that are transported with a direct bill of lading established for journeys that include the territories of at least two states and that exclusively cover lines inscribed in the list of the Central Office	• The departure point and the destination point – designated in the contract – regardless of whether there is an interruption or transhipment, are located in the territory of different High Contracting Parties • The departure point and the destination point – designated in the contract – are located in the territory of the High Contracting Party, and an intermediate stopover in a different country, even though it may not be a High Contracting Party, is planned	Applies to contracts evidenced by a bill of lading or a similar document of title, if: • The bill of lading is issued in a contracting state • The carriage is from in a contracting state • The contract states that these rules apply

Table A.1 Scope of application – *continued*

	Road	Rail	Air	Sea
Exclusions	• Carriage effected under the regulations for international postal agreements • Funeral carriage • Removals carriage • Carriage effected between the United Kingdom of Great Britain and Northern Ireland and the Republic of Ireland • Carriage subject to private agreements established between states with regard to the goods carried in cross-border trade	• All objects that can be transported by the mail authorities • Objects that, owing to their size, weight or structure cannot be adapted to the form of carriage requested • Objects whose carriage is prohibited • Materials and objects excluded from transport by virtue of the Regulations relating to the international rail transport of hazardous merchandise (IHR)	• Postal shipments	No applicable provision
State transport	Carriage effected by the state, institutions or governmental organisations is subject to the CMR	No applicable provision	Subject to the Warsaw Convention, if it complies with its requirements	No applicable provision
Mixed carriage	Circumstance The road transport vehicle, loaded with the merchandise, is in turn transferred by train, ship, or aircraft during part of its journey There is no transhipment of the freight from one means of transport to another	See Road Transport 'Mixed carriage'	See Road Transport 'Mixed carriage'	See Road Transport 'Mixed carriage'

205

Table A.1 Scope of application – *continued*

Road		Rail	Air	Sea
Legal regime	As a general rule, the rules of the CMR Convention apply, provided that there is no breakage of cargo. One exception are the rules that regulate the liability for the form of transport that is different from that carried by road, when the loss, damage or delay in delivery: – Occurs during the undertaking of another form of transport – Is not due to an act or omission by the road transport company – Is caused by a fact particular to the other form of transport When there are no rules that apply to the other form of transport, the rules of the CMR Convention shall apply			

Table A.2 Liability regime

	Road	Rail	Air	Sea
System	Liability due to culpability with the burden of proof	Liability due to culpability with the burden of proof	Objective liability Liability due to culpability with the burden of proof	Liability due to culpability with the burden of proof
Generating facts	• Total loss • Partial loss • Breakage • Delay in the delivery	• Total loss • Partial loss • Breakage • Delay in the delivery	Loss Breakage Delay • Destruction • Loss • Breakage • Delay	• Total loss • Partial loss • Breakage
Scope	Objective From receipt of the merchandise until delivery to the recipient Subjective Due to the acts and omissions of employees and other persons employed in order to perform the transport, when acting in order to carry out their duties	From acceptance of the merchandise for carriage until delivery to the consignor	While it is in the safekeeping of the carrier. This does not cover land, sea or river transport outside the aerodrome	From when merchandise is loaded onto the vessel until it is unloaded
Amount	Loss Value of the merchandise (refund: carriage and costs) Breakage Depreciation (plus refund of costs: carriage and costs) Delay Detrimental	Loss and breakage 17 SDR per kilogram of weight. Gross limits that may be necessary Delay Four times the price of carriage	17 SDR US$20 according to the conversion by IATA	Loss and breakage 666.67 SDRs per package or 2 SDRs per kilogram, whichever is higher Delay No applicable provision
Limits	Loss and breakage 8.33 SDR per kg of gross tonnage missing (carriage and costs) Delay Price of carriage		Limit that cannot exceed the threshold	Limit can be increased by agreement between the shipper and carrier and declared in the bill of lading

Table A.2 Liability regime – continued

	Road	Rail	Air	Sea
Expiry of limitations	• Misrepresentation • Fault comparable to misrepresentation In general, if the generating fact is a consequence of: • Fault by the party entitled to the merchandise • Instruction of the party entitled to the merchandise not arising from a blameworthy act by the transport company • Particular defects of the merchandise • Unexpected circumstance • *Force majeure*	• Misrepresentation • Possible misrepresentation In general, if the generating fact is a consequence of: • Culpability of the party entitled to the merchandise • Instruction of the party entitled to the merchandise not arising from a blameworthy act by the transport company • Particular defect in the merchandise • Unexpected circumstance • *Force majeure*	• Misrepresentation • Possible misrepresentation Loss Breakage • Nature or particular defect of the merchandise • Packing • Act of war or armed conflict • Act of a public authority carried out in relation to the entry, departure or transit of the merchandise • Culpability of the party that suffers detriment	• Misrepresentation • Fault comparable to misrepresentation • Act, neglect, or default of the master, mariner, pilot or the servants of the carrier in the navigation or in the management of the ship • Fire, unless caused by the actual fault or privity of the carrier • Perils, dangers and accidents of the sea or other navigable waters • Act of God • Act of war • Act of public enemies • Arrest or restraint of princes, rulers or people, or seizure under legal process • Quarantine restrictions • Act or omission of the shipper or owner of the goods, his agent or representative
Exoneration	Of a specific nature, if the generating fact is a consequence of any of the risks inherent to the following: • Use of open vehicles • Absence of or defect in the packing • Handling, loading or unloading of the merchandise effected by the forwarder or the recipient	Of a specific nature, if the generating fact is a consequence of any of the risks inherent to the following: • Use of uncovered rail. • Lack of or defect in packing • Loading or unloading operations effected by the shipper or the recipient	Delay • Proof of diligence (unexpected circumstance or *force majeure*) • Culpability of the victim or the party that suffers detriment • Nature or particular defect in the merchandise (if there is agreement in this respect)	• Strikes or lock-outs or stoppage or restraint of labour from whatever cause, whether partial or general • Riots and civil commotions • Saving or attempting to save life or property at sea • (m) Wastage in bulk or weight or any other loss or damage arising from inherent defect, quality or vice of the goods

Table A.2 Liability regime – *continued*

		Road	Rail	Air	Sea
		• Nature of certain merchandise • Insufficiency or non-completion of the markings or numbers of the packages • Carriage of live animals		• Defective loading effected by the shipper • Compliance with customs or administrative formalities by the shipper or recipient • Nature of certain merchandise • Insufficiency or non-observance of the requirements prescribed for those admitted under certain conditions • Carriage of live animals • Carriage of shipments that require escorts	• Insufficiency of packing • Insufficiency or inadequacy of marks • Latent defects not discoverable by due diligence • Any other cause arising without the actual fault and privity of the carrier, or without the fault or neglect of the agents or servants of the carrier, but the burden of proof shall be on the person claiming the benefit of this exception to show that neither the actual fault or privity of the carrier nor the fault or neglect of the agents or servants of the carrier contributed to the loss or damage
Burden of proof	General exoneration	The transport company has to establish its exoneration	General exoneration	The transport company is responsible for proving its exoneration	No applicable provision
	Specific exoneration	The transport company has to establish the concurrence of the cause of the generating fact for some specific risks, with the burden of proof being reversed	Specific exoneration		
			The railway has to establish its exoneration		
			The railway has to establish the concurrence of the cause of the generating fact for some specific risks, with the burden of proof being reversed in this case		

Table A.2 Liability regime – *continued*

			Road	Rail	Air	Sea
Claim	Losses and breakages	Apparent	At the time of delivery	At the time of delivery	Breakage 14 days from the date of delivery	At the time of delivery
		Not apparent	7 days from the date of delivery	7 days from the date of delivery		Within 3 days from the date of delivery
	Delay		21 days from the date of delivery	60 days from the date of delivery	Delay 21 days from the date of delivery	No applicable provision
	Consequences		Unless there is evidence to the contrary, delivery in conformity is presumed			
Action			Time-bar period, that can be interrupted, of 1 year (3 years in the case of misrepresentation)	Time-bar period, which cannot be interrupted, of 1 year (2 years in the case of misrepresentation, possible misrepresentation, etc.)	Expiry period, which cannot be interrupted, of 2 years from the real or expected date, or from the date of detaining the carriage	Expiry period of 1 year from the date of delivery of the goods, or the date when the goods should have been delivered

Table A.3 Content of the contract

	Road	Rail	Air	Sea
Document	Waybill (CMR) – *Consignment note*	Consignment note	• Air waybill (AWB) • Other means that record information relating to the carriage (the shipper may demand a receipt)	• Bill of lading • Other similar document of title
Obligation to ship	Not expressly established, although it can be deduced that it should be issued by the transport company	The railway is obliged to hand over a consignment note to the shipper for its completion	Shipper (the carrier is entitled to request this). If this is issued by the carrier, it is presumed that it is acting on behalf of the shipper	At shipper's request the carrier is obliged to hand over the bill of lading
Nature	• The appropriate document in terms of the existence of a contract • The appropriate document relating to the terms of the contract of transport • The appropriate document regarding the receipt of the merchandise by the transport company	• The appropriate document in terms of the existence of a contract • Proof of delivery of the merchandise to the railway company and the obligations assumed by the latter	• Execution of the contract • Receipt of the merchandise • Terms of carriage	• The appropriate document in terms of the existence of a contract • Proof of delivery of the merchandise to the carrier and the obligations assumed by the carrier • Security
Requirements	1. The contract must contain at least the following: • Date and place of drafting • Name and address of the forwarder • Name and address of the transport company • Place and date on which the merchandise was loaded • Name and address of the recipient and place of delivery • Denomination of the nature of the merchandise and the form of packing, and this should contain the usual denomination of the merchandise if it is hazardous	The contract must contain at least the following: • Designation of the station of destination • Name and address of the recipient, who shall be a private individual or any person in law • Denomination of the merchandise • The weight of the merchandise or an analogous statement • For detailed shipments: the number of bulk cargoes and a description of the packing; for complete freight: cars that contain one or more elements of freight invoiced in combined rail and sea	The contract must contain at least the following: • Departure and destination points • If the departure and destination points are located in the territory of one single High Contracting Party with one or more stopovers in the territory of another state, a stopover must be indicated • Weight of the freight	The contract must contain at least the following: • The leading marks necessary for identification of the goods as the same are furnished in writing by the shipper before the loading of such goods starts • Either the number of packages or pieces, or the quantity, or weight, as the case may be, as furnished in writing by the shipper • The apparent order and condition of the goods

Table A.3 Content of the contract – *continued*

Road	Rail	Air	Sea
• Number of packages, their particular markings, and their numbers • Quantity of merchandise, stated in gross tonnage or in another form • Transport costs (price of transport, accessory costs, Customs duties, and other unexpected costs that might accrue from the concluding of the contract until the time of delivery) • Instructions required by the Customs formalities and others • Statement that the transport is subject to the regime established by this Convention 2. In addition, as appropriate, it shall also contain the following: • Express mention that transhipment is prohibited • Costs to be assumed by the forwarder • Sum of reimbursement to be received at the time of delivery of the merchandise	• For the shipments whose freight is the responsibility of the shipper, the freight car number and in addition, the tare for private freight cars • A detailed numbering of the documents required by the Customs authorities and the other administrative authorities that accompany the bill of lading or that mention that they are at the disposal of the railway at a specific station or at a Customs office or the office of any other authority • The name and address of the shipper together with the handwritten signature. The prescriptions in force at the departure station shall determine the concepts of 'full freight car' and 'detailed shipment' for the whole of the journey		

Table A.3 Content of the contract – continued

	Road	Rail	Air	Sea
	• Declared value of the merchandise and the sum represented by special interest in the delivery • Instructions from the forwarder to the transport company concerning insurance of the merchandise • Agreed period during which carriage must be effected • List of documents provided to the transport company 3. Any other information that the parties deem appropriate			
Copies	3 original copies (signed by the forwarder and the transport company) 1st: To be delivered to the forwarder. 2nd: Accompanies the merchandise transported 3rd: For the transport company The transport company or forwarder can require the issuing of such waybills as there are vehicles used, batches or classes of merchandise.	1 original and a duplicate copy to be delivered to the shipper	3 original copies 1st: For the transport company, signed by the shipper of the merchandise 2nd: For the recipient, signed by the shipper and the carrier. This accompanies the merchandise 3rd: Signed by the transport company and forwarded to the shipper by the carrier In the case of several bulk loads, the carrier is entitled to demand an original copy, and the shipper is entitled to demand different receipts	No applicable provision

Table A.3 Content of the contract – *continued*

	Road	Rail	Air	Sea
Loss, absence or irregularity	Does not affect the validity and existence of carriage	No applicable provision	This does not affect the validity and existence of carriage	This does not affect the validity of the contract but carrier loses his rights to limit his liability
Negotiability	In principle, not negotiable	Not negotiable	Not negotiable	Negotiable
Liability	Forwarder — The forwarder is liable for all the costs and damages that the transport company suffers due to inaccuracy and insufficiency in the following statements: 1 (b, d, e, f, g, h, j), 2 and 3 (as regards the statements given by the forwarder)	Forwarder — The forwarder is liable for all the costs and damages that the transport company suffers due to irregular, incorrect or incomplete description of articles not acceptable for carriage or acceptable subject to conditions	• The shipper is liable to the carrier and third parties for the statements and declarations regarding the merchandise in the waybill • The carrier is liable to the shipper and third parties, for the statements and declarations in the receipt and other means used	• The shipper is liable for all loss, damages and expenses arising or resulting from inaccuracies of the marks, number, quantity and weight of the merchandise and shall indemnify the carrier against in such particulars
	Transport company — The transport company is liable for the omission of the statement set out in 1.k	Railway — The railway is liable for loss, damage, wastage and transit time		

Table A.3 Content of the contract – *continued*

	Road	Rail	Air	Sea
Reservations	Number of packets	The railway is obliged to verify the number of packets, weighing and state of the merchandise according to the provision in force in each state The results of the verification will be recorded in the consignment note	The waybill and the receipt certify, unless there is evidence to the contrary	• Weight • Dimensions • Packing • Number of bulk loads
	– Obligation of the transport company to review number of packets and state of merchandise – As applicable, reservations reasoned in the waybill (regarding the impossibility of checking the accuracy of the number of loads or the condition of the merchandise and packing)			
	• Apparent state of the merchandise and packing	– Any such reservations made to the forwarder must be expressly accepted in the waybill – Damages and costs due to defective packing shall be paid by the forwarder, except when this is apparent, and the transport company made no reservations	Reservations by the carrier do not certify unless there is verification	• Quantity • Volume • Condition of the merchandise, unless there is apparent evidence to the contrary
	• Gross tonnage	– The forwarder can demand verification of these aspects by the transport company		
	• Quantity	– The result of the check will be recorded in the waybill		
	• Content	– The costs of verification will be paid by the forwarder		

Table A.4 Jurisdictional competence and arbitration

	Road	Rail	Air	Sea
Jurisdiction	The claimant can choose to exercise their rights only before the court and tribunal: • Of the contracting state that the parties have expressly made themselves subject to • Of the state – contracting or not – where the claimant (note: the English and French versions of the CMR make reference to the 'respondent'): • Has their habitual place residence • Has their main domicile • Has an agency branch through which the contract of transport has been concluded • Of the state – contracting or not – of the place where: • The transport company effectively took responsibility for the freight (and not that agreed on in the contract) • It was contractually agreed to deliver the merchandise to the recipient	The courts of the state where the railway company is established	The claimant can choose to exercise their rights only before the court and tribunal: • Of the territory of the Contracting Part where the transport company: • Has its domicile • Has its main operational domicile • Has an agency branch through which the contract of transport was concluded • Of the state of place of destination	No applicable provision
Arbitration	The case can be admitted to an arbitration court provided: • That this has been expressly agreed in the contract of transport • That the clause first expressly establishes the application of the CMR Agreement by the court	No applicable provision	The case can be submitted to an arbitration court provided: • It makes reference to the transport of merchandise • The arbitration is subject to the rules of the Convention of Warsaw • It is effected in a place where a legal claim could be brought before the jurisdictional competence of the courts and tribunals	No applicable provision

Appendix 4 Analysis of the Logistics Contracts Structure

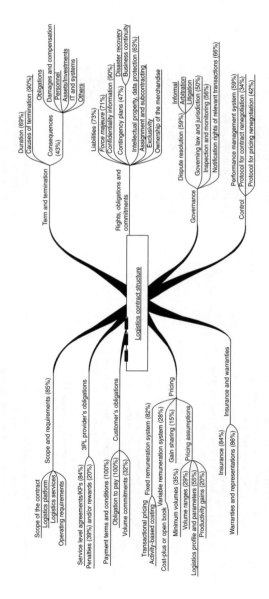

Scope of the contract
Logistics platform
Scope and requirements (85%)
Logistics services
Operating requirements

Service level agreements/KPs (84%)
Penalties (39%) and/or rewards (20%)
3PL provider's obligations

Payment terms and conditions (100%)
Obligation to pay (100%)
Customer's obligations
Volume commitments (32%)

Transactional pricing
Activity-based costing Fixed remuneration system (82%)
Variable remuneration system (28%)
Cost-plus or open book Pricing
Gain sharing (15%)
Minimum volumes (35%)
Volume ranges (29%) Pricing assumptions
Logistics profile and parameters (55%)
Productivity gains (20%)

Insurance (84%) Insurance and warranties
Warranties and representations (86%)

Logistics contract structure

Duration (69%)
Causes of termination (90%)
Obligations
Damages and compensation
Personnel
Assets/Investments
IT and systems
Others
Consequences
(43%)
Term and termination

Liabilities (73%)
Force majeure (71%)
Confidentiality information (90%) Disaster recovery
Contingency plans (47%) Business continuity (63%)
Intellectual property, data protection (63%)
Assignment and subcontracting
Exclusivity
Ownership of the merchandise
Rights, obligations and commitments

Informal
Arbitration
Dispute resolution (59%) Litigation
Governing law and jurisdiction (50%)
Inspection and monitoring (56%)
Notification rights of relevant transactions (66%)
Governance

Performance management system (59%)
Protocol for contract renegotiation (34%)
Protocol for pricing renegotiation (42%)
Control

Notes

1 Outsourcing Contracts: Outsourcing of Logistics Services

1. Contract: to enter into or make a contract. From the Latin *contractus*, the past participle of *contrahere*, to draw together, bring about or enter into an agreement: *con*, together + *trahere*, to draw *(Webster's English Dictionary)*.
2. Outsource: contract (work) out *(Concise Oxford Dictionary)*. There is no precise definition of outsourcing; however, the doctrine has generated a series of definitions, which do not greatly differ from one to another. To quote some examples, Potnis (1995) defines it as 'the purchase of a service previously performed internally'; Lacity and Hirschheim (1993, p. 34) define it as be 'the purchase of an asset or service previously produced internally'; Fiebig (1996) defines it as 'the contracting of an external supplier to provide services or products beneath the production chain of a company previously supplied or produced internally by that company'.
3. Although there is common confusion between the two terms 'outsourcing' and 'subcontracting', they are not synonymous, in fact there are great differences between them. While 'outsourcing' or 'externalisation' refers to the process of contracting out work that previously was, or would have been, done internally, 'subcontracting' only means or implies the provision by the supplier of an activity or function. From an economic, rather than a legal, point of view, the main differences between the two concepts are that the outsourcer shares the risks and responsibility for the results of any activity they carry out, and that the customer adopts a 'pro-active' attitude, while the subcontractor limits themselves to the provision of tasks and services, under the instruction and control of the customer, and without assuming or sharing any of the risk or responsibility in respect of the outcome.
4. In the public sector, examples of outsourcing can be found in prison management, road maintenance and collection of public revenue and rubbish collection. By the eighteenth century, street lamps in England were made, fixed, cleaned and lit under contract. Private contractors also operated the early convict fleets that left Portsmouth in 1787. Similarly, in early nineteenth-century France, the rights to build and operate railways, water storage and distribution facilities were auctioned by competitive tender. Industry Commission, 1996, reviewed by Domberger (1998).
5. The following text transcribed by Sir Arthur Bryant in *Triumph in the West* summarises this graphically:

> Mr. Churchill ... complained about the use of a new word that everybody used and of which he did not understand the meaning. This word was 'logistics', and although he preferred to talk about supply, the Association of Directors insisted that the term logistics was wider than that of simple supply, since it implied planning of what was needed, when and where to have it and how to move it. (Bryant, 1959, cited by Budgen, 1999)

6. The supply chain has been defined as 'the network of organisations that are involved, through upstream and downstream linkages, in the different processes and activities that produce value in the form of products and services in the hands of the ultimate customer' (Christopher, 1998). A further definition of the supply chain is 'the global process that has to satisfy the demands of the consumers and which includes obtaining the raw ingredients, distribution of the manufactured products, and any other process of transport and storage' (Budgen, 1999).

7. The continuous appearance and development of new *logistics tools* modify the concept of what, in earlier times, was also called logistics, but was a long way off modern logistics. Thus, 'Logistics management … goes beyond the traditionally accepted concept of management of the flow of products managed by a company in order that the appropriate quantity arrives at the right time for the clients.' Also, '… we contemplate the supply chain on a global scale, from the supply of raw materials until the delivery to the final client to ensure the highest level of service for the total cost. This includes the consideration within the "supply chain" of the suppliers of our suppliers and the clients of our clients' (Cuartero, 1999).

8. In Spanish legislation, without expressly referring to the logistics activity, we find an indirect definition (which to our minds is completely inadequate) in Article 125.1 of Law 16/1987, of the *Ordenación de los Transportes Terrestres* (LOTT) [Inland Transport Law] where the 'warehouse owner-distributor' is defined as '… the natural or legal persons who receive on deposit (in their warehouses or premises), other people's merchandise or goods, carrying out the functions of their storage, load splitting, or other complementary services that may be necessary, and execute or manage their distribution, in accordance with the depositors' instructions'.

9. As Navas Navarro (1999) points out, what is referred to as a logistics contract is actually the legal coverage of an increasingly common and important management technique in the field of business organisation, which consists of externalising specific services.

10. *Terminology in Logistics* (1991), cited by Paul Budgen (1999).

11. As Verhaar (1998) points out, the form of logistics contracts varies greatly.

12. Whom we refer to as the 'user'. Other titles that are frequently used to define the counterpart of the logistics service operator are 'customer' or 'client' (Burnet, 1998).

13. There are other contractual types present in the legal relationship of providing logistics services, which we will return to later: the commission, agency, appointment, leases of things, works and of services, IT, etc.

14. Transport of merchandise is the logistics case par excellence, to the point that some authors think that we only need to talk about 'legal logistics' when presented with the provision of transport as the main activity, and accompanied by other subordinate provisions, such as conservation in stores or warehouses, packaging, conditioning, labelling, Customs procedures, quality and quantity control.

15. It is quite common, however, that instead of using this structure, the parties limit themselves to concluding separate contracts for each of the countries in which the services are going to be provided. This often proves to be of little use, in addition, it can be prejudicial and even seriously prevent the

services being performed correctly. This results from the fact that, if the services are interrelated and entirely independent elements, the separate contracts can cause a lack or complete breakdown of the flow of information between operators. This in turn can result in uncoordinated services and, ultimately, the complete loss of control over the services and the products, because each operator limits themselves to dealing with their own section and does not concern themselves with other operators, which they consider to be third parties. This is particularly significant when the operators chosen in the various countries do not form part of the same corporate group (whether because the main operator was not represented in some countries, or by choice or at the request of client). In this case the client should take additional care and attention in preparing the individual contracts with each operator.

16. It is important here to highlight the fact that the activities carried out by bodies such as: in Spain the Asociación Española de Codificación Comercial (Spanish Association of Commercial Codification, AECOC) tend to substitute for the mentioned lack of regulations, in so far as possible. In this respect it is worth mentioning the so-called AECOC Recommendations for Logistics (ARL) which – while not constituting any form of legal regulations – do constitute an instrument that, in many situations, the parties can draw on when it comes to defining their obligations through contractual reference to the same. In England we can mention the British International Freight Association (BIFA) or the Road Haulage Association (RHA) which have executed general terms and conditions.

17. This does not intend to discard the logistics activity that is carried out by *transport agents* and *forwarding agents*. In our view, logistics operators as we understand them, are better embodied within the entity of a *warehouse owner-distribution company*. See section 125.1 of Act 16/1987 of 30 July on Land Transport Arrangements.

18. See section 1.2 of the Royal Decree 255/1999 of 7 July.

2 Contract to Provide Logistics Services: a General Overview

1. Alternative titles for the 'letter of intent' (i.e. 'gentlemen's agreement', etc.) are the French *protocol d'accord*, the Italian *lettere di intenti* or *acordo di principio*, and the German *Absichterklärung*.

2. The main characteristic of a letter of intent is that it arises from the traders' daily practice, lacking, as such, both national as well as conventional or customary regulation.

3. The doctrine understands that for a letter of intent to be considered as being not binding on the parties, and as having a merely declarative effect, it must fulfil at least the following requirements: (i) it must lack the essential and constituent elements of a contractual obligation, and (ii) it must be formed as a starting point, it being necessary that after it is signed and accepted, the parties must continue negotiating the essential elements of the contract. In practice, as well as this double requirement, a *contractual clause* or express clause negating binding effects is often included, in this way eliminating any risk of binding contractual or pre-contractual obligations which may be derived by either of the parties from the actual content.

4. In contrast to the previous explanation, the letter of intent will be understood to be of a pre-contractual nature when the following elements are present: (i) the desire of the parties to be bound to sign a future contract is perfectly reflected in its content and (ii) the essential elements of the future contract are perfectly determined.

5. For example, see the requirements that must be met by refrigerating warehouses destined for general and food products regulated by the Medical–Technical Regulations.

6. Each activity, considered individually, does not cease to be a typical activity of a lease of works or services, transport, deposit, agency, appointment, etc. It is the provision as a whole that gives each and every one of them the qualification of a 'logistics' service.

7. By virtue of the principle of liability *ex recepto*, and in accordance with the principles set out in the majority of applicable national regulations and international conventions.

8. As a guide, a manual of operations may refer, for example, to the following circumstances:

    (i) *Delivery phase to the 3PL provider at the platform*: information regarding the delivery of the merchandise; the moment of delivery of the merchandise (working days, delivery times, etc.); determining the unloading bay; the person responsible for the unloading of the merchandise (delivery at vehicle, at loading bay, etc.); the delivery note, if appropriate, to be signed against delivery of the merchandise (details concerning the merchandise that should be included being: number of pallets, boxes, content of the boxes, etc.); if appropriate, information about the daily volume in order to have the platform prepared for the location of new merchandise; packaging of the delivered merchandise (boxes, pallets, etc.); etc.

    (ii) *Storage phase at the platform*: operations to be carried out by the 3PL provider (whether the pallets should be deconsolidated, opened and the contents of the boxes handled, etc.); the period within which the 3PL provider should inform the customer of any lack of or damage to the delivered merchandise or boxes; location of the merchandise at the platform (location in shelf space, etc.); how to request the preparation of orders (whether by an IT system, etc.); request to prepare orders (day and time) and identification of the product to be distributed (reception before specific times, during working days, etc.); whether the 3PL provider should open the boxes, and determining the packaging to be used in preparing the orders; timescale for preparing orders; etc.

    (iii) *Sub-frontloading phase*: period of transport (according to destination, quantity, etc.); delivery time at destination (days and time); liability for any delays in delivery; who is responsible for unloading at destination; delivery note of the 3PL provider (identification of the packages, merchandise, etc.); period during which the recipient can claim against the 3PL provider for lack of or damage to boxes or merchandise; timescale and manner of notifying the customer in the event of unjustified rejection by the recipient; etc.

9. For example, creating annual budgets, periodic budgets, etc., defining the budgeting periods, settling differences between the budgeted costs and

those actually incurred, approving costs and investments to be made by the 3PL provider, etc.

10. We are using this title to refer to public liability, and not any employment, administrative or criminal liability that may arise from the contractual relationship between the parties. We are also not referring to any liability that may arise for either parties in the case of any breach of contract, as mentioned in section 2.4.14.2.

11. We refer here to shortages, although we cannot assimilate this term to *splitting of stocks* because this cannot be attributed, logically, to the 3PL provider, whenever the cause of the shortage or absence of supply is due to the customer's supplier or the customer himself.

12. We are limiting ourselves here to differentiating the liability regime solely in relation to transport by road, and of an international ambit, although other means of transport may be used to be able to provide a more effective and efficient service at a lower cost.

13. The specific nature of a contract of collaboration and cooperation, however, will require the parties to collaborate in such a way as so to minimise, in the operative event of *force majeure,* the damage for both parties. Likewise, in our opinion, strikes or riots that are not attributable to the 3PL provider should be expressly considered as an operative event of *force majeure.*

14. Generally the damages for which a debtor in good faith is liable are those foreseen or that may have been foreseen at the time of constituting the obligation, and which may be a necessary consequence of its non-fulfilment. Therefore, consequential or indirect damages can be defined negatively as those that are not specifically foreseen in the contract but originate from those specifically foreseen therein.

15. The concept of 'integration' is essential in logistics. This concept supposes:

> (i) internal integration between all the links of the supply chain in each company; (ii) integration with suppliers and customers beyond that of the frontiers of each company; (iii) integration/collaboration even between competitors to take advantage of synergies which allow the reduction of costs on a sectorial level – sharing distribution networks, means of transport, etc. – and making possible the differentiating of strategies of access and service to the customer; and (iv) integration between the strategies of the company, the operative processes, the IT systems and the groups of people affected by the logistics function. (Cuartero, 1999)

16. In the case of a 'cost-plus' contract, aside from having the right of inspection and monitoring, because the customer has rights that extend, beyond those merely granting control over the contracted services being carried out correctly, to extensive rights to control the logistical operation as a whole (the contract compliance by the 3PL provider), we can say that the customer in fact has the right of 'auditing' the contract.

17. From this arises the importance of finding, from among the vast range of possible contracts of employment, the appropriate type of contract of employment, in order to avoid unsustainable situations that could arise from its termination.

18. Thus, the complexity of the contracted logistics activity may suppose – and most of the time it does – that the 3PL provider needs extra personnel in

addition to his own resources. These additional resources could be provided by workers previously employed by the customer who carried out his own logistics activity – the 3PL provider subrogating, in this way, the contracts of employment that bind the customer – or could be obtained by employing new workers to carry out the undertaken services – in this way, concluding new contracts of employment. Similarly, it may occur that the 3PL provider is not interested in integrating all of the customer's employees, given that in principle, the speciality of the 3PL provider allows him to optimise results with fewer resources – due to which it would be necessary to contractually determine the distribution of the 'restructuring costs'. All of this must be conducted in accordance with the labour laws.

3 Contract to Provide Logistics Services: Carriage of Goods

1. The Brussels Convention was assumed by the general group of the states with maritime interests that ratified it or became members: Algeria, Angola, Antigua and Barbuda, Argentina, Australia (and Norfolk Island), Bahamas, Barbados, Belgium, Belize, Bolivia, Cameroon, Cape Verde, Cyprus, Croatia, Cuba, Denmark, Dominican Republic, Ecuador, Egypt, Fiji, Finland, France, Gambia, Germany, Ghana, Goa, Greece, Granada, Guyana, Guinea-Bissau, Hungary, Iran, Ireland, Italy, Ivory Coast, Jamaica, Japan, Kenya, Kiribati, Kuwait, Lebanon, Malaysia, Madagascar, Mauritania, Monaco, Mozambique, Nauru, the Netherlands, Nigeria, Norway, Papua New Guinea, Paraguay, Peru, Poland, Portugal, Macao, Romania, Russia, Solomon Islands, São Tomé and Principe, Sarawak, Senegal, Seychelles, Sierra Leone, Singapore, Syria, Somalia, Spain, Sri Lanka, St Kitts and Nevis, St Lucia, St Vincent and the Grenadines, Sweden, Switzerland, Tanzania, Timor, Tonga, Trinidad and Tobago, Turkey, Tuvalu, the United Kingdom of Great Britain and Northern Ireland (and Anguilla, Ascension, British Antarctic Territories, British Virgin Islands, Cayman Islands, Gibraltar, Bermuda, Falkland Islands, Hong Kong, Montserrat, St Helena, Turks and Caicos Islands), the USA and Zaire.
2. The states that have ratified or become members under this Protocol of 23 February 1968 are: Belgium, Denmark, Ecuador, Egypt, Finland, France, Greece, Georgia, Italy, Lebanon, the Netherlands, Norway, Poland, Russia, Singapore, Syria, Sri Lanka, Sweden, Switzerland, Tonga, the United Kingdom of Great Britain and Northern Ireland (Isle of Man, Gibraltar, Bermuda, Hong Kong, Falkland Islands, Turks and Caicos Islands, Cayman Islands, British Virgin Islands, Montserrat, British Antarctic Territories).
3. The states that have ratified or become members under this Protocol as of 21 December 1979 are: Australia, Belgium, Denmark, Finland, France, Greece, Georgia, Italy, Japan, Mexico, the Netherlands, New Zealand, Poland, Spain, Sweden and Switzerland and the United Kingdom of Great Britain and Northern Ireland (Gibraltar, Bermuda, Hong Kong, Falkland Islands, Turks and Caicos Islands, Cayman Islands, British Virgin Islands, Montserrat, Antarctic British Territories).
4. The states that have ratified or have become members under the Hamburg Convention of 31 March 1978 are: Austria, Barbados, Botswana, Burkina Faso, Burundi, Cameroon, Chile, Czech Republic, Egypt, Gambia, Georgia,

Guinea, Hungary, Jordan, Kenya, Lebanon, Lesotho, Malawi, Morocco, Nigeria, Romania, Saint Vincent and the Grenadines, Senegal, Sierra Leone, Syria, Tunisia, Uganda, Tanzania, Zambia.

5. The 1924 Brussels Convention established a limitation on liability of 100 gold pounds per load or unit, unless the value and the nature of the merchandise is declared in the bill of lading (section 4.5); and the 1968 Protocol introduced a limit stated in the 'Poincaré franc' coinage, specifically 10,000 francs per load or unit.

6. Hague 1955, Guadalajara 1961 (Supplementary Convention for Carriage by Air Performed by a Person other than the Contracting Carrier), Guatemala 1971, Additional protocol No. 1 Montreal 1975, Additional protocol No. 2 Montreal 1975, Additional protocol No. 3 Montreal 1975, and Additional protocol No. 4 Montreal 1975.

7. Convention for Unification of Certain Rules for International Carriage by Air (Montreal Convention) 1999.

8. Notwithstanding, the concept of 'wilful misconduct' will still apply to the handling of passengers and baggage under MP4 and MC.

9. The International Air Transport Association. Originally founded in 1919, it brings together approximately 280 airlines, including the world's largest.

10. *The Tai Ping Insurance Company, Ltd and Jetergar Ltd*, v. *Northwest Airlines, Inc.*, d/b/a Northwest Orient Cargo, United States Court of Appeals, Case No. 1520 August Term, 1995.

11. Such an action is known as 'subrogation', when a cargo insurance company sues to obtain reimbursement for claim payments to the cargo interests. Most of all cargo claims litigation today are in 'subrogation' by insurance companies against air forwarders and carriers.

12. In addition and in relation to passenger death or injury, art. 33(2) of the MC contains invaluable supplementary 'fifth' jurisdictional provision: the permanent residence of the passenger from or to which the carrier operates its services. It is considered very important to facilitate the litigation over death and injury compensation for passengers since it was the first time the victim and/or their family could sue foreign carriers in the victims' home countries.

13. According to the UNCTAD report (UNCTAD/STDE/TLB/2003/1) published on 13 January 2003, the world port container throughput, i.e. the number of movements taking place in ports, has grown from zero in 1965 to 225.3 million moves in 2000. Container traffic is forecast to more than double until 2010 to almost 500 million moves; this represents an annual growth rate of 9 per cent. While globally the major container flows are between Asia, Europe and North America, there are significant flows within all regions. According to the same report, the world seaborne trade in containerised cargo is estimated to more than double from 1997 to 2006 to around 1 billion tonnes. Most of this containerised cargo will involve transportation by more than one mode before reaching its final destination. In particular the first and the last leg of any door-to-door transaction will usually involve transportation by another mode, such as road or, to a lesser extent, rail.

14. Article 1 (1) of the United Nations Convention on International Multimodal Transport of Goods 1980.

15. Article 1 (2) of the United Nations Convention on International Multi-modal Transport of Goods 1980.
16. Abbreviations used here refer to *The Hague rules 1924; The Hague-Visby rules 1968*, as amended in 1979; *Hamburg rules 1978; CMR 1956*, as amended by Geneva Protocol 1978; *COTIF/CIM 1980; Warsaw Convention 1929*, as amended by the Montreal Protocols 1975.
17. The first attempt was made by the International Institute for the Unification of Private Law (UNIDROIT) and dates back as far as the 1930s. The work within UNIDROIT resulted in the approval, by its Governing Council in 1963, of a 'draft convention on the international combined transport of goods', which was later revised by an ad hoc committee of experts. This was followed by the preparation and adoption by the Comité Maritime International (CMI) of a 'draft Convention on Combined Transport-Tokyo Rules' in 1969. The draft conventions prepared by UNIDROIT and CMI were combined into a single text in 1970, under the auspices of the Inland Transport Committee of the UN Economic Commission for Europe (UN/ECE), known as the 'Rome draft'. This draft was further modified by meetings of the UN/ECE and the Intergovernmental Consultative Organisation (IMCO) during 1970 and 1971, and came to be known as the 'Draft Convention on the International Combined Transport of Goods', better known as the 'TCM draft', using the French acronym for 'Transport Combiné de Marchandises'. The TCM draft never went beyond the drafting stage. Its provisions were, however, subsequently reflected in standard bills of lading such as the Baltic and International Maritime Conference's (BIMCO) Combiconbill and in the 'Uniform Rules for a Combined Transport Document' of the International Chamber of Commerce (ICC). The UNCTAD was set up by the Trade and Development Board (Decision 96) and, following an extensive investigation, eventually prepared the draft convention leading to the adoption of the United Nations Convention on International Multimodal Transport of Goods 1980 (the MT Convention). In 1986 while pending into force of the UN Convention on International Transport of Goods 1980, a joint UNCTAD/ICC (the United Nations Conference on Trade and Development and the International Chamber of Commerce) working group was created to establish a new set of rules for multimodal transport documents.
18. The unit of account is the Special Drawing Rights as defined by the International Monetary Fund (IMF).

4 Contract to Provide Logistics Services: Warehousing and Resources

1. *Cheesman* v *Brewer Contracts Ltd* [2001] IRLR 144 (EAT).
2. It was held to be a 'transfer' by the European Court of Justice in case C-234/98, *G.C. Allen and others* v *Amalgamated Construction Co. Ltd*, ECR 1999.
3. *TGWU* v *Mckinnon* [2001] IRLR 597.
4. *Alamo Group (Europe) Limited* v *Tucker and Twose of Tiverton* (EAT/994/01).
5. *Martin* v *Lancashire County Council* and *Theresa Bernadone* v *(1) Pall Mall Services Group (2) Harringay Health Care NHS Trust (3) Independent Insurance Limited* [2000]

6. By virtue of the Employers' Liability (Compulsory Insurance) Act 1969.
7. In the case of *Betts and others* v *Brintel Helicopters Ltd*.
8. Vidal (C-127/96), Santner (C-119/96), Montana (C-74/97) [1997] IRLR 132, Hidalgo (C-173/96) and Ziemann (C-247/96)[1999] IRLR 136 and a more recent decision *Temco Service Industries* v *Imzilyen* [2002] IRLR 214.
9. *RCO Support Services* v *Unison* [2002] EWCA Civ 464.
10. *Williams* v *Lockhart Security Services Ltd* (EAT/1395/01).
11. *Ministry of Defence* v *Carvey* (EAT/202/00).
12. *Oy Liikenne AB* v *Liskojarvi and Juntunen* [2001] IRLR 171.
13. The Spanish Penal Code has adopted a new system of fines. Under this system, in some cases the material and financial circumstances of the convicted person are taken into account. This system is based on two methods: the first one defines the time – the law stipulates a minimum and a maximum time limit, and the judge then decides, from between these limits, the specific duration for a given case on the basis of the gravity of the crime committed; the second method defines the quota that the judge has to decide on for each case, on the basis of the economic resources of the convicted person. This means that the final amount of the fine will be based on the daily quota, which cannot be known a priori.

Bibliography

Ackerman, K.B., 'Pitfalls in Logistics Partnerships', *International Journal of Physical Distribution and Logistics*, Vol. 26 (1996).

Ajani, Gianmaria, *The Action Plan on a more Coherent European Contract Law: Response on Behalf of the Acquis Group*, May 2003.

Alba-Ramírez, A., 'How Temporary is Temporary Employment in Spain?', *Journal of Labor Research*, Vol. 19, No. 4 (1998).

Anderson, D., 'Logistical Alliances and Structural Change', thesis No. 470, Linkoping University, 1995.

AT Kearney, 'Strategic Partnerships in Logistics: a Key to Competitive Advantage', EPCA Distribution Meeting, Monaco, 23 October 1995.

Bagchi, Prabir K. and Virum, H., 'European Logistics Alliances: a Management Model', *International Journal of Logistics Management*, Vol. 7, No. 1 (1996).

Barrenechea, J. and Ferrer, M.A., *El Estatuto de los Trabajadores. Texto comentado y concordado con legislación complementaria y jurisprudencia*, Bilbao, Deusto, 2002.

Blanpain, R. (ed.), *Private Employment Agencies: the Impact of ILO Convention 181 (1997) and The Judgment of the European Court of Justice of 11 December 1997*, The Hague, Kluwer Law International, 1999.

Boyson, S., Corsi, T., Dresner, M. and Rabinovich, E., 'Managing Effective Third Party Logistics Relationships: What Does It Take?', *Journal of Business Logistics*, Vol. 20, No. 1 (1999).

Bryant, Sir Arthur, *Triumph in the West 1943–1946*, Alanbrooke diaries, London, Collins, 1959.

Budgen, P., *Freight Forwarding and Goods in Transit*, London, Sweet & Maxwell, 1999.

Burnet, R., *Outsourcing IT. The Legal Aspects*, Aldershot, Ed. Gower, 1998.

Burnett, A., 'Commission Publishes Amended Proposal on Transfer of Undertakings', European industrial relations observatory on-line – eiroline, 1997.

Byerly, John R., Deputy Assistant Secretary for Transportation Affairs, US Department of State, 'Aviation Policy: the Montreal Convention and the Hague Protocol', testimony before the Senate Foreign Relations Committee, Washington, DC, 2003.

Camps Ruiz, L.M., *La nueva regulación del mercado de trabajo*, Valencia, Atelier, 1994.

Carlos Bertrán, J.M., 'El Outsourcing como técnica de gestión alternativa y su regulación contractual', *Derecho de los Negocios*, February 1998.

Casa Baamonde, M.E. and Palomeque Lopez, C., 'La ruptura del monopolio público de colocación: colocación y fomento de empleo', *Relaciones Laborales*, Nos. 5–6 (1994).

Cavalier, S., Dandridge, N., Jenkins, B., Phillips, V. and Stacey, M., 'TUPE – What Next?', *Thompsons Labour and European Law Review*, No. 17 (December 1997).

Cavalier, S., Arthur, R., Leydon, W., Stacey, M. and Phillips, V., 'TUPE plus ça change?', *Thompsons Labour and European Law Review*, No. 24 (July 1998).

Christopher, M., *Logistics and Supply Chain Management, Financial Times*, Pitman Publishing, 1992.

Christopher, M., *Strategies for Reducing Cost and Improving Service, Financial Times*, Pitman Publishing, 1998.

Clarke, Malcolm A., *International Carriage of Goods by Road: CMR*, London, Sweet & Maxwell 1991.

Coia, A., 'Distributors and CMs Ramp Up Logistics Roles', *Electronic Business*, Vol. 29 (2003).

Cruz Villarón, J., 'El nuevo régimen jurídico de la colocación de trabajadores', *Temas Laborales*, Madrid, Vol. 32 (1994).

Cuartero, A., 'Una visión global de la cadena de suministro, Logística y Transporte', *Expansión* (20 December 1999).

Davidow, T.H. and Malone, M.S., *The Virtual Corporations: Structuring and Revitalizing the Corporation for the 21st Century*, New York, HarperCollins, 1992.

De Wit, R., *Multimodal Transport: Carrier Liability and Documentation*, London, Lloyd's of London Press, 1995.

Dimichael, Nicolas J. and Booth, Karyn A., 'Comparison of the Hamburg Rules, Hague-Visby Rules and the MLA Proposal to Reform the Carriage of Goods by Sea Act (COGSA)', counsel for the National Industrial Transportation League, Reading, 1996.

Dolado, Juan J., García-Serrano, C. and Jimeno, Juan F., 'Drawing Lessons from the Boom of Temporary Jobs in Spain', *The Economist*, 112 (June).

Domberger, S., *The Contracting Organization: a Strategic Guide to Outsourcing*, Oxford University Press, 1998.

Drucker, P., 'The Network Society', *Wall Street Journal*, March (1995).

Duran López, F., 'Las empresas de trabajo temporal', *Revista de Trabajo*, No. 69 (1983).

Escudero, R. and Mercader, J., 'Las agencias de colocación y los servicios integrados de empleo', *Relaciones Laborales*, No. 14 (1995).

Fiebig, A., 'Outsourcing under the EC Merger Control Regulation', *17 European Competition Law Review*, No. 123 (1996).

García Fernández, M., 'Posición del trabajador ante la empresa de trabajo temporal y ante la empresa cliente: puntos críticos', *Actualidad Laboral*, No. 34 (1994).

García Murcia, L. 'Una primera aproximación a la ley 10/1994 y normas concordantes: las nuevas normas sobre colocación y cesión de trabajadores', *Temas Laborales*, No. 31 (1994).

García Villaverde, R., 'Tipicidad contractual y contratos de financiación', in *Nuevas entidades, figuras contractuales y garantía en el mercado financiero*, 'Contractual Classification and Contracts of Financing' in [*New Entities, Contractual Types and Guarantee in the Financial Market*] Civitas, 1990.

Glass, David A., *Introduction to the Law of Carriage of Goods*, London, Sweet & Maxwell, 1989.

Gordon, Benjamin H., 'The Changing Face of 3rd Party Logistics, Armstrong & Associates, BG Strategic Advisors Analysis', *Supply Chain Management Review*, March/April (2003).

Gould, Stephen A., 'How to Source Logistics Services Strategically', *Supply Chain Management Review*, Sept/Oct. (2003).

Handy, C., *The Age of Unreason*, Boston, Harvard Business School Press, 1989.

Hannon, D., 'Line Blurs between 3PLs and Contract Manufacturers', *Purchasing*, Vol. 131 (2002).

Hardy, E.R., *Ivamy, Payne & Ivamy's Carriage of Goods by Sea*, 13th edn, London, Butterworths, 1989.

Hertz, S. and Alfredsson M., 'Strategic Development of Third Party Logistics Providers', *Industrial Marketing Management*, Vol. 32 (2003).

Howitt, R. (PSE) 'Written Question P-2200/02' to the Commission, *Official Journal of the European Communities*, C 301 E/265 (12 July 2002).

Jané, J., 'The Effectiveness of Logistics Alliances: a European Research on the Performance Measurement and Contractual Success Factors in Logistics Partnerships between Third-party Logistics Providers and Customers', thesis, Universitat Politècnica de Catalunya, 2005.

Jarrillo, J.C., *Strategic Networks: Creating the Borderless Organization*, Oxford, Butterworth-Heinemann, 1993.

Kaar, R. van Hent, 'New Regulations on Transfer of Undertakings', European industrial relations observatory on-line (February, 2003).

Lacity, M. and Hirschheim, R., 'The Information System Outsourcing Band-wagon', *Sloan Management Review*, No. 34 (1993).

Lambert, Douglas M., Cooper, Martha C. and Pagh Janus D., 'Supply Chain Management: Implementation Issues and Research Opportunities', *The International Journal of Logistics Management*, Vol. 9, No. 2 (1998).

Leahy, S.E., Murphy, P.R. and Poist, R.F., 'Determinants of Successful Logistical Relationships: a Third-party Provider Perspective', *Transportation Journal*, Vol. 35, No. 2 (1995).

Les, Dwight R., 'Why Is Flexible Employment Increasing?', *Journal of Labor Research*, Vol. 17, Fall (1996).

Lewis, J.D., *The Connected Corporation*, New York, Free Press, 1995.

Lieb, R.C., Millen, R.A. and Wassenhove, L.V., 'Third Party Logistics – from an Interorganizational Point of View', *International Journal of Physical Distribution and Logistics Management*, Vol. 30, No. 2 (1993).

Lieb, R.C. and Randall, H.L., 'A Comparison of the Use of Third Party Logistics Services by Large American Manufacturers, 1991, 1994 and 1995', *Business Logistics*, Vol. 17, No. 1 (1996).

McDaniel, Michael S., 'A Presentation of Montreal Protocol 4 to the Warsaw Convention', a presentation to 24 national delegates of the 5th Air Cargo Americas International Congress, 26 October 1999, Miami, Florida.

McDaniel, Michael S., 'A Presentation of the Montreal Convention 1999', a presentation to 190 nations assembled for the FIATA (International Federation of Freight Forwarding Associations) World Congress 2000, 27 September 2000, Rotterdam, The Netherlands.

McMullen, J., 'TUPE Update for In-house Lawyers', C&I Group, 1995.

McMullen, J., *Business Transfers and Employee Rights*, London, Butterworths, 2000.

Martín Valverde, A., 'La superación del monopolio y cesión de trabajadores', *Temas Laborales*, No. 31 (1994).

Mercader Uguina, J., 'La intermediación en el mercado de trabajo tras la reforma laboral: realidades y respuestas', *Revista de Trabajo*, No. 14 (1994).

Murphy, P.R. and Poist, R.F., 'Third-party Logistics Usage: an Assessment of Propositions Based on Previous Research', *Transportation Journal*, Vol. 37, No. 4 (1998).

Murphy, P.R. and Poist, R.F., 'Third-party Logistics: Some User versus Provider Perspectives', *Journal of Business Logistics*, Vol. 21, No. 1 (2000).

Navas Navarro, S., 'El "contrato de logística": una nominación social para un contrato atípico', *Derecho de los Negocios*, May (1999).

Nollen, Stanley D., 'Negative Aspects of Temporary Employment', *Journal of Labor Research*, Vol. 17, No. 4 (Fall 1996).

Peters, Thomas J., and Waterman, Robert H., *In Search of Excellence: Lessons from America's Best-run Companies*, New York, Harper & Row, 1982.

Potnis, A., 'Managing IT Outsourcing Contracts: Issues and Concerns', Working Paper Series of the Computer Security Research Centre, 1995.

Prahalad, C.K. and Hamel, G., 'The Core Competence of the Corporation', *Harvard Business Review*, May–June (1990).

Ramírez Martínez, J.M., 'El proceso de colocación: intervencionismo público e iniciativa privada', *AA.VV La reforma laboral de 1994*, Madrid, 1994.

Razzaque, M.A. and Sheng, C.C., 'Outsourcing of Logistics Functions: a Literature Survey', *International Journal of Physical Distribution and Logistics Management*, Vol. 28, No. 2 (1998).

Rodríguez-Pinero Royo, M., *Las empresas de trabajo temporal en España*, Valencia, Tirant lo Blanch, 1994.

Schulze, R., 'The *Acquis Communautaire* and the Development of European Contract', in Reiner Schulze, Martin Ebers and Hans Christoph Grigoleit (eds), *Informationspflichten und Vertragsschluss im Acquis communautaire* [Information Requirements and Formation of Contract in the *Acquis Communautaire*], COM (2003) 68 final.

Tetley, Q.C., *Marine Cargo Claims*, 4th edn, McGill University Faculty of Law, Montreal, Quebec, Canada (to be published 2008).

Tversky, A., *The Psychology of Risk; Quantifying the Market Risk Premium Phenomenon for Investment Decision Making*, Charlottesville, Institute of Chartered Financial Analysts, 1990.

Valdes Dal-Re, F., 'Las empresas de trabajo temporal: notas sobre un debate no tan lejano para un próximo debate propio', *Relaciones Laborales*, La Ley (1993).

Verhaar, A., 'Logistics Contracts Need Standard Rules', *The American Shipper*, March (1998).

Weber, T., 'Commission Issues Memorandum on Transfer of Undertakings', European industrial relations observatory on-line – eiroline (March 1997).

Index